THE DECISIVE MIND

THE DECISIVE MIND

HOW TO MAKE THE RIGHT CHOICE
EVERY TIME

Sheheryar Banuri

HODDER &
STOUGHTON

First published in Great Britain in 2023 by Hodder & Stoughton
An Hachette UK company

1

Illustrations by Cali Mackrill @calimackdesign

A CIP catalogue record for this title is available from the British Library

Hardback ISBN 978 1 529 34409 7
Trade Paperback ISBN 978 1 529 34413 4
ebook ISBN 978 1 529 34411 0

Typeset in Adobe Jenson by Hewer Text UK Ltd, Edinburgh
Printed and bound in Great Britain by Clays Ltd, Elcograf S.p.A.

Hodder & Stoughton policy is to use papers that are natural, renewable and recyclable
products and made from wood grown in sustainable forests. The logging and manufacturing
processes are expected to conform to the environmental regulations of the country of origin.

Hodder & Stoughton Ltd
Carmelite House
50 Victoria Embankment
London EC4Y 0DZ

www.hodder.co.uk

Contents

PART I:
BEHAVIOURAL INSIGHTS

PART II:

THE ROADMAP

PART III:

THE DECISIVE FRAMEWORK

For Ilyana

'It is not the mountains we conquer but ourselves.'

– Sir Edmund Percival Hillary (1919–2008)

Man vs Mountain

Polepole

The man: Christmas Day, 2013. He's been walking now for about four hours. He has felt the pressure of every heartbeat for the last three hours. He senses the blood pulsing through his body, enduring thoughts of how a blood vessel rushing through his head might burst at any moment. He keeps pressing his index and middle fingers on his neck, not so much to check his pulse but to reassure himself that he isn't experiencing cardiac arrest. He's wearing a heart monitor, the rate displayed on his wrist, but he doesn't trust the readings. They have been steadily hovering around 140 beats per minute all day. It feels like his heart wants to leap out of his chest. He puts his fingers on his neck again, just to double check. Is it too high? He's not sure. But it feels like it.

Polepole

The uncle: It was a lovely autumn day in Washington, DC when the man got the call. It was his uncle, calling to wish him a happy birthday. Ever since he was a young boy, he'd absolutely adored his uncles. They had effectively raised him. This one had taken him on his first ever trek when he was a teenager.

This uncle was an avid trekker, and now, as he was closing in on retirement, his trekking plans were becoming bolder and more extreme, almost as if he were ageing in reverse. The uncle wishes him a happy birthday, but then swiftly moves on to plans for the winter break. He was planning a trip unlike any he had attempted before: to trek the fabled Mount Kilimanjaro in Africa.

When asked why, he spoke of a Yūichirō Miura, who had, just a few months ago, scaled Mount Everest at the age of 80. An incredible feat as he was the oldest man to do it; an exceptional story. His uncle had thought to himself, 'Why not do it as well?' After all, he was much younger, albeit without any climbing experience. He looked into taking on mountain-climbing, and found Kilimanjaro to be a great start.

The man thought it sounded exciting, but there was a problem: there was little time, and he was . . . to put it kindly . . . unfit. He had gained a little . . . well, actually, a lot of weight. Now, as his uncle was talking through the offer to summit Kilimanjaro, it sounded like he didn't really believe that the man would come along. Almost as if he didn't think that someone of his fitness could, or would, do this. As soon as he sensed this doubt in his uncle's voice, he made up his mind. He *would* do this! And he would do it right. He would train for it, make himself ready. No matter how difficult it might be, he would do it.

Polepole

The man: The headaches are the worst. They began earlier this morning, just as he left camp. He remembers turning around to take one last look at the campsite. He could have headed back and just called it quits right then. The headaches foretold what was to come. But he didn't. He can't understand why he made that decision, but here he is.

The headaches now feel like he is being hit with a hammer, not at full force, but a sort of repeated tapping, just enough to hurt but not enough to make him shut down. He tries to recall a time when he had experienced a similar sensation. Grad school. The day when he slipped and his backpack pushed his head onto the ground as he fell. It had been a sharp pain as his face met the pavement, followed by a dull thud every second for the next few hours. It coincidentally ended exactly at the moment the lecture he was supposed to be attending finished too.

He thinks back to that day. That pain of his head meeting the ground . . . that was not as bad as the pain that he is feeling now. Every few seconds, he stops to let it pass. To let it calm down. He knows the pain is temporary, but he wonders if he is causing lasting damage to his brain. He buries the thought and continues.

Polepole

The guide: The guide has been running his adventuring company for a number of years. He was born and bred in Moshi, first working as a guide for another company and then as a business owner, running his own company.

Rather than ascend with every party, he would typically join them for a day to make sure they were well taken care of and then send his crew to take them further. On this occasion, however, he sensed that one of the trekkers needed him. So he stayed.

The guide had more experience than most, and a degree in psychology, which gave him the skills to get a sense of motivation, and to provide mental support as and when it was needed. It was important to his business to guarantee the success of each party. He used what he could to ensure that people would complete the trek.

Polepole

The man: Every breath is a struggle. He draws in air, but it's not clear where it is going. Breathing becomes more and more laboured with each step. He pauses to suck it down. Rationally, he knows that air is going into his body because he can hear himself gulping it. But somehow, it doesn't help. He still feels breathless.

He remains still, hoping, willing, demanding that his body will take in the air that it needs. His mind wanders back to the time he fell into the sea. He has flashbacks of that day, falling into the water, taking in a big gulp of what he desperately needed to be air but was actually seawater. He remembers the feeling of helplessness, of needing to be rescued. This feels like that. Like drowning. He shakes it off, tries to inhale another deep breath, and takes his next step.

Polepole

The guide: The guide stays back with the group. One of the members was clearly not fit: the man. The guide had seen this before, the rest of the group deciding to wait for the unfit member to catch up, making the entire group more fatigued than they should be.

He felt that spending another day to observe the group was necessary. He wanted to be home for Christmas, but he had a nagging feeling that he was needed. He also could see that the unfit person was getting frustrated with his lack of pace. He decided to intervene.

He spoke to each group member, one person at a time, and explained to them how their instinct to be supportive was counterproductive. In other words, what felt right for them would lead to achieving the opposite of the outcome they wanted. He told each group member that they needed to continue at their own pace.

Polepole

The man: His legs are on fire. They have been screaming for relief for at least 98 per cent of the day so far. Each step leads to another jolt in a never-ending cavalcade of pain. His knee hurts, exactly at the spot where a cricket ball slammed into it decades ago. He feels that pain over and over, but intermittently, enough so that he can't anticipate it, can't mentally prepare for it.

In his hands he carries two walking sticks, presumably designed to take the load off his legs and distribute it through his body. Rationally he knows that this is their purpose, but somehow he can't get the rhythm right so that the sticks are effective. Every so often they don't fall the right way and jarring vibrations strike across his entire body. He does not know how long he can keep this up.

Polepole

The uncle: The uncle is in the middle of the pack. He has lost sight of other members that are younger and fitter and are keeping a higher pace than him. Truth be told, he could also keep up with the faster bunch, but is feeling guilty about leaving his nephew behind. He had asked him to train for this, and yet somehow he was still lagging. He felt that the right thing to do was to pause for his nephew to catch up. So he found a tree trunk on the ground and waited. And waited.

Rounding the corner he sees the guide. It is odd because the guide had said he might leave. Furthermore, he is usually following his nephew, bringing up the rear. The uncle fears something has happened.

He speaks to the guide and understands the need for continuing ahead, but is still a little sceptical. He decides to listen to the expert advice and goes at his own pace. He plans to bring this up at the camp later in the day, but for now, he continues.

Polepole

The man: Boxing Day. The day of the climb to the summit. He had been dealing with all manner of pains and aches for four days now, what was another one? The guide woke him up at 5am. It was cold. The type of cold where it feels like it is cutting through your skin. The type of cold that comes at 4,600 metres. In December. What else did he expect?

So far, he has already climbed 2,800 metres. That is nearly 16,000 stair steps. Nearly 850 storeys. He was feeling sweaty and muggy just a few days ago, but now has to wear thermals, sweaters and thick jackets to stay warm. Another 1,400 metres, all in one day. This was the day he would conquer the mountain. In total darkness he starts walking, with just a little headlamp to illuminate the way. A darkness that is alien to city-dwellers with all the light pollution. A darkness which he has never seen. In its own way, it was completely fascinating. An experience that he has not had very often and likely will not have again. Every now and then he turns off the headlamp to get a sense of how dark the environment truly is.

Polepole

The man: Ascending higher, he leaves uncovered ground behind, transitioning into trails covered in snow. The sun is really close and very bright. The reflection of the sun's rays off the snow is blinding. He finds himself struggling to see, squinting as much as his eyes will let him. He remembers his sunglasses. He remembers his balaclava. He had no idea why he was asked to bring these items, why he needed to weigh down his backpack with them, small as they were. Well, now he knows and wonders why he was not more prepared.

He cannot see for more than a few seconds, even through squinted eyes. He looks in his pack for a split second and finds what he needs. He puts on his sunglasses, but they can only be worn over the balaclava. His breath rises from the fabric and fogs up the glasses. He has nowhere to wipe them. He alternates between looking just above the glasses to map out the next few steps and walking. His stick hits a rock and he falls to his knees. The snow is deep enough to slow his walking to a crawl. He would crawl, but his gloves are too wet. He gets up and takes off his foggy glasses, and squints to see the next few steps while wiping them. He continues.

Polepole

The man: He hears voices. Cheering and yelling. He hears his guide's muffled voice behind him. He looks, but can't quite see him. It's too bright. He imagines that the guide is proud of him.

He tries to look into the distance, in the direction of the yelling voices. He can sense that the voices are getting closer. The wind is slicing right through him. He can feel every metre of this climb. He takes off his glasses to chart his route for the next few steps. He can't do it. He knows, in his heart of hearts, he can't. But he keeps walking forward. He takes a step. Two. Three. Four.

No more – his heart is going to beat out of his chest. His head is going to explode. The cramp in his legs is almost normal now. Every couple of steps, he needs to catch his breath. Any more than four steps and a stitch comes. He isn't supposed to be doing this, he thinks. It's not for him. He's too unfit. He's not built for this kind of ordeal. And yet, here he is.

Polepole

The man: How much more? They are yelling out to him. His family, his friends, all there already, egging him to keep going. He looks. Maybe ten steps. Maybe five seconds away. On a normal day. With his normal stride. But not today.

He inches closer but has to stop. Four steps. Then three. Then two. Then one laboured step after another, until he feels an embrace. Hugs. Yelling in his ear. *How do you feel?* How does he feel? Has he done it?

He's done it! Has he done it? There are congratulations. He is asked to stand and pose for a picture. Standing, what utter luxury. He collapses in a big heap but doesn't pass out. He feels a wave of relief wash over him. He's done it. He's peaked. He's reached the summit. He is at the top of the highest point of the entire continent of Africa. He has done it. By himself. Right?

Polepole

Climbing the mountain

It might not surprise you to learn that the 'man' was yours truly.

Summiting Kilimanjaro is quite achievable. Many people attempt it each year and most of them succeed. In mountaineering, Kilimanjaro is unique because it does not have many steep climbs. It can be largely hiked. Hence, many that attempt it complete it.

However, two ingredients are important. The first is fitness. Anyone attempting the climb must prepare accordingly, including regular visits to the gym and climbing stairs, because it really feels like five straight days of that particular activity. The second is motivation: you must want to do it.

I had plenty of motivation, but my fitness was lacking. Lack of preparation is perhaps the most critical reason for not completing the trek. This made my summiting Kilimanjaro more difficult than it needed to be.

Of course, while on the mountain, I couldn't change my fitness. I had to play the hand I had been dealt (even if it was me that had done the dealing). My motivation also wavered at various points. However, my guide was a critical ingredient in my success: without targeted interventions by him, Emmanuele, I would never have reached the top. As it was, Emmanuele was able to use my motivation to compensate for my low levels of fitness and get those oh-so-critical extra bits of effort out of me to keep me on track.

Emmanuele had been involved in a series of world records, serving as guide to a recent record-breaking ascent. His wise words, and a few clever tips and tricks, changed the outcome of the whole experience for me.

This book is a kind of Emmanuele for your life. We all have mountains to climb – big ambitions, goals, dreams. Climbing the mountain is hard. We may not all be Yūichirō Miuras. But we can, with a bit of training and the right motivation, succeed.

I study human decision-making for a living. My research focuses on why high performing people (including doctors, teachers, development and policy professionals, college students) make the decisions that they do, the manner in which these decisions are undertaken, and what motivates them to go above and beyond. In my professional life, I've worked all around the world, conducting field research in Burkina Faso, Indonesia, Pakistan, the Philippines, the UK, Germany and the US, and my work has provided guidance to various government agencies. My work is multi-disciplinary – I'm an economist by trade, but I also look at different fields, especially psychology, to provide the answers to why we achieve (or don't) what we set out to achieve.

Over the course of my career, I have had numerous successes. But many more failures. I have learnt a lot from working on large, long-term projects which require a consistent amount of effort even when the ultimate rewards are uncertain. Undertaking these kinds of multi-year projects with lots of moving parts has informed my research. Through both behavioural science and lived experience, I have developed an understanding of why we don't reach our goals, and devised strategies to help counter some of our instincts that keep us from achieving what we want.

This book takes everything that I've learnt as a behavioural scientist, everything that the different academic disciplines tell us, and couples it with my own experience, all in one place. With a greater understanding of human behaviour (including your own), and with a series of direct interventions, you can use what is here to set an aspiration, understand your behaviour and achieve what you want to achieve.

And, by extension, you can change your life.

But if I were to sum up this book, to simplify all of its insights, research and experiences into a single idea, I would have to return to the briefing I received from my guide on Kilimanjaro, Emmanuele. There was one thing he told me that was essential to remember: *Polepole polepole*. Swahili for *Slowly slowly*.

It's all about you

Consider Jack. Jack is generally a good person. He tries to do the right thing. He works hard, loves, and is loved by, his close friends and family. He is respected by his colleagues. Overall, things are pretty good for Jack.

However, Jack has a problem. Like most people, he has dreams and ambitions. They aren't anything too extraordinary, like climbing K2 in winter or sailing around the world, but they are his. He thought he would have achieved them by now, or be well on the way. But they seem insurmountable. Over time they've been replaced. Replaced by meetings, by work, by random aimless scrolling online, by things that seemed more achievable ... more realistic. He's lowered his aim. Jack has settled.

Jack isn't alone. We've all been Jack at some point. Something seems off in your world. You're not content with how things are working out for you. You have a vague sense of what life *should* be like, and a sense that what you have is different from what you envisioned. You feel doomed to accept the worst kind of disappointment – disappointment in yourself. You're settling.

But why? Why is that the case? Is there something you can do about it? Is it too late? Should you have started earlier? Can you start again?

The Decisive Mind is going to help you understand why your dreams become disconnected from reality. It provides a framework for you to put a plan into action so that your dreams can become reality. Using insights from behavioural science, we are going to discuss all the ways you work against yourself. We'll look at how you can reduce that kind of behaviour. And we'll start replacing it with behaviour that works for you.

This book will not tell you what your goals and aspirations in life should be. I don't mind what you want to use this book for – your career, your family life, your hobbies. Its principles are applicable to any area where you set a target but have trouble reaching it. The goal of this book is to help you understand yourself, how to optimise your behaviour, and how, slowly but surely, to get you closer to the life you envision for yourself.

The good news is that change isn't beyond you. Real, lasting, profound change comes down to the kind of small decisions you make every day. The bad news is, it isn't automatic and it isn't easy. But then, if it was, you wouldn't need this book.

Throughout, I'm going to talk about building a decisive mind. I mean something specific by that. A decisive mind, in the context of this book, refers to somebody who sets an aspiration and achieves it. It doesn't matter what that aspiration is – whether it's your daily to-do list, or the greatest ambition of your life: a decisive mind sets an aspiration, develops goals, identifies decisions and executes. Being able to do this is the secret sauce that you *really* want to sprinkle on your life. You don't need to be extraordinary. You don't need to be different, or be someone you are not. You just need to know yourself and work within your limitations.

Let's return to Jack and his problems to make this a bit more specific.

Scenario 1: Jack has a problem . . . he's overweight. He knows he's overweight. He keeps telling himself he needs to get fitter. Everyone tells him he should. He's starting to have health problems. He knows what he needs to do. It's simple: eat the right kinds of foods and do some exercise. He has tried lots of diets; he's even joined a gym. But the weight stubbornly stays on. It's *hopeless*.

Scenario 2: Jack has a problem . . . he's broke. Again. This happens so frequently that you'd think he would be better at dealing with it. It's not as though there is a specific reason for it, he just doesn't seem to save enough, spends too much on stuff he doesn't need and ends up living paycheque to paycheque. He promised himself that he would be more careful this month . . . and yet he's dipped into his overdraft yet again. It's *crazy*.

Scenario 3: Jack has a problem . . . he gets so stressed that it stops him in his tracks. He knows what causes him to feel so stressed out – his job – and yet it's not as though he can stop going to work. Sometimes it's the little things that get to him, and sometimes it's big things. He hates his daily commute. He knows he shouldn't doomscroll. He knows that constantly ruminating on how best to care for his elderly parents isn't going to help him care for them. But it is so hard for him to come down from the state he gets into; stress and anxiety are ruling his life. It's *ridiculous*.

Scenario 4: Jack has a problem . . . he smokes. In 2023. He still smokes, even though the link to health problems has been shown again and again. He just can't seem to quit. He's wanted to. Many times. He remembers stubbing out his 'last cigarette', wondering why he was doing this. And yet, here he is, standing in the rain, alone, on his lunch break, sparking up. It's *insane*.

Jack's problems weren't selected by me at random. A look at the self-help industry tells us that the most common topics are weight management, finances, stress and addiction – physical, mental and financial challenges. But if we know what these challenges are, then why is it so difficult to resolve them?

To a greater or lesser extent, we are all Jack. You may have identified strongly with one of those problems. But you are not *hopeless, crazy, ridiculous* or *insane*. You certainly aren't alone. And you can definitely do something about it. Any change that you make will be down to your choices. Over the course of this book, we will think through many decision-making scenarios together, and based on your responses, we will figure out how to optimise your decision-making so that you can start living the life you really want.

There are hundreds of books that you can buy on any one of the issues that Jack has above. Learning to have a decisive mind causes you to look past the specific experience. At the core of it all, what we are talking about when it comes to smoking, dieting, stress and finances is decision-making. This is where behavioural science comes in.

Decision-Making: A Framework

Each decision we make, from the smallest to the most significant, can be plotted on two axes: frequency and impact. What to wear on any given day isn't a very impactful decision, but it's one you must make all the time; whether to get married, on the other hand, is a decision you may only make once or, perhaps, a handful of times. Regardless, clearly it has an enormous impact on your life.

This framework, tracking the frequency and impact of every decision we make, is the guiding principle of this book. If you allow it to be a guiding principle in your life, you'll be amazed at what change is possible. We're going to look at this idea from many angles, but if you were to put this book down right now, you have already learnt one essential principle that you can use to start changing your decision-making: **every decision can be situated on a grid of frequency and impact.** Here's a graph to help it stick.

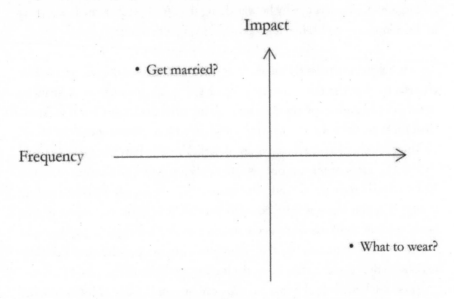

Once we understand the scientific principles underpinning decision-making behaviour, we begin to recognise how we can go about making small changes which allow us to get closer to what we want. If all decisions can be plotted somewhere on this frequency-impact grid, then our ability to make the best choice becomes a matter of resources: how healthy our levels of motivation, effort and patience are.

You need to balance your inner resources against the external costs of the kinds of decisions you make. Looking again at the above graph, we can see that there are four quadrants. This corresponds to four types of decisions: high frequency and high impact, high frequency and low impact, low frequency and high impact and, finally, low frequency and low impact. Learning what type of decision you are making halves the battle. It allows you to pinpoint the sorts of resources you need to dedicate to that decision. Doing so allows you to free up resources by not dwelling on decisions that don't contribute to your goals. Should you choose to, you can then put resources towards decisions that *are* contributing to your goals.

It might be a matter of taking energy away from low impact decisions – whether I should wear the grey suit or the blue suit for a job interview – and putting them into high impact decisions – seeking a professional to help me with my interview technique – so we have a better chance of getting them right. Or it might be a question of turning high frequency decisions – what to eat for lunch – into low frequency decisions, which don't require any thought or will-power once you've made an initial choice – the giant dal you batch-cooked on Sunday evening. Whatever you're aiming for, once you understand what kinds of decisions you need to make to get you there, you can use my framework to optimise your decision-making and align them with your goals.

If this idea seems abstract right now, don't worry. Throughout the book, we'll use stories to illustrate the science and provide you with enough context to internalise the message.

We will also make things practical. You're going to think about aspirations and goals. You will think about decisions that build towards those goals and decisions that work away from those goals (we're often our own worst enemies). Setting an aspiration and a goal are only a single step on the path to reaching it, and we're going to help you see why. By the end, you will come away with a deeper under-standing of yourself, what you want and why you behave in the way you do.

Once we've absorbed the decision-making framework, and realised why we so often get confused over the kind of decision we're making, we will look at techniques to counter these tendencies. We will focus on taking control of your time and your life and using these resources to make your life work for you. With a deeper understanding of your decision-making processes, your aspira-tions, your goals and your limitations, all things are achievable. The most important factor is already growing within you: awareness.

If you read this book carefully and integrate its message, you'll understand why good intentions may not have worked for you in the past. Furthermore, you will develop the tools you need to get the most out of your life. So, let's begin building our decisive mind.

We start with the story of Bill W. and how he overcame the biggest chal-lenge of his life.

CHAPTER I

Just One More Drink . . .
Introducing the Decisive Framework

In 1927 the stock market was hurtling towards the Great Depression. But no one knew it. Wall Street was booming and traders were busy making unprecedented amounts of money. Among them was an unusually driven young man, Bill, whose professional successes hid a growing problem.

Bill was from a humble background. He had grown up with a healthy scepticism of alcohol consumption, not least because his grandfather had been an alcoholic. Bill was conscripted into the US Army in 1916 and commissioned as an officer a year later. Bill had an unusual gift for leadership and being in the military opened doors for him. He was introduced to people with money and status. In 1917, during a dinner at a highly influential household, Bill drank liquor for the first time. Bill found the effects of alcohol quite amazing: the social barriers between him and his hosts dropped, allowing him to have a great time, free of social anxiety. Almost instantly, Bill found that he felt inferior and nervous around others when he hadn't had a drink. This was where Bill's love of – and addiction to – alcohol began.[1]

Fast forward to 1927. Bill had become a margin trader and was making more money than he knew what to do with. He was popular as well, having made many friends, and many small fortunes for those friends. However, Bill's drinking habit was well known. It had crept into more and more of his life, straining relationships, including his marriage. When the stock market closed at 3pm, Bill would hit the bars. He often spent 500 dollars in a single evening. That's more than 7,000 dollars in today's money. Bill's wife, Lois, told a story about him leaving her at the US-Canada border with no money or mode of transport, so that he could go across the border to drink, away from her concerned gaze.

In the stock market crash of 1929, Bill lost everything. He went from being rich to being nearly 60,000 dollars in debt. However, he didn't lose his taste for drinking. Bill continued to drink alcohol in quantities that led to delirium and mental impairment. Lois had long been concerned about his drinking, but it was his repeated lies (even breaking an oath sworn on the Bible) that left her feeling helpless.

In 1932, two Wall Street contacts offered Bill a generous share in a speculative trading firm, but with a stipulation that if he started drinking again, he would lose his share. Bill had hit rock bottom and he knew it. He thought this was precisely the motivation he needed. He signed the contract.[2]

For the first few months, Bill remained sober. Word spread that he was back. His reputation on Wall Street began to improve. He found that he wasn't even *tempted* to drink during this time. However, everything changed during a business trip with some engineers in New Jersey. After dinner, the engineers invited Bill to a poker game. He declined to play but joined them in the room.

The engineers offered him a local drink, an apple brandy known as Jersey Lightning, which he also turned down. As the evening wore on Bill refused further offers of the liquor, even disclosing his problem with alcohol to his companions. As midnight approached, however, Bill's resolve weakened. He reasoned that he had never tried this drink before and the others were enjoying it so much, he was likely depriving himself of an experience. Plus, surely just one drink couldn't hurt. Eventually he gave in to temptation – his one drink turned into a three-day bender. Bill lost everything. Again.[3]

In 1933, Bill found himself in hospital with alcohol addiction for the fourth time. As the year began, he and his wife were penniless, living with Bill's sister and her husband. His brother-in-law was an osteopath and upon witnessing Bill's struggles with alcohol, admitted him to Charles B. Towns hospital, run by a Dr William Silkworth, a noted psychologist specialising in the treatment of alcoholics. Bill's brother-in-law paid for his treatment. Even this show of family solidarity wasn't enough, however – Bill would improve under the hospital's care, but then relapse on being released. He was hospitalised four times and eventually told he would end up either dead or permanently institutionalised, such was the depth of his addiction to alcohol. His case seemed hopeless.

And yet . . . Bill took his last drink on 11 December 1934. He remained sober for the rest of his life. It was an incredible achievement – many had given up on him. However, Bill did not accomplish it alone. He had help and support from an organisation which he himself founded, following a spiritual epiphany during his final bout of hospitalisation. That organisation was Alcoholics Anonymous.

The 12-step programme and the decisive mind

Few of us struggle with such a serious addiction or make such bad decisions that we ruin our lives. Repeatedly. And yet, just like Bill, many of us, despite our other accomplishments, have goals that we fail to reach, dreams that we can't make real. This chapter will teach you how you make decisions, help you to look more closely at them and show you a path to making better ones. The stakes may not be life and death, as in Bill's case, but there are things in each of our lives that could be improved if we develop the ability to follow through on our choices, if our thoughts align with our actions. That is, we don't simply decide something, we then act decisively. This is what I mean by a decisive mind – somebody who sets a course and follows through.

There are a few lessons in Bill's story that are worth highlighting.

First, Bill had strong motivations for quitting alcohol, but most of them were external. The effects they were having on his spouse and his business partners were driving him to stop. But it was not until signing the contract in 1932 that he internalised the true reality of his problem.

Second, while Bill was able to make the right decision many times during the poker game in New Jersey, he eventually gave in. His resistance – and the clarity of his reasoning – waned over the course of the night. Importantly, his prediction about the impact of his decision was very different from the impact the decision actually had. He had decided 'one little drink can't hurt'.

These issues of motivation, effort, patience and perceptions are critical behavioural factors, which affect our decision-making at every level. Over the course of this book, we'll look at how our minds navigate them and what balance makes for better decisions. By understanding how our minds work, and getting a clearer sense of what we're really doing in the moment, we can take the next step and improve our decision-making: we can make it easier to make good decisions and harder to make bad ones.

For now, though, in this chapter we're going to look at the key principles that establish the decisive mind. Firstly, there are **Four Insights** from behavioural science, heavily backed by rigorous evidence, that allow us to think about why we do the things we do. Taking these Four Insights together, I provide a **Roadmap** that allows us to navigate changing our behaviour. Finally, I'll go into more depth on the decision-making framework, which we will call the **Decisive Framework**. This is the chief innovation of this book, introduced in the last chapter. It will help you bridge the gap between naming an aspiration, setting some goals and achieving them. At its heart, the Decisive Framework is a tool that helps you make better decisions, whether that's what to eat for breakfast or whether to marry your partner.

Taken together, the Four Insights, Roadmap and Decisive Framework are the engine driving everything that's happening in this book, and by extension in your life. We're going to spend the whole of the rest of the book looking at them in detail. But in this chapter, I'm going to show you them in precis, ensuring you are familiar with the basic shape of the ideas, so you can start thinking about how they might apply to you and the challenges that you're facing.

Once we've grasped these principles, set our aspirations, established our goals and identified our decisions, nothing is insurmountable.

Bill W. wouldn't have got sober without the organisation he helped to found. To this day, AA is often the frontline defence against addiction problems. It is likely, if you go to your local GP to seek help with alcohol addiction, that they will point you towards the nearest AA meet-up group. But how is it that a programme like AA helps people to achieve sobriety and turn their lives around? What's going on beneath the surface? What does the science say? Why does it work?

AA presents a 12-step plan to recovery. Bill W. warned individuals against trying to apply these principles to other problems. Also, AA uses spiritual beliefs as a form of motivation. I don't replicate the 12 steps in my decision-making matrix in any way. Nor, indeed, do I specifically endorse any single step in the AA programme. Furthermore, this book doesn't have a spiritual component. Still, there are certain truths about human behaviour that underpin the steps and help us to understand the decisive mind.

I want to draw out those behavioural lessons here. We understand better now, with advances in behavioural science, why the programme has had such remarkable success. We will end the book with our own seven steps, with exercises along the way to help internalise each of the messages and insights.

Firstly, here are the Alcoholics Anonymous steps in full:

The 12-step programme by Alcoholics Anonymous	
Step 1:	We admitted we were powerless over alcohol – that our lives had become unmanageable.
Step 2:	Came to believe that a power greater than ourselves could restore us to sanity.
Step 3:	Made a decision to turn our will and our lives over to the care of God as we understood Him.
Step 4:	Made a searching and fearless moral inventory of ourselves.
Step 5:	Admitted to God, to ourselves and to another human being the exact nature of our wrongs.
Step 6:	Were entirely ready to have God remove all these defects of character.
Step 7:	Humbly asked Him to remove our shortcomings.
Step 8:	Made a list of all persons we had harmed, and became willing to make amends to them all.

Step 9:	Made direct amends to such people wherever possible, except when to do so would injure them or others.
Step 10:	Continued to take personal inventory and when we were wrong promptly admitted it.
Step 11:	Sought through prayer and meditation to improve our conscious contact with God as we understood Him, praying only for knowledge of His will for us and the power to carry that out.
Step 12:	Having had a spiritual awakening as the result of these steps, we tried to carry this message to alcoholics and to practice these principles in all our affairs.

The 12 steps anticipate many findings from behavioural science. The first thing to note is the focus on motivation. The steps encourage the user to uncouple their motivation to get sober from external factors and instead anchor that motivation on internal ones. The second point is that the programme asks the user to exert effort to achieve sobriety. They recognise that the journey to sobriety requires effort at various stages. It doesn't just happen; it's the individual who must 'make direct amends'. The repeated calls to a higher power seek to bolster personality characteristics through increasing patience and confidence, and to shift perceptions of what is possible and achievable. These are important behavioural considerations that contribute to success in long-term projects and underpin our framework in the same way. Finally, the steps encourage self-awareness – we have to take an inventory of ourselves, to figure out where we are going wrong and make a plan for the future.

It is also important to note that the process of improvement is slow and operates on thin margins. To achieve lasting change in our lives, we need to start by making modest changes in our behaviour – changes that are small enough to be sustainable. After all, the big change you are looking for isn't easy to implement because if it was, you would have implemented it already! But change is possible. Bill W.'s story illustrates that.

The programme I outline in this book is not based on AA, but it's worth showing the strong behavioural foundations underpinning that programme. These are the sorts of techniques that the evidence shows helps people overcome even the most ingrained behaviours – life-destroying addictions. Drawing on the same foundations will aid us in cultivating a decisive mind.

Four insights from behavioural science

The literature on behavioural science has four important insights for our purposes. These Four Insights underpin the framework that this book is built on. Understanding them (and the evidence behind them) makes it easier for us to understand why the framework is so powerful and how we can best use it to achieve the goals we set for ourselves.

Over the next four chapters that comprise Part 1, we'll explore these insights in depth. We're going to look at the scientific evidence, and we're going to see how the literature in psychology and in economics complement and complicate each other. I think it's incredibly important that you fully understand the science if you're going to make the framework work for you.

But I also think it's important that you have a primer. So, the Four Insights that a decisive mind is built on are as follows.

Insight # 1: Decisions take effort

In perhaps the most famous book on behavioural science, Daniel Kahneman writes about two systems of thinking: System 1 and System 2. System 1 is the automatic decision-making process: decisions are made without any consideration or deliberation. You get up in the morning and you make a cup of coffee, whilst drinking it you read the news on your phone. You've made two decisions there – to drink coffee and to read the news on your phone. But you haven't deliberated, you haven't consciously thought about making these decisions. They just sort of happened. These types of decisions are effortless, you make them numerous times a day.

In contrast, System 2 is the deliberate decision-making process: decisions made via this system are thought-out and considered. You would hope that a decision such as who to marry, or whether to take a job in a new city, are made via deliberation, that is System 2. The distinction between these two systems is dealt with in more detail in Chapter 2, but for now it is important to note that System 2 decisions (those that contribute to behaviour change) take more effort and are harder to make when you are low on energy.

This is critical for our purposes – when you think about your daily routine, most decisions you take are made without deliberate thought. If we want to make changes in our lives, we must acknowledge and internalise the fact that there are difficult decisions that will need to be made, and that to make those decisions, and to follow through on them, takes energy and effort. Because of the effort involved, you are likely to make better decisions when you are rested and relaxed, as opposed to when you are tired and stressed. Take effort into account, meaning that you plan for it. Time decisions so that they can be made when your energy levels are high, rather than when they are low. This gives you the best possible shot at making the right decision.

Imagine you have just arrived home from work. You had to skip lunch because of some important meetings in the early afternoon, and then you had to work late. You have the ingredients for a healthy stir fry in the fridge, but it'll take time to prepare. You quite like the idea of making a stir fry for dinner, but it'll take *ages* and you're hungry *now*. Perhaps you can get a healthy dinner from a takeaway food app. But when you open the app, there's a flashing advert for fried chicken and chips. 30 per cent off!

This situation is all about effort. Because you're more tired and hungry than usual, the effort needed to make dinner looms larger than it otherwise would. Whilst you are consciously aware that the stir fry is the best option, your ability to stick to the plan slips when you think about an alternative. Because hunger is already present, you are more suggestible when a new option presents itself in the moment. Finally, this fast-food experience takes minimal effort: you don't need to get off the couch. If you were to boil it down, the choice was between a meal that required effort, with an uncertain short-term outcome – you might burn the stir fry – and a meal that required no effort, with a known short-term outcome – fried chicken and chips is fried chicken and chips. Thought about in this way, it's no contest – the food delivery app wins every time.

Insight # 2: Why am I doing this again? Motivation

The second, and perhaps the most important, insight is how necessary it is to understand your motivation. If you are working on something that won't pay off until a long time in the future, you need to ask yourself 'why'.

Motivation is complex. It comes from many different places, but we broadly categorise it as 'external' or 'internal'. Internal motivation stems from the task itself; the pain of the effort is offset by the enjoyment from doing the task. A typical example comes from fitness. Some people jog every morning because they enjoy it. They're engaging with the task for its own sake. We call these psychological rewards or intrinsic rewards.

External motivation may come from material rewards (buying yourself something nice because you did well throughout the week) or social rewards (demonstrating your achievements to others). We will cover each of these different types of motivators/rewards in depth in Chapter 3.

Insight # 3: When do we want it? Now!

The third important insight is a question of patience. Patient people persevere with tasks for longer because they are willing to wait for a reward. However, many of us aren't that patient. We want rewards *now* in exchange for as little effort as possible. In general, we seek to maximise pleasure and minimise pain.

The trouble with this is that we can get into the habit of prioritising easy things that pay out straight away (like working our way through our inbox) over harder things that take a long time (like writing a long, but essential, report). We understand intellectually that pain is sometimes necessary to achieve pleasure, but the extent to which we are willing to engage in painful activities depends on both the intensity and the frequency of the reward. The important thing to remember is that when you set your eyes on the long term, you must be aware of your patience threshold and the extent to which you can sustain effort without reward.

A fascinating illustration of this point is shown by our behaviour around saving money. When people do a job that they don't particularly enjoy, chances are they are more likely to spend the money than save it, particularly on items or experiences that they enjoy. There's a reason that pubs the world over are fuller on payday. On the other hand, people who are paid for pursuing their passions are much more likely to make savings from their paycheque. Their need for a reward is lower. This will be covered in detail in Chapter 4.

Insight # 4: Your perceptions shape your decisions

The fourth important insight from behavioural science is that what we think is going on, very often, isn't what's going on at all. Our perceptions differ from objective reality. A lot. This kind of distortion is usually called a 'bias' in the field of behavioural science. The idea here is simple (and will be covered at greater length in Chapter 5): what we think is happening is different from what's really happening, usually because our response is filtered through our mental models.

Sometimes, relying on our instincts is a good policy. But our perceptions can often lead us to make decisions that are not in our best interests. When dealing with uncertainty – where the consequences of our actions aren't easy to know – our perceptions help guide our decision-making. Importantly, our perceptions are generated based on our preferences and emotions. For instance, have you ever checked your bank account and found that there's less money than you expected? That's because your preferences and emotions led you to have a gut feeling about how much you were spending. Of course, you would *prefer* it to be different.

These Four Insights provide the scientific underpinning for everything that I'm going to teach you about cultivating a decisive mind. If you get stuck, or you feel unsure, please come back to the above precis.

These insights lead naturally to three steps we need to undertake when figuring out where to go and how to get there. These three steps are a shorthand for a practical guide to optimising behaviour. We're going to look at the **Roadmap** in greater detail in the chapters that make up Part 2. But let's start by getting a sense of what's in store.

The Roadmap

Step # 1: Set a goal

What do you want to do? What would you like to achieve? At this first stage it's important to reflect on two things: motivation and impact. Where does your motivation come from? How do you think your life will be different when you're on the other side?

If your motivation is coming from within, your perceived rewards are likely to be a lot stronger than if the motivation is coming from others. Then there's impact: this is the primary reward that you will have to focus on, your guiding star.

I make a distinction between an aspiration and a goal. An aspiration is a big picture goal, something that you want out of life, but does not specify any means to achieve it. Get richer. Get healthier. Write a book. Learn a skill. Something like that. Goals, however, are much more precise, much more specific, and include details such as timelines and steps. Chapter 6 will give you all the details.

Step # 2: Check in

The next step on the Roadmap is to structure feedback – that means checking in with yourself. Over the long haul, you're going to need to figure out how, and how often, you'll get feedback about your progress towards your goals. This is a more important step than we tend to realise because feedback is more than just data.

Feedback can be both positively and negatively motivating. If not structured appropriately, feedback that is too frequent can be demoralising, but feedback that is too rare is also demoralising. An optimal level of feedback, based on the type of goal you've set, your levels of patience and confidence, and your motivation, will help you keep striving towards your aims. The more patient you are, the more flexible you can be with structuring feedback. For those that are less patient, setting the right intervals for getting feedback is key. Chapter 7 will give you the science behind structuring feedback.

Step # 3: Cash out

The last step, prior to embarking on our journey to success, is to think very carefully about your rewards. Remember, working towards your goal takes effort, and your brain doesn't want you to make any. No matter how strong your will, you need to balance effort with shorter-term gratifications, ones that are enjoyable to you but do not work against your goals. Here again, creating a structure that works for you is the most important thing. Your patience determines how frequently you'll need to reward yourself for efforts exerted towards your goal – if you are impatient, you'll need to structure your rewards closer to each decision. On the other hand, if you have a strong, internal motivation for doing whatever it is that you are doing, you won't need as many rewards along the way. Chapter 8 will detail these and specifically ask you to think about rewards in three categories: psychological, social and material, and ask you to specify these ahead of time.

Again, I'm going to go into more detail on the Roadmap in Part 2 of the book, but if, in the months and years after reading this book, you feel unsure about the Roadmap, here is a good place to return to.

So, there are four key insights from behavioural science that underpin our process. We have a three-stage map to help guide us to where we want to go.

But there will be bumps along the way that we can't necessarily control for. It's all very well in theory saying that you will set a goal, check in and offer yourself adequate rewards. But how do you actually go about doing that in practice? How do you get by day-by-day? What happens when something unexpected comes up? We need the decision-making framework. The **Decisive Framework** allows us to understand what sort of a decision we are making, in the moment that we are making it, and from there we're able to, hopefully, make a better decision, or, indeed, not bother with making an energy-sapping decision.

In Part 3 of the book, we will put the Decisive Framework together with the Roadmap so that we can go about building a decisive mind.

The Decisive Framework

Having considered our motivation, confidence and patience levels, set our goal(s) and structured feedback and rewards, we need to do the hard part: start doing things that will get us along the path to our goal. At every moment, we will be faced with decisions that contribute to, or detract from, our progress. If you can reliably make the right choice, you, my friend, have a decisive mind.

But how do you make the right choice? This is where the framework comes in.

Every decision you make can be classified along two dimensions: impact and frequency. Decisions can be low or high impact – meaning they do more or less to move you towards your goal or aspiration. And they can be frequent or infrequent – that means we might need to make the decision multiple times a day, or just once in our lifetime.

Taking impact and frequency together allows us to broadly group our decisions into just four categories. That means we only ever make one of four decisions. In order of importance:

Type I: Low impact high frequency decisions
Type II: Low impact low frequency decisions
Type III: High impact low frequency decisions
Type IV: High impact high frequency decisions

Type I decisions are the least important (and less worthy of deliberation), while Type IV decisions are the most important (and worthy of repeated, in-depth deliberation).

For now, the most important thing to understand is that our decisions are often misclassified. That means we waste time and energy making unimportant decisions that don't contribute to our goals. Doing so has the knock-on effect of reducing time and energy that should be spent on those decisions which really matter. Chapters 9 and 10 discuss these misclassifications in detail.

You can classify *any* decision you make within this framework. A large proportion of the problems we face with follow-through and self-control arise from misclassification and the wasted effort that ensues.

So, before we move on, let's look at the decision types in detail. Now, I love food. To help you remember the difference, and hopefully to help you classify your decisions, I'm using a food metaphor.

Low impact-High frequency: TYPE I (APPLES OR ORANGES)

It's mid-morning and you're feeling peckish. You wander into your kitchen and look in the fruit bowl. You have a choice: apple or orange. This is a Type I decision. Apples and oranges are both fruit, both roughly as good for you as each other. Whilst you wouldn't want to eat just apples, or just oranges, at 11am every day forever, whether you have an apple or orange in the grand scheme of things doesn't matter.

Type I, Apples or Oranges, are the daily decisions that we make without even thinking about them: what to wear, what route to take to work, how to greet people, what and when to eat, when to go to the bathroom, when to floss, when to chew gum, when to have coffee, etc. Most of these decisions are made instinctively, with little to no deliberation. When you are making this kind of decision, automatic thinking process is to be encouraged. Sure, maybe you could tweak the impact a little bit, but, in general, don't sweat the small stuff.

Low impact-Low frequency: TYPE II (CHINESE OR KOREAN)

You are organising a dinner for some old friends you haven't seen in a while. But where to go? There's a great Chinese restaurant in town. But a new Korean BBQ place just opened up, too. Reviews of the latter have been good, but you've been to the Chinese place before and you love their Peking Duck. On the other hand, if you've been there before, chances are your friends have, too, and wouldn't it be more fun to try somewhere new?

Chinese or Korean? That's a Type II decision because, whilst it's not a decision you have to make all that often, ultimately, in the grand scheme of things, it won't matter that much which restaurant you go to.

Type II, Chinese or Korean decisions, are made occasionally: whether to buy tickets for a concert, where to go for your next vacation, what kind of washing machine to buy, what kind of computer to get, etc. These decisions have little impact on your life and well being in the long term. However, they're often made with a great deal of deliberation and reflection. These decisions occupy mental resources in part *because* they are less frequent. Reducing the energy invested in these decisions will help you to dedicate more effort towards the remaining decision types.

High impact-Low frequency: TYPE III (VEGAN OR CARNIVORE)

You've read the reports on the health and ethical impacts. You've watched documentaries and have followed a vegetarian diet for six months. But now, after lots of research and experimentation, you've decided to take the plunge. You're going vegan. This is a Type III decision – it has a high impact on your life and on those around you. There are health implications, financial implications and even environmental implications. Most people don't choose to go vegan repeatedly – they do it once, and it informs lots of the other higher frequency decisions that they must make.

Type III, Vegan or Carnivore decisions, are decisions about things like where to live, investing money, whether (and how much) to contribute to a pension, what career to choose, whether to go for that promotion, whether to obtain an advanced degree, whether to get married or have children, etc. These are decisions that we make occasionally but have a high impact on our lives and our well being. Typically (and ideally) these decisions are made with deliberation and controlled thinking. Unfortunately, we are often too bogged down by 'other things' to make these decisions rationally. Some people may become vegan to fit in with friends. Some might eat meat for the same reason. This is not the best way to come to a big decision!

High impact-High frequency: TYPE IV (CRISPS OR NUTS)

The working day is done. You've had your evening meal and you've put your feet up to watch some television. But you could do with a little snack. You have a choice between healthy unsalted, unroasted nuts and significantly less healthy salt and vinegar crisps. Classic Type IV decision. Type IV, Nuts or Crisps, are daily decisions that have enormous impact on our well being, particularly over the long haul. Things like how much sleep to get, whether to buy a high-calorie chocolate bar at the checkout, whether to smoke a cigarette, whether we buy a coffee at the shop or make one at home, etc.

As with Apples and Oranges, you might choose crisps over nuts unconsciously, with little to no deliberation. But, unlike Type I decisions, Type IV decisions have the potential to affect our well being tremendously, particularly due to their frequency. If you eat crisps every night, over the long course of the years you are likely to suffer from all sorts of health problems – heart disease, high blood pressure, obesity. This category is particularly relevant for us as we seek to develop decisive minds: it's the area we are most likely to overlook, but just a little extra effort and planning can make an enormous difference. In this instance, you can make the decision to not buy crisps and so, when you feel a bit peckish, the choice is between healthy, unsalted nuts or . . . nothing.

We'll return to the framework in significantly more detail in Part 3. But again, the above provides a good primer for you to return to if you get stuck or if you haven't read this book in a while.

In the meantime, this chapter has given you a sense of the different kinds of thinking we engage in, a recognition that our decisions can be classified and the insight that we can be strategic in how much effort we put into making them. The Four Insights are a good primer on the science that underpins everything else in this book. The Roadmap explains how we might go about changing our behaviour, and the framework is a method of classifying decisions in a simple, yet highly effective, manner.

Along the way I will get you to do a number of exercises at the end of each chapter. I designed these to make life as easy for you as possible, but remember, you will get out of this book what you put in. So, please pick up a pencil and get ready to mark up the pages. Chapter 11 will make you run through the entire steps (given below) to build your decisive mind around your aspiration. However, it is critical for your understanding to engage in these reflection exercises. You might even enjoy doing these along with a friend who will act as a social motivator! So, without further ado, here is your decisive mind programme:

The 7-Step Decisive Mind Programme
Step 1: Write down your aspiration
Step 2: Write down concrete goals that feed into your aspiration
Step 3: Break up the goal into a series of repeating decisions
Step 4: Classify decisions according to whether they are low or high frequency
Step 5: For each high impact decision, specify a low impact decision
Step 6: Structure rewards (i.e. cash out)
Step 7: Set out your feedback and revision plan

Looks a little daunting? Well, all of these steps are covered in each of the next chapters. So all you have to do is keep reading!

Staying quit

On 11 December 1934, Bill bought and consumed his last drink. Following a spiritual experience, Bill never touched alcohol again for the remainder of his life. He turned his energy towards supporting others who were going through the same experience: this was the genesis of the Alcoholics Anonymous 12-step programme. What is instructive in Bill's story is his journey: finding the motivation to achieve sobriety, acknowledging his weaknesses, understanding why he succumbed to temptation and ultimately mobilising resources towards achieving his goals. It's a remarkable story, but it's one that is shared by millions of people who have achieved sobriety through the AA programme.

Whether you aspire to cut alcohol, save a certain amount, get fitter, or something else entirely, the lessons that underpin this book are universal. They apply to all sorts of aims and individuals. They require an explicit focus on the motivation behind the goal, a clear statement of the perceived reward once the goal is achieved, and deeper understanding of both patience and confidence, to be able to structure feedback and rewards and optimise resources in the service of achieving the goal.

This book is going to take us on a step-by-step journey. We'll learn about the mechanisms behind each step and in so doing give ourselves a greater understanding of what works and what doesn't. At the same time, it's no good just reading. I want you to engage in this book, and engage with the decision-making framework. So, to nudge you in the right direction, at the end of each chapter I'm going to turn things over to you. There's an assignment and a place for you to make note of your thoughts. Over the course of this book, if you work through each of these assignments, you're going to have come a long way towards building a decisive mind.

Box: Your turn!
Assignment # 1
Please put down three things that you aspire to. These should be big-picture aspirations, so write down something broad, which you would like to achieve over a long time horizon (say five or ten years). You might consider aspirations like 'get fit', 'save more' or 'be happy' at this stage. As

we work through the chapters, you will become much more specific and precise. But for now, it is important to simply think about the big aspirations, things that you think would improve your life.

For each aspiration, I would like you to answer three Ws: What, Why and When. At this stage don't think too much about whether it is achievable or not, just write it down. Aim to answer the Ws based on your instincts and feelings as well (the space is limited for a reason!). Over the course of the book, we will transform these into tangible, achievable goals, but for now I want you to put down three reasons that made you pick up this book.

Aspiration 1:	
What do you want to achieve?	
Why do you want to achieve this (how will it change your life)?	
When do you want to achieve this by?	

Aspiration 2:	
What do you want to achieve?	
Why do you want to achieve this (how will it change your life)?	
When do you want to achieve this by?	

Aspiration 3:	
What do you want to achieve?	
Why do you want to achieve this (how will it change your life)?	
When do you want to achieve this by?	

When you've done this, read on – the next four chapters (Part I) are going to get deep into the science that underpins this book. If we understand why we do the things we do, we can figure out how to change.

References

Anonymous. 'Pass It On': The Story of Bill Wilson and How the A.A. Message Reached the World. Alcoholics Anonymous, 1984.

Kahneman, Daniel. Thinking, Fast and Slow. Macmillan, 2011.

PART I:

BEHAVIOURAL INSIGHTS

CHAPTER 2

Long Shifts and Fatal Errors . . .
Decision-Making, Effort and Fatigue

Key lesson: Insight # I: Decisions take effort

If you were to imagine a typical suburban American street, it would be Long Street, in upstate New York. It's nice and clean, with two-storey detached houses on either side. The houses themselves are typical Americana: white picket fences, well-manicured lawns, clapboard houses. Instantly recognisable were one to see them on the screen. Residents, too, are typical middle-class Americans – teachers, white-collar workers, professionals – often young families with children. They enjoy their quiet neighbourhood away from the hustle and bustle of larger cities like the nearby city of Buffalo, New York.

But this picture of calm changed forever on the night of 12 February 2009. It was a cold Thursday, with temperatures just above freezing (33 degrees

Fahrenheit, 0.5 degrees Celsius), but that's not unusual for upstate New York in winter. Just after 10pm, many residents of Long Street were turning in for the night; having got over the hump of the week, they were setting their sights on 5pm the next day, and with it, the weekend.[1]

At 10.15pm, Douglas Wielinski, aged 61, left the family room and went to the dining room to do some work. Doug was a marketing manager at Luvata Buffalo, a Finnish metallurgical company. He was a Vietnam War veteran who occasionally lectured in history at Clarence Central High School.[2] The school superintendent later recalled how committed Doug was to the students, how much he enjoyed sharing his experience. He was husband to Karen, also at home that night, and father to four daughters, only one of whom, Jill, was also in the house.[3]

Then, just off the corner of Long Street and Maple Street, there was an incredibly loud crash. Next, a great fireball lit the street as though it was daylight. People rushed out of their homes. Was it an earthquake? Terrorists? Nuclear war?

What the residents of Clarence Centre were greeted with was nothing short of astounding. The massive fire that lit up the entire neighbourhood emanated from 6038 Long Street. Residents were shocked to see what appeared to be the tail of a plane sticking out of the ground where once a house stood. Just above the ground, the logo of Continental Airlines appeared on the tail. The plane had sheared the tops off two trees, before slamming into the south side of the house. Doug died from multiple blunt force trauma, while Karen and Jill escaped with minor injuries. A pathologist hired by the family stated that, based on the autopsy, Doug's death was comparable to being put in an oven.[4]

How could this have happened?

After a long investigation, the airline concluded the crash was down to pilot error. What error? Why was it made?

Marvin Renslow was aged 47 at the time of the crash. An experienced pilot, he worked out of Newark, New Jersey, but lived near Tampa International Airport, in Tampa, Florida. Company records showed that he had been a commuting pilot since joining the company. By all accounts Renslow was a hardworking man, who had to fit his flight training around other work, often moonlighting in grocery stores and working in travel reservations and sales. He was a family man, living with his wife and two children. He was described as a 'by the book' sort of guy.[5] It was shocking to those that knew him that the cause of the crash was ascribed to pilot error.

By the day of the crash, Renslow had accumulated 3,379 hours of total flying time, 1,030 hours as the pilot in command, and 111 hours on the Q400 airplane.[6] While his path to becoming a pilot had been long and difficult, he was experienced and professional. There had been no recent pause in his flying – he wasn't rusty. Records show he had flown 116 hours in the 90 days preceding the crash. He had no history of accidents or incidents, and no record of driving licence revocation or suspension. His decision-making had been characterised as 'very good' during simulator and flight training, with his greatest strength noted as his 'methodical and meticulous' nature.[7]

On the days immediately preceding the accident, his first officer stated that Renslow handled the airplane well, used checklists and adhered to callouts. Specifically, on the Q400, officers that had flown with Marvin stated he was competent. He created a relaxed cockpit atmosphere but was strict when it came to the sterile flight deck rule, which states that during critical phases of a flight, all non-essential activities in the cockpit are forbidden. There was little to question about his decision-making abilities.

Turning to his health, Marvin's wife reported that he did not have any serious illnesses preceding the crash. He had a little hypertension and he took nutritional supplements. He was also a good sleeper, typically getting eight to ten hours of sleep each night.[8]

A good sleeper. Typically, eight to ten hours a night. Let's wind the clock backwards on the night of the crash.

At 6pm that February night, at Liberty International Airport in Newark, New Jersey, Continental Airlines issued a dispatch for flight 3407, estimated to depart at 7.10pm to Buffalo-Niagara International Airport. It's a short haul flight typically lasting just under an hour. The plane used for this flight, a Bombardier DHC-8-400 (Q400). The flight eventually departed at 7.45pm, a delay caused by the plane arriving in Newark at 6.53pm. So far, so good.[9]

At 1.30pm, the pilot (Marvin) and first officer of flight 3407 reported for work having arrived early. They had been asked to report at that time as their first two flights of the day were from Liberty International Airport to Rochester International Airport, but these had been cancelled due to high winds in Newark, which led to ground delays.

At 12pm, the regional chief pilot met the pilot of flight 3407. He offered to do some office work, which is part of the administrative duties of pilots.

At 11.30am, a flight attendant for another flight reported the pilot eating lunch in the crew room.

At 7.26am, the pilot logged into the online system.

At 5.25am, crewmembers reported seeing the pilot asleep in the crew room.

At 3.10am the pilot logged into the online system.

At 9.51pm on 11 February (the day preceding the crash), the pilot logged into the online system.

No records are available of where the pilot slept that night, but, as we can see, he was at one point asleep in the crew room.

The night of 10 February the pilot had spent sleeping in a hotel. He checked out at 5.15am on 11 February and reported to work shortly after. He had a report time of 6.15am and worked on his shift for 9 hours and 49 minutes.[10]

A long shift. Not much sleep. And then: a fatal error.

By all accounts, Marvin Renslow was a careful, conscientious and dedicated pilot. He was meticulous, a family man, a Christian. Crucially, he was not prone to making mistakes at any time throughout his long flying career. He was not the sort you'd expect to make a bad call.

Yet the flight records indicate quite clearly that the crash was due to pilot error.[11] The plane crashed into the house on Long Street just 5 miles from the end of the runway at Buffalo-Niagara International Airport. Prior to arriving at their destination, the aircraft warned of an impending stall, to which Renshaw, for seemingly the first time in his life, responded inappropriately, setting off a chain of events that led to the aircraft stalling and then crashing. The crash killed all 45 passengers along with 4 crewmembers, and Douglas Wielinski.

On the day preceding the crash, it is clear from the report that Marvin Renslow had not slept well and had been working long shifts. Furthermore, it was clear that he had been sleeping in the crew room, but his sleep was interrupted in the middle of the night when he logged into the system to check and update flight records.

Marvin was *tired* when he was called upon to make a critical decision. It cost him his life, and those of many others.

Decision fatigue

It should be fairly intuitive that when we're exhausted, our decision-making becomes more challenging. Marvin Renslow's case is an extreme one. He was, clearly, very fatigued. As we know, the energy that we expend when making a decision has a huge bearing on how good that decision is. When our energy is depleted, whether that's because we haven't slept for days on end or for far more subtle reasons, making reasoned choices becomes much trickier.

In this chapter, we're going to look at why that's the case, what the science says about it, and how it impacts us when trying to achieve our long-term goals. To do so, we need to go back through the history of my field, behavioural economics.

In 1943, the famed psychologist Clark Leonard Hull published *Principles of Behavior*. In it, he spells out the 'Law of Less Work'.[12] The law says that given the choice of two paths to achieve the same goal, people (and animals) display a marked preference for the shorter path. In other words, if people need to get to the town on the other side of the river, people prefer to take the bridge than to swim.

This simple principle has been around in many forms for over a century, in the fields of both economics and psychology. Economists like to think of things in terms of value and prices. For this reason, economists attach a cost to physical labour, and these costs must be compensated to get individuals to engage in effort. Put another way, if you want me to lug a heavy bag up a hill, you need to pay me to do it. The cost of struggling up the hill is balanced by the payment for having done so.

In simplest possible terms, action follows two rules:

- Do something if rewards are greater than the costs
- Do nothing if costs are greater than the rewards

When weighing costs and benefits, economists use a model of 'utility'. The basic idea is that any action that gives individuals pleasure (getting paid money) generates positive utility, while any action that causes individuals pain (lugging a heavy bag up a hill) generates negative utility.

Using this as our guide, and broken down into its simplest form, when you make a decision, what you are ultimately doing is weighing the benefits/rewards of the decision against the costs. Essentially, just like a business thinking about starting a new project, we engage in a simple cost-benefit analysis. The results of our projected balance sheet lead to our behaviour. If we think the pleasure arising from a decision is going to be higher than the pain of undertaking the decision, we do it (*£500 is a good deal, I don't mind lugging this heavy bag up that hill*), while if the opposite is true, we do not (*£2! You're having a laugh*).

This is a simplified framework. Nevertheless, it explains why we make many decisions we routinely undertake.

Adam Smith was an economist who picked up on this idea early on. Smith was writing way back in the 1700s, and the idea of effort for him usually meant manual labour. That is, people who exerted physical effort at work in return for wages.[13] But since the eighteenth century, economists have used these models in all sorts of labour markets. Today, work may not require much physical labour – think of Marvin Renslow flying his plane. It is not physically difficult to successfully pilot an aircraft, but it requires a huge amount of *mental* labour. Contemporary economists and psychologists have found that mental labour costs us just as physical labour does. If I asked you to design a machine that carries heavy bags up a hill, you'd want to be paid even if, physically speaking, the task was less difficult.

Even though our lives are very different today, the principle Hull put forward in 1943, the 'Law of Less Work', still holds. People minimise mental effort in exactly the same way they minimise physical effort. We always engage in mental shortcuts, regardless of how intelligent or able we are or how experienced we are. If the same reward can be achieved at lower costs of (mental or physical) effort, the human mind tends to choose the less costly action. That's true if you're crossing a river or . . . flying a plane.

A series of experiments was conducted to test the 'Law of Less Work'.[14] The basic setup was this: participants are tasked to select cards from one of two possible decks. Upon selecting a card, a number is displayed between 1 and 9, but excluding 5. The number appears in either the colour blue or the colour purple. Participants are informed that if the colour is blue, then they need to say 'Yes' if the number is above 5 or 'No' otherwise. If the colour is purple, then participants need to say 'Yes' if the number is even or 'No' if it's odd. Participants repeat this task 500 times in total.

Whichever way you cut it, the task is pretty simple – it's certainly not as hard as flying a plane. Still, if the colours stay the same, the task is easier because you only have one rule to remember. But if the colour keeps switching between blue and purple, the task becomes more challenging because participants need to remember the different rules governing the colours. This is where the experiment gets interesting.

Participants had to choose cards between two possible decks. Unbeknownst to them, however, one of the decks was less cognitively demanding than the other. In one of the decks, if a card pulled was blue, then the next card had a 90 per cent chance of also being blue. Similarly, if a card pulled from this deck was purple, the next card had a 90 per cent chance of being purple. Hence, cards chosen from this deck had a high probability of being consistent in the rule needed to solve the trial (above/below 5 or odds versus evens). For the second deck, the probabilities were reversed. The colour stayed the same only 10 per cent of the time, meaning you are flipping between rules 90 per cent of the time.

The authors found that when participants freely chose between the two decks, 84 per cent chose the low demand deck: the vast majority of people. This shouldn't be particularly surprising. Indeed, psychologists had assumed this was the case for years, but it's only recently that experiments such as these have demonstrated it.

For our purposes, though, it's worth understanding the way that this works for different people because what counts as mental effort varies substantially. Another experiment asked individuals to recall a series of letters, but they had a choice in how many they needed to recall. There were more difficult versions of the task (remembering six letters) for more money, or easier versions of the task (just one) for less money. People had to choose the level of difficulty that they were comfortable with and at what level they would be happy with being recompensed.[15]

The result? Different people valued what counted as a mental cost differently – some people were happy to take on the difficult task for more money, others weren't. The findings also suggest that self-control depends on how costly an effort is – everybody has a threshold beyond which they won't push. It's just that different people have different thresholds.

So, two main findings: people vary in the degree of mental costs, and are willing to pay to avoid the task.[16] We need to keep both these findings in mind if we're going to be successful in making the right decisions when trying to achieve our goals, whatever they may be.

Two types of decisions

As we can see, gaining self-knowledge is crucial when you are making decisions. As the purpose of this book is to bridge the gap between setting goals and reaching them, understanding whether you are somebody who is willing to pay to avoid difficult tasks is going to be important when you come to setting goals and structuring rewards. But to build the decisive mind most effectively, I think it's best to understand why we act like we do. What's happening beneath the hood?

As we heard already, Daniel Kahneman suggested that there are two types of thinking that can be applied when we make a decision. We call them systems – two distinct mechanisms operating at different times to reach different outcomes. There is the *automatic system* (System 1) or the *deliberative system* (System 2). These two systems are distinct and used at different times to work on different problems.[17]

Taking each in turn, System 1 (automatic) thinking is classified as effortless, associative and intuitive.[18] It doesn't take much effort to think like this. As we have seen, individuals tend to choose this form of thinking most of the time, and that's especially true when the rewards are low. Examples of this type of decision-making include reading emotions from faces, or catching a ball. Both are enormously complex and difficult calculations that are done in a fraction of a second. Most decision-making in our daily lives occurs this way, and it's a good job, too. After all, you'd never catch a ball if you had to sit around calculating where it was going to land ahead of schedule – there wouldn't be time.

The second is System 2 (deliberative) thinking, which is classified as effortful, reflective and based on reasoning.[19] If you're trying to make your next move in a game of chess or figuring out whether or not to buy a house, chances are you are engaging in deliberative thinking. As we saw in the previous section, our minds try to minimise the use of System 2. Why swim when there's a bridge?

Consider the following problem: A bat and a ball cost £1.10. The bat costs £1 more than the ball. How much does the ball cost?

10p, obviously.

Right?

Wrong. But don't worry if this is where your mind leapt in the first instance. Many people respond exactly the way that you do. This question is taken from the Cognitive Reflection Test.[20] It's a riddle, and it illustrates just how easy it is for our mind to trick us into not engaging with a given problem. The correct answer is that the ball costs 5p, as the bat (which costs £1.00 more than the ball) costs £1.05, for a total of £1.10.

Your brain takes a short cut. Rather than go to the effort of engaging in deliberation, it reaches for the answer that feels right.

Here is another riddle for you to take a crack at, taken from the same Cognitive Reflection Test: In a lake, there is a patch of lily pads. Every day, the patch doubles in size. If it takes 48 days for the patch to cover the entire lake, how long (in days) would it take for the patch to cover half of the lake?

Think about your gut reaction . . . Now think back over it and read the question carefully, forcing yourself to push past that first answer. Did you come up with something different?

In behavioural science, we talk about 'cognitive bias'. This is a departure from the real state of the world caused by the way our brain processes information. What this means is that for many of us, reality is subjective. The way we view the world is coloured by our life experiences, which then manifest themselves in our behaviour. For instance, a tall, heavier built person that has never been in a physical altercation may not hesitate to walk through a dark alley at 4am, while another individual may walk well beyond the shortest path to avoid such a situation. The key point here is that the world may differ for many of us, and those differences are systematic. This means that deviations are common and predictable.

In the example of the riddles, note that once you became aware of this type of thinking, you may well have read the second riddle differently. That's because simply being aware of our biases can help us to mitigate them. Importantly, once we develop a deeper understanding of System 1 and System 2 thinking, we can start working against our blind spots.

An important example of precisely this captured the attention of US sports fans when a study demonstrated racial bias among referees in the National Basketball Association (NBA) in the USA.[21] The authors collected data at the player level for each NBA game played between 1991 and 2003. These data contained performance statistics, as well as minutes played and the number of fouls committed per game. The authors also studied the referee teams that were calling the fouls in each game. The NBA uses teams of three referees for each game. They observe the racial composition of each team, as well as the racial composition of the team of referees. Specifically, they focus on African-American players and white players, as well as African-American referees and white referees.

What they found was striking: referees typically favoured their own race when making marginal calls on fouls. They found that players had up to 4 per cent fewer fouls and scored 2.5 per cent more points when their race matched the race of the refereeing crew. In other words, referees were shown to be biased in favour of their own race.

What is especially interesting about these results is that referees are highly trained officials. They are under incredible pressure and enormous scrutiny in their daily work. Due to the level of training they undergo, and the speed at which they need to make these calls, we can reasonably expect them to be using System 1 processes to make quick decisions in many cases. When relying on such processes, systematic biases creep in. Due to the high level of scrutiny, it is unlikely they are making these decisions when the calls are more straightforward, but the use of System 1 processes, and particularly intuition, can allow a bias that we call 'group-based favouritism' to creep in.[22]

The results of the study were publicised widely, even before the study was published. It's a bombshell finding and received widespread media attention, including front page coverage in the New York Times, and comments from well-known former basketball players such as Charles Barkley.

But this didn't stop the scientists from gathering more data. The authors go on to show that during the 2007–10 period (in the immediate aftermath of the media coverage), the result of referee teams favouring players of the same racial composition disappeared.[23] The results from the new study were electric – they conclude that simply being aware of bias has the effect of reducing biased behaviour.[24]

Trying to decide

So, what does all this mean for us as we go about trying to build our decisive mind? Well, the first point to note is that decisions require effort. That's Insight

1, after all. More specifically, though, decisions that require objective judgements, rather than subjective feelings and intuition, require effort. These decisions are taxing in the same way that physical effort is taxing. By extension, it also means that deliberating over something over and over again can be (and often is) exhausting. That's why, so much of the time, your brain relies on a short cut. Otherwise, you'd be standing in front of the bathroom mirror every morning earnestly thinking over the pros and cons of washing your face before brushing your teeth.

The second point to note here is that, in general, people are cognitive misers.[25] It costs a lot to use your brain and so people are stingy. This means that for a given reward, we always try to take the path of least resistance. The action that brings about smaller cognitive loads is consistently taken. Why cross the cognitive river by swimming if you can take the bridge?

Third, in order to take an action or decision that requires a higher cognitive load, the reward must be seemingly commensurate. That is, higher-effort decisions require higher levels of rewards. You'll swim rather than take the bridge if somebody pays you enough money to make it worth it.

The reason *why* we do this is because our brain has two distinct systems for processing problems and coming up with solutions: the System 1/System 2 framework. According to this, most decisions are taken using System 1 processes because it's easier on our brains. Some decisions are taken using System 2 processes however, and it is important to recognise when and where these decisions are being triggered.

To preserve cognitive resources, our minds take mental shortcuts, which we call heuristics, to solve complex problems. We rely on System 1 processes, meaning that we might overlook information, or only process that information which is easily accessible to us. Think back to our riddles – it's the most accessible information from the questions that makes its way into our answer. We think that the question is asking us something slightly easier than it is. This forms the basis of subjective reality; our world is just that – ours. We're not always operating with an accurate picture of what's going on around us. In fact, most of the time when we make a decision, we do so with incomplete information. A lot of the time, that doesn't matter. But when there's an absence of information, our brain will fill in the blanks. And that's where systematic biases start to build up.

The fact that biases are systematic means that they apply to you and you need to consider them. You shouldn't feel bad. They apply to me too, and to everyone else. What this means is that, in certain contexts, the way you behave is pretty predictable. You rely on System 1 processes and take many decisions based on intuition and gut feelings.

In terms of building the decisive mind, that has huge implications. If your goal is to eat more healthily, you may have thought, when you were setting the goal, that all you have to do is remind yourself to eat healthily when the time comes. But the burden of all this evidence is to show that the healthiness, or otherwise, of your dinner is typically *not* based on your long-term health goals or on what your healthcare provider recommends. It's based on how hungry you feel when deciding on what to eat. You suffer from what scientists call the intention-action divide: you intend to make the right decision, but you often falter when the time comes to make it. The same way the referees in the NBA, with all their years of training and the constant scrutiny, never *intended* to make biased decisions when reprimanding certain players, but when the time came, they did.

You have willpower. You can restrain impulses. You can push decision-making from System 1 towards System 2. But there are limits. Doing so, restraining impulses, pushing decision-making from System 1 to System 2, is limited to the amount of mental effort you can exert without reward, and this level of effort is different for different people. You may happen to be on the lower end of this scale. Don't panic. That's not the end of the world. You just need to find ways to preserve your cognitive resources. That means you need to look through all the many choices that you make and actively consider which choices are taking up a lot of energy, or whether there are ways you can minimise the number of decisions you might take. In Part III of the book, we'll go into much more detail on this, but it's worth starting to think about it now.

For instance, using the healthy eating example, instead of choosing what to eat when you're hungry, when you're tired from a hard day at work, can you make the decision when you are in the right frame of mind? Can you choose what you're going to eat on Sunday morning, just after breakfast? Can you then cook your midweek meals on Sunday evening when you are refreshed from the weekend, and reheat in the microwave when the time comes?

Your brain naturally makes it difficult for you to align your behaviour with your long-term goals. Your intentions with your actions. Your wants with your needs.

But there is hope. As we have seen, simple awareness can help to mitigate these tendencies. If you reflect for a moment on how the first riddle tripped you up, you were probably more careful when coming across the next one. You looked to push past your first instinctual answer. This is awareness in action. It's the first step in recognising that those split-second decisions you routinely make may not be serving your best interests. And, having read this chapter, you are now significantly more aware than you were just an hour or so ago.

Here's a final riddle to ponder: If it takes five machines five minutes to make five widgets, how long (in minutes) would it take 100 machines to make 100 widgets?

If your first answer is 100, it's time to get out of System 1!

The fatal heuristic

We know that Marvin Renslow made a bad call. His plane was stalling and he made the wrong decision. The mistake was his. It cost him his life, and those of everyone on board. A deadly mistake indeed.

Renslow would have faced a stall condition before. Pilots drill their response to stalls from their earliest training, to ensure that they make the right decision when they need it most. In the case of the crash, though, the instruments had been adjusted for icy conditions. Renslow, because he was tired, neglected to account for this when undertaking the decisions during the stall event. Instead, he made a split-second decision based on his previous experience of flying in slightly different conditions. All those drills during his training, those innumerable stalls he had faced before, caused him to think he saw one situation, but actually he was faced with a slightly different one. He was relying on a heuristic. Just like thinking that if it takes five machines five minutes to make five widgets, it'll take 100 machines 100 minutes to make 100 widgets, Renslow carried those previous decisions over, looking only at the most striking information and not accounting for the change in context. A tiny error in thinking. An enormous error in outcome.

The trouble with System 1 processes is that while the processes do a superb job in preserving resources, they are not necessarily 'right'. Designed to be accurate enough for most situations, they leave out context and nuance. This means that they introduce biases, which cause us to make errors in judgement. Thankfully, for most of us, these decisions are not as dangerous as the one faced by Renslow, but many such decisions over a long period of time contribute quite substantially to the difference between what we intend to do and what we actually do.

In the aftermath of Flight 3407, the Federal Aviation Authority recognised pilot fatigue as one of the contributing factors in the crash.[26] In December 2011, the rules included a maximum amount of time pilots could be on duty (between 9 and 14 hours, reduced from 16 hours). Furthermore, pilot flight times were limited to eight or nine hours. In addition, the rules added a minimum rest time of ten hours a day (up from eight hours) before duty day, as well as mandating airlines develop a pilot fatigue plan. This case was notable in bringing pilot fatigue to the forefront of the policy agenda and recognised the effect that fatigue had on decision-making. Aviation experts suggest that the heightened safety in the United States is directly attributable to flight 3407.[27] Just like you, institutions become more effective by becoming aware of their blind spots.

Our brains are lazy and they'll look for ways to conserve energy, doubly so when we're tired. That means that if you are expecting to force yourself to eat healthily through sheer strength of will, it's not going to happen. At some point, you're going to be tired and your brain will rely on a heuristic that takes you away from your goal. You do it automatically. But, once we are aware of this, we can identify triggers which cause the intention-action gap to widen.

In the next chapter, we build on this idea by introducing the role of motivation and how it can enhance the use of deliberative systems in keeping us focused on our goals.

Box: Your turn!

Assignment # 2

Referring to your three aspirations that you put down in Chapter 1, I would like you to think about a time when you had to make a decision that would have contributed to the aspiration, but you chose not to. This might not have been an active choice, but a situation when you went in the exact opposite direction of what each aspiration would have suggested you do.

Think about moments where you gave up. Think about moments where you 'couldn't be bothered'. Where you didn't go for a run, or where you ate that chocolate bar that was crying out to you. Try to figure out what the context was when you made the decision that cut against your aspiration.

Don't feel bad about this! In the past you may have tried to rely on willpower alone, but without an awareness of the behavioural science running in the background, this was bound to fail. This exercise is to aid you in gaining awareness, which, as we saw with those basketball referees, is a huge step in the right direction.

Aspiration 1:	
What was the decision?	
Why did you make the choice that you did?	
What would you change?	

Aspiration 2:	
What was the decision?	
Why did you make the choice that you did?	
What would you change?	

Aspiration 3:	
What was the decision?	
Why did you make the choice that you did?	
What would you change?	

References

Hull, Clark L. *Principles of Behavior: An Introduction to Behavior Theory.* Appleton-Century-Crofts, 1943.

Smith, Adam. *The Wealth of Nations.* Edited by Edwin Cannan, 1776 [1904]. https://www.econlib.org/

Kool, Wouter, McGuire, Joseph T., Rosen, Zev B and Botvinick, Matthew M. 'Decision making and the avoidance of cognitive demand.' *Journal of Experimental Psychology: General* 139, no. 4 (2010): 665.

Westbrook, Andrew, Kester, Daria and Braver, Todd S. 'What is the subjective cost of cognitive effort? Load, trait, and aging effects revealed by economic preference.' *PloS One* 8, no. 7 (2013): e68210.

McGuire, Joseph T. and M. Botvinick, Matthew. 'Prefrontal cortex, cognitive control, and the registration of decision costs.' *Proceedings of the National Academy of Sciences* 107, no. 17 (2010): 7922–7926.

Botvinick, Matthew M., Huffstetler, Stacy and McGuire, Joseph T. 'Effort discounting in human nucleus accumbens.' *Cognitive, Affective, & Behavioral Neuroscience* 9, no. 1 (2009): 16–27.

Posner, M. I. and Snyder, C. R. R. 'Attention and cognitive control.' In R. L. Solso (Ed.), *Information Processing and Cognition.* Hillsdale, N. J.: Erlbaum, 1975.

Stanovich, Keith E. and West, Richard F. 'Individual differences in reasoning: Implications for the rationality debate?' *Behavioral and Brain Sciences* 23, no. 5 (2000): 645–665.

Kahneman, Daniel. 'Maps of bounded rationality: psychology for behavioural economics.' *American Economic Review* 93, no. 5 (2003): 1449–1475.

Evans, Jonathan St BT. 'Dual-processing accounts of reasoning, judgment, and social cognition.' *Annu. Rev. Psychol.* 59 (2008): 255–278.

Frederick, Shane. 'Cognitive reflection and decision making.' *Journal of Economic Perspectives* 19, no. 4 (2005): 25–42.

Price, Joseph and Wolfers, Justin. 'Racial discrimination among NBA referees.' *The Quarterly Journal of Economics* 125, no. 4 (2010): 1859–1887.

Pope, Devin G., Price, Joseph and Wolfers, Justin. 'Awareness reduces racial bias.' *Management Science* 64, no. 11 (2018): 4988–4995.

Banuri, Sheheryar, Eckel, Catherine and Wilson, Rick K. 'Does cronyism pay? Costly ingroup favoritism in the lab.' *Economic Inquiry* 60, no. 3 (2022): 1092–1110.

Axt, Jordan R., Casola, Grace and Nosek, Brian A. 'Reducing social judgment biases may require identifying the potential source of bias.' *Personality and Social Psychology Bulletin* 45, no. 8 (2019): 1232–1251.

Fiske, Susan T. and Taylor, Shelley E. *Social Cognition.* McGraw-Hill Book Company, 1984.

CHAPTER 3

Wisdom of the Crowds . . .
Decision-Making and Motivation

Key lesson: Insight # 2: Why am I doing this again? Motivation.

1906, Plymouth, England: Francis Galton is attending the West of England Fat Stock and Poultry Exhibition. Galton is a polymath. He is already a renowned statistician, credited with inventing the concept of correlation and psychometrics – the science of measuring mental faculties. He is also the inventor of the dog whistle, which he used at the time to test for hearing ability. In nearly all respects, Galton is as close to the idea of a genius as it gets.[1]

On this day, Galton is simply out for a day at the fair, but he happens upon a contest that intrigues him. At the exhibition, a weight judging contest is being held, where a fat ox has been selected and participants are asked to provide estimates of how much the ox will weigh after it has been slaughtered and dressed. The correct guess will receive prizes, though there is a small cost to participate. Galton notes that guesses are written on pieces of paper and submitted individually by participants – meaning that nobody can see what others are guessing. Furthermore, the cost of participation deters random guessing. Galton could see that the individuals providing guesses were experts: butchers and farmers, with considerable experience in judging the weight of various farm animals.[2]

Galton got access to the results and discovered something astounding (which he termed 'Vox Populi' or the 'Wisdom of Crowds'). When he arranged all the guesses in order, he found that the median guess (1,207 lbs) was just 9 lbs shy (0.8 per cent) of the actual weight (1,198 lbs).[3] While each guess was incorrect, the fact that the median was so close to the true value indicates that the sum of all information from a large enough (and appropriately motivated) sample of experts yields the truth – even though nobody was privy to the truth at the time of the competition.

The Wisdom of the Crowd suggests that the collective opinion of an independent group of individuals gets closer to the truth than the opinion of a solitary expert. While Galton was able to empirically demonstrate the existence of such an effect, the idea goes back to Aristotle, who writes: 'It is possible that the many, though not individually good men, yet when they come together may be better, not individually but collectively, than those who are so.'[4] But how do you get the crowd to offer their opinion?

Fast forward to September 2001. Larry Sanger, a philosophy PhD from Ohio State University, declared on Usenet: 'Long live the Wikipedia,' signalling the beginning of the mainstreaming of Wikipedia, itself birthed on 15 January 2001. Sanger was employed by Jimmy Wales and worked for Bomis, the company credited with founding Wikipedia. Jimmy Wales created Bomis with a vision to provide a free peer-reviewed encyclopaedia (called Nupedia). This was a reaction to the expense of owning a set of physical encyclopaedias, which Wales believed the internet would render obsolete (in this, he was right).[5]

However, Nupedia had a problem. Sanger was hired to take the project forward, but Nupedia was difficult to work with. There was a multistep editorial process, which was difficult for the contributors of Nupedia (who worked on a volunteer basis) to use. Growth in Nupedia was extremely slow. A solution presented itself in the form of the new 'Wiki' technology, which allowed web browsers to directly edit pages, making proofing a published article a lot easier. Sanger decided to create a Wiki, to which Jimmy Wales objected, recognising that contributors to Nupedia would resist the Wiki format. To address this, Wikipedia was given its own webpage and was officially birthed on 15 January 2001.[6]

Joseph Reagle documents how many predicted the death of Wikipedia many times over. But the success of the platform is nothing short of remarkable. It is one of the great wonders of the online world. In July 2001, Sanger predicted that Wikipedia would have over 100,000 articles (a little more than print encyclopaedias) in seven years. By September 2007, Wikipedia had reached *two million* articles. The growth of such an open source, volunteer-driven platform is nothing short of incredible. But it wasn't just the growth. Much like Galton's heavyset ox, the Wisdom of Crowds has meant that, over time, Wikipedia has become an accurate source of information. Is it 100 per cent accurate? No. But it is significantly more accurate than its critics could ever have imagined. And we can assume, as more people become involved in the project over time, that it will continue to converge on the truth. Making an encyclopaedia isn't easy. Just ask Microsoft. Their fully funded effort, Encarta, was a costly flop.[7]

So how did Wikipedia obtain so many contributors? Even though the Wiki technology made contributions easier, why did so many decide to contribute? Some editors are compensated, but the vast majority are not. Critics assumed Wikipedia would fail because no one believed that volunteers would be willing to contribute so much time and effort for free. But they did. Why?

William Beutler writes that '[e]veryone involved in Wikipedia has some kind of interest in what it says.'[8] Some of the motives behind participation are intrinsic to the individual (i.e. it appeals to their personality and sense of justice, or they get an ego boost from the demonstration of knowledge). So, most of these people are not getting paid with money. But they are being rewarded. Older economic theories don't predict such collaborative behaviour. But Wikipedia stands as a monument to decentralised crowdsourced effort, a testament to non-monetary incentives.

The science of rewards

This chapter will take a deep dive into the science of rewards. We're going to look at how and why people exert effort even when there is no material interest in doing so. Obviously, there are lots of times when the reward for doing something is fairly straightforward – they may be getting paid for it, for example. This is essential for us because, oftentimes, when you set a goal in your life, the financial reward might be the last thing on your mind. Want to learn a new language or master the trumpet? It's unlikely that anyone is going to pay you. Indeed, if you want to eat healthily, you might find that it's more expensive than subsisting every day on a diet of baked beans and white bread. So, what compensates us for our efforts when we aren't getting paid?

Again, all of this background science is essential to understand if we are to have the best shot at building a decisive mind and making the right choice time and time again, over the long haul. In brief, this chapter is going to focus on three distinct types of rewards, which will each contribute to our achievement of goals and aspirations:

- Psychological rewards – referring to intrinsic incentives, rewards coming from within. Critical, but unstable.
- Social rewards – referring to social incentives, rewards coming from others in the form of competition, feedback and support. Useful, but can be unstable.
- Material rewards – referring to extrinsic incentives, rewards coming from things that we provide ourselves or others provide for us. Useful, stable, require additional resources.

Sounds good? Let's begin.

The science of motivation has a history. An early, and very well-known, example is Abraham Maslow's 'Hierarchy of Needs', which Maslow put forward in 1943. The idea is that human beings have a series of basic, psychological and self-fulfilment needs. These needs follow a distinct hierarchy. Only upon the fulfilment of basic needs (the need to eat and sleep, the need for safety) do psychological needs become noticeable.[9] Maslow's work on the hierarchy of needs has been useful for organisations to think about what trade-offs employees make when they sign a contract. For example, the need for emotionally fulfilling work is all well and good, but it's lower down the list of priorities than more basic needs, such as pay.

A further refinement is Alderfer's ERG theory which takes the same idea and collapses the categories into three main ones: Existence (needs associated with physical and psychological survival), Relatedness (the need for community) and Growth (the need for fulfilment and self-development). These needs are set in the form of a pyramid, just like with Maslow. Basic needs are highly motivating if they are lacking, but if not, higher needs step in.[10] In order to motivate employees, organisations must identify which needs are being fulfilled by the work that is on offer and structure rewards accordingly. That means that if people are using their job to fulfil existence needs, the rewards need to focus on pay and career progression. But if they are using the work to fulfil a need for personal growth or community, then good work should be rewarded by opportunities to spend time with family, or the chance to master a skill.

In Chapter 2, we introduced the concept of utility. It means that when we do something, some effort is exerted which causes displeasure, which must then be balanced by some form of reward. Lug a heavy bag up a hill, get paid £500. When viewing the world like this, rewards generate motivation. A simple way to represent this is:

- Do something if rewards are greater than the costs
- Do nothing if costs are greater than the rewards

In the real world, though, rewards can be more complicated. They might take on the obvious, external incentives like a paycheque, for example. But there are internal incentives, too. People might decide that it pays to do a difficult task if they feel happier afterwards. People may decide to learn a language or play the trumpet because getting good at something brings them satisfaction. We might join a sports club because we want to lose weight, but we stay because we become friends with our clubmates.

Individuals differ in their motives. It's not just a case of internal or external. And it's not simply a case of having needs met. A more contemporary theory of motivation comes from the psychologists Richard Ryan and Edward Deci, which is labelled Self-Determination Theory (SDT).[11] This research has been extensively covered in popular psychology books, but often at a fairly surface level. According to SDT, motivation can be broadly classified into three categories: Amotivation, Extrinsic Motivation and Intrinsic Motivation. Within the category of Extrinsic Motivation, further subcategories are based on how the behaviour is regulated – how a person stays on task. Regulation of behaviour can stem from outside the individual, via a paycheque, for instance. But perhaps more interestingly, the individual can motivate and reward themselves, too.

What's startling is that different types of motivation have different impacts on our behaviour. Clearly this insight will be enormously helpful to us as we go about trying to build a decisive mind. SDT, then, is an important contribution from psychology not simply because it differentiates external and internal forces of motivation, but because it allows us to understand the effects that they have on our behaviour.

Outside of psychology, economics has come up with some slightly different explanations for the same problems of motivation. Researchers have traditionally focused on financial incentives. But as we've seen, effort can be both physical and mental, and therefore rewards can too.

To better understand what's going on here, we are going to look more closely at the three main types of rewards. These are: (1) Material (extrinsic) rewards, (2) Psychological (intrinsic) rewards and (3) Social rewards.

Material (extrinsic) rewards

The first and most basic form of incentives are extrinsic. They come from outside of ourselves. Economists tend to use a narrow definition of extrinsic incentives: money.

At the heart of the study of economics is the study of how incentives affect behaviour. In the 1960s and 1970s, a series of classic economic experiments was conducted in a lab.[12] They used cash incentives to study individual behaviour. The conclusion that emerged was that putting a financial incentive on a certain behaviour gave it a *value* – a measurable amount of benefit to a person. Cash rewards work for three very straightforward reasons. They are 'monotonic'. That means that more reward is preferred to less reward, or £10 is always better than £5. They are 'salient', meaning that they are a reward that is dependent on behaviour – your paycheque comes when you've completed your work for the month. If you don't turn up, you'll get fired, meaning no payment. And they are 'dominant', meaning that they are the most important way that you are rewarded – you'd rather take a bad boss and a paycheque than a good boss and nothing.[13]

These experiments kicked off a revolution within economics. Researchers started testing incentives in all kinds of topics, but for our purposes we're going to focus on just one area: labour markets. The first rigorous investigations into labour economics were the so-called 'gift-exchange' experiments. Employers needed to publicise wages and based on these wages, employees select who to work for and how much effort to put in. Wages are costly for employers and effort is costly for employees.

What was striking about these experiments was that they started to suggest why employers would often offer wages that were higher than what might be expected for a particular job. Employers offered higher wages because they attracted better employees: employees who put in more effort. When wages were higher than predicted, effort was also higher than predicted. The authors interpreted this to mean that employers and employees were exchanging 'gifts'. If one party offers a gift, the other reciprocates.[14] Or, put more simply, treating people well motivates them to work harder. We might call this a carrot.

But that's not the whole story. There is a carrot. But there is also a stick. A more recent study looked at a real-world situation.[15] Experimenters paid people to alternately press a and b on a keyboard for ten minutes. Participants amassed one point for each a-b alteration they successfully completed. Some workers were provided a salary and were informed that their score in the task would not affect their payment in any way. In this situation, there are no monetary incentives to go the extra mile. Over the course of ten minutes, participants successfully completed 1,521 button presses on average. What slightly astonishes many economists is that it was so many! They could have got away with just pressing a, then b, and then walking off!

But other participants were provided with a different contract. They were paid by how many points they scored. In one version of the experiment, participants were given an extra 1 cent for every 100 points scored. In another, participants were given 4 cents for every 100 points scored, and, finally, 10 cents for every 100 points scored. Each of these conditions increased effort, with the 1 cent version generating an average of 2,029 button presses (a 33.4 per cent increase), the 4 cent version generating an average of 2,132 button presses (a 40.2 per cent increase) and the 10 cent version generating an average of 2,175 button presses (a 43 per cent increase). Note, however, that while effort increases with the pay rate, the effort does not increase at the same rate as pay. Going from 1 to 4 cents for every 100 points (a 300 per cent increase), effort increased by only 6.8 per cent. Going from 4 to 10 cents (a 150 per cent increase), effort increased by 2.8 per cent. Increasing pay increases effort, but at a diminishing rate, displaying a phenomenon known as 'diminishing returns'.

That means that effort does not rise linearly with reward. You can't just continuously reward people and expect ever increasing amounts of effort on their part. And that goes for you, too. You can't endlessly reward or punish yourself into exerting more effort. Thankfully, carrot and stick are not the only methods to motivate.

Psychological (intrinsic) rewards

The SDT definition of intrinsic motivation is narrow: it focuses on our motivation to do a task for the sake of the task itself. But why might you be doing it? It's one thing to take up running because you like running. But it's quite another to take up running because you want to raise money for a charity dear to your heart. Scientists have therefore expanded this to also include the output of effort, i.e. the mission or purpose.

This is an area of focus for me as an academic. Along with my co-authors, I conducted an experiment to test mission-based motivation. We worked with a group of university students in Indonesia. They were asked to perform a simple but boring task. But, instead of being paid, we told the students that for each unit of effort they provided, we'd donate a certain amount of money to the Indonesian Red Cross Society, a well-known charity in Indonesia.[16] We also measured students' voluntary donations to charity. Perhaps unsurprisingly, we found a positive relationship between those who donated voluntarily and the amount of effort they put into the task when they knew a charity would benefit. In other words, doing a task becomes easier when the task has a purpose behind it that aligns with their values.

We also tested task-based motivation. We conducted an experiment with healthcare workers in Burkina Faso. We believed that workers are more likely to try hard on tasks that they like, which for healthcare workers tends to involve diagnosing and treating patients. On the other hand, we also believed that tasks that people don't like doing, they're less likely to bother with – for instance, for our workers, pointless-feeling admin (the bane of healthcare professionals the world over). We assigned our healthcare workers randomly to one of three conditions.[17] In the first, we forced them to sit and stare at a blank screen. I know. Cruel. In the second, we made them move sliders across a screen. And in the third, we had them diagnosing and treating computerised medical cases. We found that relative to the unmotivating tasks (black screen and sliders), participants exerted nearly three times more effort when the task was intrinsically motivating.

In the examples given above, the mission is pro-social, meaning that the effort is generating some sort of public good. But that doesn't need to be the case. Effort can be meaningful to you but have no effect on wider society. Two experiments demonstrate that the mission need not improve society or wellbeing to be motivating. It just needs to serve some purpose. It doesn't even have to be a particularly useful one!

In a particularly interesting experiment, researchers asked participants to build Lego sets for pay. They split the participants into two groups, each getting paid based on the number of sets they built. However, one group saw each set they built dismantled in front of them, while with the other group, the set was kept intact. This experiment simulated purpose. The first group's effort served no purpose; it was being dismantled right in front of them. The second group's effort served a purpose as the sets were being kept intact. The researchers reported that participants in the condition with no purpose built an average of 7.2 Lego sets, while those in the condition with a purpose built an average of 10.6 – a 47.2 per cent increase.[18] Like I said, it doesn't have to be a useful purpose. Any kind of purpose seems to work.

In some of my most recent research, my co-authors and I asked participants to decode a five-character word for a fixed wage. It was a meaningless task that they got paid for. In parallel, we had another group solve the same puzzles, but doing so filled in the gaps to a short story, and thus provided the task with some purpose. We were astonished to find that adding purpose to the task – even the fairly flimsy purpose of reading the short story – nearly *doubled* the amount of effort the participants were willing to put in.[19] In short, whether the task is imbued with a purpose that is prosocial or not, individuals respond to this source of motivation by increasing their effort.

All of this is to indicate that motivation that comes from within is critical. You don't always need some external factor, like a payment, or a treat, to motivate yourself. Material rewards are useful in conjunction with psychological rewards, but psychological rewards are your primary reward mechanism. This will prove to be an essential ingredient in building our decisive mind.

Social rewards

The third and final category is social motivation. That's the role other people play in making you put some effort in. There are all kinds of ways others can play this role. Perhaps there are social norms that motivate us – we don't want to look a certain way, for instance. There is social approval or disapproval – we might do something because it will make others think well of us. There's even competition – there's a reason that athletics world records are most often broken during competition rather than in training: running, throwing or jumping in competition with others spurs the athletes to new heights.

My co-authors and I have added competition to experiments that we've run to study its effect on motivation. We did so in the computerised decoding task that I described earlier. In one condition, participants were provided with no additional incentive. But running in a second treatment, participants had their effort benchmarked against their peers on a 'leaderboard'. Now, again, this competition was meaningless. The winner didn't receive any additional financial incentive. They just won bragging rights. Bragging rights in their totally meaningless code-word solving skills. Furthermore, bragging rights stated to no one in particular (the participants were not allowed to communicate or discuss). Still, the results showed that even though the financial incentives were identical, the presence of a leaderboard induced much more effort. Individuals exposed to the leaderboard treatment increased output by 56.8 per cent over the baseline.[20] Perhaps unsurprisingly, though, this effect was strongest in people that demonstrated high levels of competitiveness. Not everybody responds well to competitive environments, just as not everybody will find purpose and meaning in pro-social causes.

Just as some people are motivated by helping charities, others are motivated because they like winning. For our purposes, layering in lots of different types of rewards gives you the best opportunity to pay your effort dues when it matters.

What does this mean for you?

Humans are motivated by several factors. I've offered a broad category based on Deci and Ryan's self-determination theory. These categories are important to know and consider when you think about how to offset the costs of effort. All types of rewards can be powerful: even the founders of Wikipedia struggled to anticipate the sheer volume of content produced by their contributors in the absence of financial incentives. These sources of motivation provide rewards that individuals use to offset costs. In later chapters we will learn to structure different rewards for actions in service to goals and aspirations.

The three forms of motivation are incredibly important. Without at least one of them driving you in each decision, you aren't going to be able to do the things that you want to do over the long haul. Whilst we will go into much more depth in Parts II and III of the book, for now it's worth thinking about how you might use these three forms of motivation when trying to achieve the life that you want. Remember:

Material (extrinsic) rewards are crude, but very useful and straightforward. If you want to give yourself a material reward, look for a way to **pay yourself**. It doesn't have to be with money, you might reward hitting your workouts every week with a trip to the movies, or even a day off!

Psychological (intrinsic) rewards are more subtle, critical but unreliable. They need to be present, but also need to be maintained. They're related to imbuing what you are doing with **meaning, or making it fun**. If you want to get fit and you hate running, don't force yourself to do a marathon! Do something you enjoy. To further your motivation, tie it to some deeper purpose – make your fitness goals align with your aim to raise money for a charity, or to inspire your partner or children to live healthily, too.

Social rewards matter enormously. We use the performance of others to improve our own performance. Sticking with our fitness theme, join a club or a group and **get competitive!**

The great thing about motivation and rewards is that they aren't fixed – you can do things to hack them. Over the course of weeks, months and years, sometimes that might mean doing something to boost your material rewards, sometimes it might mean doing something to boost social rewards. But, when motivation is running low, there's almost always another lever that you can pull. Remember, **Insight # 2: Why am I doing this again?** The answer to this might be as simple as 'because if I do I'm going to get paid' or as complex as 'to show my kids how much I love them'. It doesn't really matter how, but to motivate yourself, there needs to be an answer to the question.

In Part II of the book (the Roadmap), we're going to look at how you can schematise this process, but for now, just as in the previous section, allowing yourself to get to grips with these ideas, to become more aware, will begin the process.

The people's encyclopaedia

The safe bet back in the early 2000s was that the Wikipedia experiment was doomed. And yet, here we are. As I write in 2023, Wikipedia has about 6.5 million articles in the English language alone. It has faced numerous challenges, but it's still standing, still growing and still improving. There were no external motivations to help Wikipedia grow – hardly anyone was getting paid, no one was getting wealthy. That meant that intrinsic factors had to lead the way. People wanted and enjoyed contributing their knowledge to a grand project that they believed in. They were encouraged by social motivations, too. Egos were engaged and flattered, or ruffled, as different users competed to show who knew the most about a subject. Slowly but surely, the quality and number of articles improved over time.

For economists and psychologists, the classic motivational device is financial. Financial rewards compensate the costs of effort, so we work in exchange for money. Money brings pleasure, work brings pain. Lug a heavy bag up a hill, receive £500. But this is far too simple a story. Looking at the example of Wikipedia with everything that we've learnt during this chapter in mind, it's obvious that psychological factors bring pleasure – including doing the work itself. Presumably lots of people edit Wikipedia articles because ... they like it.

Others edit articles because they believe in the project – the contributions they are making are a single brick placed in the giant wall of public knowledge. Others might use it for virtue-signalling: when they turn up to work on a Monday morning, they tell everybody who'll listen that they spent their whole weekend editing articles on Wikipedia. Others may quietly correct historical inaccuracies, believing that telling the true story of past atrocities is an act of justice.

There is a lesson contained here that is essential for our purposes. The Wikipedia project is, from the outside, a seemingly impossible task. Make an accurate encyclopaedia from scratch for free. You would imagine it couldn't be done (and many did). And yet, even such a seemingly impossible task can be overcome when the appropriate motives are tapped into.

Box: Your turn!

Assignment # 3

For this assignment, I would like you to look over your aspirations again, but this time think about the different types of motivation that currently apply to them. Think a little more deeply about your motives. You can look over what you wrote for Assignment # 1 in Chapter 1. What I want you to do next is think about the three types of rewards that you expect to gain upon achieving each aspiration.

Don't worry about how realistic these are at the moment, the main thing you want to focus on is the perceived rewards across each of the three domains.

Aspiration 1:	
How will it change your life (from Chapter 1)?	
Extrinsic rewards:	
Intrinsic rewards:	
Social rewards:	

Aspiration 2:	
How will it change your life (from Chapter 1)?	
Extrinsic rewards:	
Intrinsic rewards:	
Social rewards:	

Aspiration 3:	
How will it change your life (from Chapter 1)?	
Extrinsic rewards:	
Intrinsic rewards:	
Social rewards:	

References

Brookes, Martin. *Extreme Measures: The Dark Visions and Bright Ideas of Francis Galton.* Bloomsbury Publishing PLC, 2004.

Galton, Francis. 'Vox populi (the wisdom of crowds).' *Nature* 75, no. 7 (1907): 450–451.

Herzog, Stefan M. and Hertwig, Ralph. 'Harnessing the wisdom of the inner crowd.' *Trends in Cognitive Sciences* 18, no. 10 (2014): 504–506.

Landemore, Hélène and Elster, Jon, eds. *Collective Wisdom: Principles and Mechanisms.* Cambridge University Press, 2012.

Reagle, Joseph M. Jr. *Wikipedia @ 20: Stories of an Incomplete Revolution.* MIT Press, 2020.

Maslow, A. H. 'A theory of human motivation.' *Psychological Review* 50, no. 4 (1943): 370–396.

McLeod, Saul. 'Maslow's hierarchy of needs.' *Simply Psychology* 1, no. 1–18 (2007).

Alder, G. S. 'Employee reaction to electronic performance monitoring: A consequence of organizational culture.' *Journal of High Technology Management Research* 17, no. 6 (2001): 323–327.

Deci, Edward L., Olafsen, Anja H. and Ryan, Richard M. 'Self-determination theory in work organizations: The state of a science.' *Annual Review of Organizational Psychology and Organizational Behavior* 4 (2017): 19–43.

Smith, Vernon L. 'An experimental study of competitive market behavior.' *Journal of Political Economy* 70, no. 2 (1962): 111–137.

Smith, Vernon L. 'Experimental economics: Induced value theory.' *The American Economic Review* 66, no. 2 (1976): 274–279.

Fehr, Ernst, Kirchsteiger, Georg and Riedl, Arno. 'Gift exchange and reciprocity in competitive experimental markets.' *European Economic Review* 42, no. 1 (1998): 1–34.

DellaVigna, Stefano and Pope, Devin. 'What motivates effort? Evidence and expert forecasts.' *The Review of Economic Studies* 85, no. 2 (2018): 1029–1069.

Banuri, Sheheryar, and Keefer, Philip. 'Pro-social motivation, effort and the call to public service.' *European Economic Review* 83 (2016): 139–164.

Banuri, Sheheryar, Keefer, Philip and De Walque, Damien. 'Love the job . . . or the patient? Task vs. mission-based motivations in health care.' *Policy Research Working Papers* (2018).

Ariely, Dan, Kamenica, Emir and Prelec, Dražen. 'Man's search for meaning: The case of legos.' *Journal of Economic Behavior & Organization* 67, no. 3–4 (2008): 671–677.

Banuri, Sheheryar, Dankova, Katarína and Keefer, Philip. *It's Not All Fun and Games: Feedback, Task Motivation, and Effort* (No. 17–10). School of Economics, University of East Anglia, Norwich, UK, 2017.

CHAPTER 4

Good Things for Those Who Wait . . . Decision-Making and Time

Key lesson: Insight # 3: When do we want it? Now!

Marie Curie won the Nobel Prize in Physics in 1903. But the first woman to win the Nobel Prize in Economics did so more than 100 years later, in 2009: Professor Elinore 'Lin' Ostrom, a remarkable woman. Lin investigated how societies shared 'the commons' – resources like water, land and energy. When she began her research, academics believed we faced a 'tragedy of the commons' – that collective resources would inevitably be depleted when there was no obvious way to police their use. Lin showed us why this wasn't true.

The 'tragedy of the commons' is where an individual puts their interests ahead of those of the group. The most famous example describes a group of cattle herders grazing their animals on 'common ground'. From the perspective of each individual herder, it makes sense to increase the size of their flock. If you have more cattle, you can make more of whatever you sell – meat, milk or leather. But if all the herders did this, they would ruin the common ground because it only supports so many animals. The 'tragedy' is that individuals acting in a rational, self-interested way will ruin things for everybody in the long run. People put short-term profits ahead of shared, longer-term goals.[1]

But Lin's research overturned this idea. She demonstrated that, in the real world, people solve the problem through cooperation, communication and trust. They don't act out of pure self-interest; they figure out a way to manage the commons.[2]

It was this research that won her the Nobel Prize. But, for our purposes, Lin's journey is equally as interesting. Her patience and resilience led her to the highest honour an academic can achieve. And it is patience and resilience that we are interested in finding out more about here.

Lin was born in 1933 in Los Angeles, California. Her parents separated at a young age and her mother raised her alone. This meant that, while she did not grow up in poverty, she was not well off either. She attended the affluent and successful Beverly Hills High School but was a 'poor kid in a rich kid's school'. This was an enormously important factor in her later career, though, as around 90 per cent of Beverly Hills High School students went on to college. Lin was one of them. She attended UCLA, paying for her tuition by working at the bookstore and library.[3]

At the time, women were treated very differently from their male counterparts. There was marked discrimination against women in the study of mathematics. Women without top marks in algebra and geometry were *not allowed* to take trigonometry. Lin, despite being an excellent mathematician, had a gap in her mathematical knowledge – and this meant she was unable to study economics. At UCLA, she studied political science, graduating with honours in 1954.[4]

After graduation, Lin began looking for work. There were primarily two roles for educated women at that time: schoolteachers or secretaries. To that end, employers requested information about her typing and shorthand skills. She had none – she hadn't studied shorthand or typing at college. But Lin persisted: she went about learning shorthand through a correspondence course simply to get a first position within a firm. She joined a business that had never hired a woman for any position other than a secretary. Despite this tough environment, after a year of working at the firm, she was promoted to a managerial position.

Around this time, Lin became interested in pursuing a PhD in Economics at UCLA. However, she was discouraged as, once again, she did not have the required mathematical training due to the discrimination she had faced in high school. She approached the political science department where she had completed her undergraduate degree. At the time, the department was reluctant to admit women as the faculty felt that women with PhDs could only get jobs at a city college – this was not a good look for a department intent on building a strong reputation. Still, after much-heated discussions within the faculty, they admitted four women (out of a class of 40). Lin was one of them.

Lin defended her dissertation and obtained her PhD in 1965. She studied the water industry in Southern California, working with her (eventual) husband Vincent Ostrom, an associate professor. After graduating, however, she struggled once again. Just as the faculty had predicted, prestigious universities were reluctant to hire women. Vincent, now her husband, received an offer to become a full professor at Indiana University and Lin decided to go too. At Indiana, they offered her a visiting assistant professor position – they needed someone to teach a course on American Government. After a year, they offered her a role as a graduate advisor. Lin had managed, just, to land a permanent position.[5]

At Indiana, Lin returned to the study of the commons problems. She travelled and conducted extensive field research – often sitting in on local council meetings where commons-type problems were being discussed. One of her many research trips took her to a small farming community in a developing country. It was here that Lin spotted a lone cow, standing in a small field, surrounded by a barbed wire fence. This was odd. Why was it separated from the herd? Why put it in such a small enclosure?

She enquired about the cow among the villagers. The local farmers informed her that this cow had been placed in ... 'cow jail'.[6]

Any villager caught violating the commons rules – taking too much water, grazing their cattle where they shouldn't – would have their cow incarcerated.

Whilst in cow jail, anyone from the village could milk the cow, apart from the villager who had abused the rules of the common. This, Lin recognised, was a bespoke punishment that made sense for that community, which they readily implemented and enforced to solve the commons problem. It also highlighted just how difficult it would be for a central government to devise a solution to a commons problem when the commons is as vast and as vague as something like a welfare state. Nevertheless, the fact that Lin showed that the 'tragedy of the commons' isn't inevitable changed the course of the world we live in.[7]

It's an amazing insight, and one that flew totally in the face of the orthodoxy at the time. Lin was working in a competitive field – she was not the only brilliant researcher investigating commons problems. Yet why did her insights point in the opposite direction to those of her colleagues?[8] Why, when they had similar or better levels of access, did they argue precisely the opposite?

Besides her intellect, which was self-evident for any who interacted with her, Lin had a key skill that her largely male contemporaries lacked. Other researchers sat in on meetings. They listened. They absorbed. They took notes. And later they'd come back to these notes, and their recollection of the meetings, and write up their discoveries. But Lin had trained to write shorthand in order to obtain that secretarial position many years previously.[9] She didn't need to recollect the meetings – a process which was highly sensitive to bias. Lin could generate entire transcripts from the meetings due to her shorthand skills. While others would come back from meetings with only their understanding of what had been discussed, Lin returned to her office with hard data!

Lin's story is instructive for two reasons. Even though she faced considerable discrimination to simply enter her field, even though that hostility seemed only to intensify as she took her place among the ranks of academics, and even though she faced an endless parade of challenges due to her gender, Lin Ostrom rose to become one of the most important economists of the twentieth century. The very same discipline that rejected her as a young woman bestowed their highest honour on her over 50 years later. Her story is a par excellence example of toughness. She was never discouraged. No matter what was thrown at her, she overcame it.

If there is one word that I would use to describe Lin Ostrom, it is this: resilient.[10]

Patience and present biasedness

The question we're going to look at in this chapter is: how do we deal with recurring adversity? How, when the universe appears to be telling us to give up, do we ignore the signals and plough ahead? How, ultimately, do we learn to power through? And what role does it have in developing a decisive mind? How do we develop Lin Ostrom levels of resilience? How can we learn to be patient?

To set about answering these questions, we first have to figure out what patience *is*, and how people like Lin Ostrom cultivate it.

In a seminal paper on the topic of self-control, researchers wrote that infants are 'ruled entirely by a pleasure principle that demands immediate satisfaction'.[11] Any parent of very young children knows this to be true and will have experienced precisely this in the howling demands for affection, food or a nappy change. Over time, as a child grows into an adult, they manage to learn self-control. They learn to delay immediate rewards for future (often larger) rewards.

However, there is considerable variation across people in the extent to which they can exert self-control. Some seem able to delay rewards consistently, others almost never. In addition, individuals vary in what they apply self-control to, with some able to do so across multiple domains and decisions, while others are only able to do so in some domains but not in others. For instance, a person may always be able to maintain militaristic discipline when it comes to their work life and yet transform into a tiny baby ruled by the pleasure principle when in the presence of ice cream.

It may seem self-evident that those that are able to suppress their infantile tendencies are more successful than those that do not. But is there any data to back this up? A classic experiment authored by Walter Mischel and others on how delayed gratification works seems to show this. Young children (typically pre-schoolers) are given a choice between a small immediate reward and a larger reward with a time delay. The rewards are typically things the children value, most famously a marshmallow placed in front of them – hence the name of Mischel's bestselling book: *The Marshmallow Test*. The delay can be large (a week) or small (ten minutes).[12]

This example offers a simple way to measure delayed gratification: those that take the smaller immediate reward struggle to delay gratification. Follow-up studies showed that children who prefer to delay rewards demonstrate higher intelligence, are more likely to delay gratification in other areas, and exhibit greater tendencies towards helping others.

Overall, the studies reported that those children who were able to delay gratification experienced better life outcomes as they age.[13] Willpower really seems to be one of life's silver bullets – if you can delay gratification and stick out doing something you don't particularly want to do for longer, chances are you're going to be happier and more successful than your peers who struggle. Clearly then, being able to delay gratification is an essential skill to cultivate.

Our ability to delay gratification is broadly defined as 'patience'. Very young children exhibit a wide variety in patience – some children are extremely patient, willing to wait, and some . . . less so. But if children exhibit such diversity in their levels of patience, what does that mean for patience itself? Is it something that's innate? Or is it something that we can learn? What's the psychology of patience?

If it's something that we learn, it will be an essential tool as we try to build a decisive mind.

Studies in patience are not just related to children and adolescents. Patience has also been studied in adults. Results from a study involving delaying a financial reward showed that patience is significantly related to having a lower body mass index, lower likelihood of smoking and higher levels of exercise.[14] One study gives an extremely clear indication that patience is helpful in our ability to set goals and stick to them. Whilst trying to understand different types of patience, researchers split domains where patience was exercised into interpersonal, life hardships and daily hassles. Patience here is understood to be a personality trait, defined as the likelihood an individual will 'wait calmly in the face of frustration, adversity, or suffering'. The author correlates how patient the subjects were in the lab with self-reported measures of goal pursuits and found that individuals high in patience exerted more effort in pursuit of their goals, and furthermore reported higher satisfaction from achieving their goals.[15]

Building from what we learnt last chapter, this implies that the intrinsic rewards we receive from attaining a goal are higher in those individuals who are also more patient – a double whammy. Overall, the results show that individuals with higher degrees of patience are more likely to exert effort to achieve a goal, likely driven by higher perceived rewards for goal attainment. Clearly then, patient people are more likely to develop decisive minds. They may even have them without reading this book, the gift of some mix of environment and genetic factors. Unfortunately, the majority of people aren't especially patient. We need to learn patience. Can we?

The author of this study went on to report the results of an intervention designed to increase patience. This intervention was intended to help the participants boost their levels of patience, like doing a guided meditation.[16] This is critical to our project, but controversial, too. Some researchers believe that patience is a personality trait – it's fixed, innate and can't be changed. Those pre-schoolers who were able to resist the delicious marshmallow would continue to be more patient than their peers who could not. But that might not be the whole story. The scientific results are promising, but still early. They show that in the immediate aftermath of an intervention, patience levels increase; there is at least some evidence that you can cultivate patience.

Measures of patience, in both the lab and the field, are associated with impulsive behaviours. Other studies show that patience is predictive of credit card borrowing and financial literacy, smoking, alcohol consumption and nutrition.[17]

But if you feel you are low in patience, there is hope. Evidence suggests it can be a malleable trait – certain interventions, such as meditation and cognitive behavioural therapy, can aid you in boosting your levels of patience.[18] And the simple practice of being patient, necessary for all of us at various times in our lives, would, it seems likely, give rise to improving patience.

So, remember, patience really is a virtue.

The waiting game

Economists have also studied the problem of delayed gratification. Through their own experimentation, they have shown that we apply a discount on future rewards to make them more comparable with immediate rewards. The higher this discount factor is, the smaller the future reward becomes. Their experiments were very similar to Mischel's marshmallow tests: they asked participants to choose between a smaller payment now and a larger payment later. The experiment asked participants to undertake several choices, with each choice varying the size of the later reward. This constitutes a measure of 'time preferences'. Or, to put it more simply, it puts numbers on where our 'patience' actually is.[19]

These experiments returned fascinating results. We might reasonably assume that we discount future rewards consistently. Take a simple example: suppose someone offered you £50 today or £51 tomorrow. Chances are that you (like me, and most other people) would lump for the £50 right now. Now consider the following situation: someone offers you £50 in a year or £51 in a year and one day. Chances are, when faced with this situation, you would take the £51. In both instances, you would get £51 on the same day. But why is the reasoning different?

Here's another example: imagine that someone asks you to choose between doing seven hours of physical labour in four weeks' time and eight hours of physical labour in six weeks' time. Most people would choose to engage in seven hours of work in four weeks' time. However, if you are asked to choose between seven hours of hard work today or eight hours' hard work in four weeks' time, the data suggests that most people choose the longer days' work about a month in the future.[20]

What is going on here? We can see clearly that these aren't logical decisions, but they probably feel familiar to us. This phenomenon is broadly labelled present biasedness: the tendency to assign greater value to 'now', or the near future. Getting right down to brass tacks, what this means is that self-control is difficult. If we value the present much more than the future, clearly we are going to struggle to delay gratification. 'A bird in the hand is better than two in the bush' is an idiom written into the human psyche at the deepest level.

So, the evidence suggests that we gravitate towards immediate smaller rewards over longer-term but higher rewards – just like Walter Mischel's infants who lunged for the marshmallow that was right in front of them. But our present biasedness might shift depending on what it is that we are doing. One experiment asked participants to choose when to do jobs at work – in the present or in the future. Participants could change their plans to shift work from the present into the future, or to shift work from the future into the present. The authors found that upon getting this choice, participants tended to move work from the present to the future, rather than from the future to the present. Why do today what can wait until tomorrow? Clearly, there's a strong present biasedness indicated. But, when they conducted a similar task with monetary rewards, the authors found less evidence for present biasedness, indicating that individuals tend to be more present-biased when making effort decisions rather than monetary ones.[21]

This idea of individuals having different degrees of present biasedness over different domains has generated considerable interest among economists. Research has shown that individuals display more patience for monetary rewards than for food, alcohol, chocolate and fizzy drinks, and other primary goods, such as sugar or beef.[22] That's probably because monetary rewards are easier to quantify than goods and effort, which are harder to convert into units of pleasure and pain. Ten pounds is ten pounds. But what is the value of a chocolate bar? Is it its cost? Or is it how it makes you feel?

What all of this is telling us is that our *perceptions* of the costs and benefits of the activities we undertake affect our decisions, and that time is one way we modulate those perceptions. We tackle the issue of perceptions in Chapter 5 but for now, when thinking about the way in which we can build a decisive mind, it is important to understand that we have a bias towards the present, and this manifests more strongly in some areas (for instance, food) than in others (like money). Furthermore, between individuals, there is considerable variation in their ability to delay present rewards for future rewards.

Patience and the decisive mind

Patience is the virtue of those who 'wait calmly in the face of frustration, adversity or suffering'. It is the delaying of immediate gratification in favour of a larger reward at some later date, rewards that in real life, rather than lab experiments, may never come. Patience varies between individuals, and within individuals: you might be patient in one area of life but not in another. We've learnt that patience is an uphill battle – we tend to be present-biased, preferring small rewards now rather than big rewards later.

In terms of the message of this book, and in terms of attempting to set a goal and stick to it, we need to internalise the idea that our future can be affected (and often is affected) by our tendency to prefer earlier rewards. Impatience is correlated with a slew of undesirable behaviours such as unhealthy eating, greater smoking and alcohol consumption, gambling and other types of impulsive behaviours. If you have picked up this book because you want to start a business, it's clear that having very high alcohol consumption is going to distract from that goal. But this principle works itself through in more subtle ways, too. The fact is, what you do today has an enormous bearing on your life in a year, two years or five years. It just doesn't *feel* like it.

In Part III, we'll talk about the Decisive Framework, but for now, it's important that you understand simply that your brain tricks you into believing that any reward that you are about to get is more valuable than the rewards you might get in the future. This is the challenge before us: to resist!

While we will deal with this in greater detail later, note that there are ways to help. Acknowledging and understanding the problem is the biggest step in the right direction. Doing so can help us design temptations out of the process or build in what we might describe as positive temptations. The fact is, we are all impatient. It's better to work with this than against it.

Back to Lin

Now that we better understand patience and present bias, it perhaps comes as less of a surprise that Lin was both unusually resilient and unusually successful. Early on in her career, Lin was faced with a decision-making problem. Told that she was unable to take advanced mathematics courses because women without high marks were forbidden, she was shunted down an administrative route. However, she was denied secretarial jobs because she hadn't learnt typing or shorthand. Then, having proved her worth to a firm, she was denied managerial jobs because of her gender. She was denied admission into an economics programme because she did not have adequate technical skills – again, due to gender discrimination. She was nearly denied admission into the political science PhD programme because the administration were unsure whether she would get a job after graduating. Their fears weren't unfounded; she did have trouble finding a job, again due to discrimination, and very nearly failed to join a university as a post-doc so that she could continue conducting research.

But she overcame. Lin not only achieved all these things, she was the first woman to receive the Economics Nobel Prize, and the first political scientist to receive a Nobel Prize. At many (many) points throughout her career, she defied expectations and achieved things most people only dream of. In her biography, she highlights the impact of obtaining the managerial position early on in her career. She learnt 'not to take initial rejections as being permanent obstacles to moving ahead'. No matter how resilient we are, very few of us are going to achieve the sorts of things that Lin Ostrom achieved in her amazing life and career. But we can all take inspiration from her story. We can all learn 'not to take initial rejections as being permanent obstacles to moving ahead'.

We are almost ready to start discussing the Roadmap for the decisive mind, but there is one further behavioural insight/piece of the scientific puzzle that we need to understand first: our perceptions.

Box: Your turn!

Assignment # 4

In this task, let's break down your aspirations a little further. First, I would like you to think about one single decision that would feed into your aspiration, something that you might come across that contributes to your aspiration. For example, if your aspiration is to save money, think about a situation that you might face where you can either save money or not (so buying a cup of coffee, or some shoes that you might not really need). Think of a single decision for each aspiration (or as many as you can muster).

Next, I would like you to imagine an infinitely patient person, someone who can delay rewards endlessly. What would they do?

Then, imagine an incredibly impatient person, someone who always puts immediate rewards first. What would they do?

Finally, think honestly about what *you* would do. What would you typically do on an average day when faced with the same choice? Are you closer to the impatient person or the patient one?

Aspiration 1:	
Describe the decision:	
What would an infinitely **PATIENT** person do when facing this decision?	
What would an infinitely **IMPATIENT** person do when facing this decision?	
What would you typically do when facing this decision?	

Aspiration 2:	
Describe the decision:	
What would an infinitely **PATIENT** person do when facing this decision?	
What would an infinitely **IMPATIENT** person do when facing this decision?	
What would you typically do when facing this decision?	

Aspiration 3:	
Describe the decision:	
What would an infinitely **PATIENT** person do when facing this decision?	
What would an infinitely **IMPATIENT** person do when facing this decision?	
What would you typically do when facing this decision?	

References

Ostrom, Elinor. *Governing the Commons: The Evolution of Institutions for Collective Action.* Cambridge University Press, 1990.

Ostrom, Elinor. 'Tragedy of the commons.' *The New Palgrave Dictionary of Economics* 2 (2008).

Ostrom, Elinor. 'Collective action and the evolution of social norms.' *Journal of Economic Perspectives* 14, no. 3 (2000): 137–158.

Nordman, Eric. *The Uncommon Knowledge of Elinor Ostrom: Essential Lessons for Collective Action.* Island Press, 2021.

Harding, G. 'The tragedy of true commons.' *Science* 162 (1968): 110–117.

Mischel, Walter, Shoda, Yuichi and Rodriguez, Monica L. 'Delay of gratification in children.' *Science* 244, no. 4907 (1989): 933–938.

Mischel, Walter. 'Preference for delayed reinforcement: An experimental study of a cultural observation.' *The Journal of Abnormal and Social Psychology* 56, no. 1 (1958): 57.

Mischel, Walter. 'Delay of gratification, need for achievement, and acquiescence in another culture.' *The Journal of Abnormal and Social Psychology* 62, no. 3 (1961): 543.

Mischel, Walter, Shoda, Yuichi and Peake, Philip K. 'The nature of adolescent competencies predicted by preschool delay of gratification.' *Journal of Personality and Social Psychology* 54, no. 4 (1988): 687.

Shoda, Yuichi, Mischel, Walter and Peake, Philip K. 'Predicting adolescent cognitive and self-regulatory competencies from preschool delay of gratification: Identifying diagnostic conditions.' *Developmental Psychology* 26, no. 6 (1990): 978.

Sutter, Matthias, Kocher, Martin G., Glätzle-Rützler, Daniela and Trautmann, Stefan T. 'Impatience and uncertainty: Experimental decisions predict adolescents' field behavior.' *American Economic Review* 103, no. 1 (2013): 510–531.

Schnitker, Sarah A. 'An examination of patience and well-being.' *The Journal of Positive Psychology* 7, no. 4 (2012): 263–280.

Meier, Stephan and Sprenger, Charles. 'Present-biased preferences and credit card borrowing.' *American Economic Journal: Applied Economics* 2, no. 1 (2010): 193–210.

Khwaja, Ahmed, Sloan, Frank and Salm, Martin. 'Evidence on preferences and subjective beliefs of risk takers: The case of smokers.' *International Journal of Industrial Organization* 24, no. 4 (2006): 667–682.

Weller, Rosalyn E., Cook III, Edwin W., Avsar, Kathy B. and Cox, James E. 'Obese women show greater delay discounting than healthy-weight women.' *Appetite* 51, no. 3 (2008): 563–569.

Chabris, Christopher F., Laibson, David, Morris, Carrie L., Schuldt, Jonathon P. and Taubinsky, Dmitry. 'Individual laboratory-measured discount rates predict field behavior.' *Journal of Risk and Uncertainty* 37, no. 2 (2008): 237–269.

Kirby, Kris N., Petry, Nancy M. and Bickel, Warren K. 'Heroin addicts have higher discount rates for delayed rewards than non-drug-using controls.' *Journal of Experimental Psychology: General* 128, no. 1 (1999): 78.

O' Donoghue, Ted and Rabin, Matthew. 'Doing it now or later.' *American Economic Review* 89, no. 1 (1999): 103–124.

Augenblick, Ned, Niederle, Muriel and Sprenger, Charles. 'Working over time: Dynamic inconsistency in real effort tasks.' *The Quarterly Journal of Economics* 130, no. 3 (2015): 1067–1115.

Odum, Amy L., Baumann, Ana A.L. and Rimington, Delores D. 'Discounting of delayed hypothetical money and food: Effects of amount.' *Behavioural Processes* 73, no. 3 (2006): 278–284.

Odum, Amy L. and Rainaud, Carla P. 'Discounting of delayed hypothetical money, alcohol, and food.' *Behavioural Processes* 64, no. 3 (2003): 305–313.

Estle, Sara J., Green, Leonard, Myerson, Joel and Holt, Daniel D. 'Discounting of monetary and directly consumable rewards.' *Psychological Science* 18, no. 1 (2007): 58–63.

Ubfal, Diego. 'How general are time preferences? Eliciting good-specific discount rates.' *Journal of Development Economics* 118 (2016): 150–170.

CHAPTER 5

Did You See the Gorilla?
Perception vs Reality

Key lesson: Insight # 4: Your perceptions shape your decisions

In early 2018, shortly after returning from the Christmas break, Paul Romer was feeling perturbed. He had spent a year and a half as chief economist of the World Bank and he was growing suspicious of foul play. He was concerned about the intellectual honesty of some aspects of the Bank and was mulling these over as he headed into an interview with the *Wall Street Journal*.

The interview was to be devastating for him.

Romer was an extremely well-known and well-respected economist. He graduated from the University of Chicago with his PhD in 1983.[1] In his dissertation he had written about an important aspect of economic growth that had not been captured in models at that time: the role of innovation and technological change. Specifically, he showed that research and development was one of the primary engines of growth for a business, and by extension, for the economy. Previously, economists assumed that technological change 'just happened' – it was the natural course of events. But Romer demonstrated that technological change was the direct result of human capital – that is, the people that companies choose to invest in.[2]

Human capital differs substantially from physical capital. A great innovation, one fantastic idea, has a spillover effect that can impact the whole economy. '[T]his special characteristic of an idea, which is if [a million people try] to discover something, if any one person finds it, everybody can use the idea.'[3] Romer ran with this insight and it led him to study how growth occurs, opening up whole new fields of study within economics. This work eventually led Romer to a Nobel Memorial Prize in Economic Sciences. He was as brilliant as they come.

But on that morning in January 2018, Romer had been thinking about one of the World Bank's most influential products: the Doing Business Report.[4] This report was issued annually and ranked countries on how easy it was to work in them. It was a hugely influential product because many large organisations made investment decisions and risk calibrations based on the rankings. In addition, policymakers around the globe took credit for improvements in the rankings. Overall, the report had considerable influence within a country and internationally, and though an evaluation reported modest effects on developing countries, it carried clear political weight, with many politicians offering improvements in the rankings as evidence for their success.[5]

Due to the lack of data, authors of the report often made decisions on a set of indicators and comparison countries. As these indicators and countries change year on year, comparing rankings across years isn't accurate or fair. However, in the real world, many countries of course make comparisons and often announce improvements in their rankings as great successes. To the World Bank's credit, the methodology for calculating the rankings was always published with the report itself, so the process was transparent. But there are many choices that researchers make when developing this methodology and the process for making these is not declared – it also differs year to year. Ultimately, the researchers changed the rules to some degree each year, rather than working from a set concrete template, and therefore the rankings were subject to fluctuations caused by the biases of whoever was coming up with the rules each year. Due to this, Romer considered the rankings to be suspect. And he was right.[6]

He told the journalist from the *Wall Street Journal* exactly this, citing the treatment of the government of Chile in particular. He noted the drop in the published rankings for Chile during the tenure of Michelle Bachelet as president from 2014 to 2018. Bachelet is the leader of the Socialist Party of Chile. Her predecessor (and successor), Sebastian Pinera, was the leader of the conservative, 'National Renewal' party, under whose tenure saw an increase in Chile's ranking. The report showed that the ease of doing business in Chile reduced when the leader of the Socialist Party was in power and increased when the leader of the Conservative Party was in power.[7]

The shifting of Chile's position was not just an academic problem. The drop in the rankings during Bachelet's tenure coincided with a drop in foreign investment into Chile. But these rankings came from an institution that was also conservative in its political orientation, at least from a fiscal perspective. The journalist wrote the story accusing the World Bank of unfairly influencing their own rankings because of political bias. Romer resigned from his post shortly after, a full two years before his term was up.

The Centre for Global Development issued a blog post where they recalculated the rankings using a fixed methodology. They did not find that Chile dramatically dropped in the rankings as had been reported by the World Bank.[8] The analysis seemed to indicate something sinister going on. But an independent inquiry conducted by the bank into the Doing Business report found no evidence of maliciousness, but rather a general negligence. The Bank has now discontinued the report and the individual in charge has, like Romer, since resigned.[9]

We can't tell if anybody stacked the deck to punish Chile's socialist Premier. But even if one assumes that the mistake was purely down to negligence, it's an enormous shock. You would expect the flagship intellectual product produced by an elite institution to go through some quality checks prior to publication. Especially when the potential outcome has such huge implications for all those involved – both heads of government around the world, citizens and the World Bank itself. Furthermore, note that the pattern in question was observed by Romer over the four-year period of Bachelet's presidency and at least one term of Pinera's presidency. It seems impossible that, were quality checks being performed rigorously, they failed every year.

What is much more likely, however, is the role of cognitive biases. The World Bank is generally a conservative institution, with mostly economists in its data and research departments. That the Doing Business rankings increase with conservative policies and decrease with liberal policies may not raise an eyebrow with these individuals – it affirms their world view. However, imagine if the data went in the opposite direction. The economists would likely want to double-check the figures if every time their favoured politicians came to power, they precipitated a decline.

This phenomenon is suggestive of a specific type of cognitive bias known as confirmation bias. And it shows just how essential your perceptions can be. Sometimes, even when the facts in front of your nose suggest one thing, you may see something else if it chimes with your deeply held beliefs.

The science of perception

This chapter explains the difference between our beliefs, what we think is going on and the actual concrete facts of our reality. It's a crucial distinction to make, and one of the chief differences between behavioural science and economics. Economists have long assumed that all you need, if you are making poor decisions, is more information. But recent research makes clear that decision-making is prey to all kinds of problems with the way in which we perceive the world, regardless of the amount of data at our fingertips. Economists at the World Bank aligned the report with the way in which they believed the world *should* work, rather than the way in which it *did* work. The science suggests that the amount of evidence required to change our behaviour is much higher when the data goes against your views, in comparison to when the data conforms to your views.[10]

We might have experienced this in our lives. We may feel, for instance, that we are a fast learner. We'll seek information that confirms this is the case – you picked up how to use the new computer system at work far quicker than everybody else, for example. But it's possible that there is contradictory information out there, too – you still can't speak a word of French, despite multiple hours wasted on your favourite language learning app. You pay attention to the first piece of information because it affirms your view, whereas the second doesn't catch your attention. Which piece of information you pay attention to matters because it becomes your reality – your subjective, rather than objective, view of the world. Clearly, in this example, telling yourself the story that you are a fast learner has a bearing on how well you might learn things. It may mean that you don't put in as much effort as somebody who thinks that they are not a good learner. On the other hand, it may fill you with confidence that you can pick up a new skill, meaning that you begin the hard work sooner than others and are buoyed throughout by a positive outlook. Either way, neither of these behaviours is built on a rigorous analysis of whether or not you are a good learner. Truthfully, you've no idea how well you learn in comparison with others. When building a decisive mind, when trying to set a goal and then stick to it, this matters enormously. The fact that we don't perceive the world accurately has to be built into our plans.

So, to get a better understanding of all of this, we're going to dive into the science of perception.

When we make a decision, we use the data that we have to divine the best possible choice. But there's an issue: we have limited attention. That means that we sort, often unconsciously, the information that we are presented with and only pay attention to that which this sorting process shuffles to the top. This is related to something we covered in Chapter 2 – the idea of our brain making shortcuts to preserve cognitive resources. Here, though, it is a distinct phenomenon. Everybody carries an image of the world around with them in their head (what some behavioural scientists call 'construals' or 'mental models').[11] The decisions they take are based on this image. But it's an image constructed in your brain – it's not the full picture. It's not the real world. Therefore, we often make decisions based on limited information, or, perhaps more accurately, on our *perceptions* of the situation, rather the situation itself.

Here's an easy way to think about it. Imagine that one day you're wandering through the jungle. On the ground ahead of you, out of the corner of your eye, you see a red-and-black striped creature, long and thin, coiled up and you're about to tread on it. Your heart leaps out of your chest, it's beating nineteen to the dozen, and before you know what's going on, you're sprinting in the opposite direction. You took several pieces of information. Your location in the jungle, the shape, size and colour of the thing that you briefly saw, and they fit a story that you tell yourself about the world: it's a snake. This information caused you to decide: run! It's only when you get back to camp and you tell somebody about this experience that you are informed of new information: Somebody left their climbing rope earlier that day on the trail that you were walking along – it's finished in a Dennis the Menace-style red and black stripe.

Essentially, we do this to preserve cognitive resources. Our brains are wonderful tools that help us organise and make sense of the world. But taking in all the information that the world provides is far too much for any one brain to handle. So, we often pick and choose the information that we pay attention to, or the information we retain, which over time, leads to biases in decision-making. As a reminder, a bias is not a random error. A bias is a systematic departure from objective reality. The fact that these deviations are systematic means that they are predictable and can be overcome. We will discuss strategies to overcome them in a bit more detail in Part III, but for now it's more important for us to come to a deeper understanding of the science of attention and perception.

Selective attention

The idea behind selective attention is simple: when our attention is focused on some specific task, we tend to miss out on other information that occurs at the same time. There is fairly robust evidence for this, some of which has gone viral on the internet.[12] The most famous version of the experiment features a video of a group of people playing a simple game of basketball. In total, six players are visible on screen, split into two teams, one team wearing white shirts, the other wearing black shirts. The players of each team pass a basketball to each other in a simple order repeated over the course of the video, from player 1 to 2 to 3 back to 1 and so on. The task for the participants was to mentally count the number of passes made by a particular team (either black or white, randomly assigned).[13]

Halfway through the video, a remarkable event occurs. A person wearing a gorilla suit emerges. They enter, dressed as a gorilla, on the right side of the screen, dodge the players, beat their chest whilst facing the camera, before ambling out of shot. Participants are asked to report the number of passes they counted. They are then asked whether they noticed the gorilla. Overall, the results find clear support for selective attention: across all conditions, nearly half of the participants failed to notice the gorilla. These findings replicated earlier ones reported by a series of papers. What is even more notable is that the event was what a researcher might describe, somewhat bathetically, as 'highly salient'. That is, it's hard to miss a person dressed as a gorilla under normal circumstances. The authors also reported that many of their participants who missed the gorilla did not *believe* that they had missed the gorilla until they rewatched the tape. They thought the researchers were tricking them.

When attention focuses on one area, details from unrelated events occurring in the same space get missed. This leads to a divergence between our perceptions and objective reality. Essentially, our perceptions are based not on the information that enters through our senses, but which information we're concentrating on.[14] This divergence between perceptions and reality yields what we understand as a bias in our cognition: a systematic deviation of our perception from objective reality. We can imagine how this can wreak havoc in our lives and on our ability to build a decisive mind. For instance, if you are focused on your career, you might take your eye off the ball in your closest relationships and then, seemingly without warning, an argument erupts. But of course, the warning signs were there – just like the gorilla – yet your attention was elsewhere.

Psychologists have documented a huge number of cognitive biases. But for our purposes, there is one that's particularly pertinent: confirmation bias. Confirmation bias is a type of selective attention. It's when we use information to confirm what we think we know, rather than evaluate it objectively. We are subject to confirmation bias both when we search for information, but also when we try to remember information, or when we are presented with two competing pieces of information.

Confirmation bias is stronger in those views that we hold more dearly. Consider the following situation: when was the last time you tried to convince someone about something they held strong views about (which political party they should vote for), versus something they held weak views about (whether *Strictly Come Dancing* is better than *The Great British Bake Off*)? Chances are that the evidence you needed to persuade someone to change their mind in the former was a lot higher than for the latter. Labour vs Conservative, Republican vs Democrat, Left vs Right – these are views that are strongly held. Some people don't simply vote for a party, they consider themselves 'of' that party. It becomes part of their identity. This fact may have far greater consequences than simple living room discussions. For example, one study found that the political composition of judicial panels influenced their opinions: when judges sat on a panel with ideologically consistent judges, they were far more likely to offer ideological opinions, as opposed to sitting on a panel with mixed views.[15]

Another study offered an interesting test of this phenomenon. A representative sample of the US population was asked to evaluate a simple table of data. It provided participants with data on the effectiveness of a skin cream on a rash – the point being that participants were not expected to have strong opinions on the effectiveness of a skin cream. Questions were then put to the participants to test their comprehension of the data – most evaluated the data correctly. However, for another subset of participants, the authors changed the framing of the exact same table. To these participants, they said that the data was on the effectiveness of gun control laws on crime. This frame was used because, unlike skin cream, they expected participants to have strong opinions on the effectiveness of gun control laws.[16]

And so it proved – far more people interpreted the data incorrectly when it was over an issue they had a strong opinion on. Moreover, in the paper they show that individuals with strong beliefs were more likely to interpret the data in line with their priors, relative to individuals that had weaker beliefs about this particular topic. People rely on their instincts because thinking too hard about things takes up energy. That means that if they strongly believe that strict gun control laws reduce crime and they see a number in a table that confirms their belief, they stop right there and do not consider the rest of the evidence in front of them.

My co-authors and I have studied this phenomenon further, surveying a sample of development professionals at two heavily influential development agencies. We asked some of the participants to evaluate the effectiveness of a skin cream on a rash (just like the prior experiment), while others were asked to evaluate data on the effectiveness of minimum wage laws on poverty (something development professionals have strong views about). The results showed confirmation bias: participants were less accurate when evaluating data framed as a topic they have strong views about (minimum wage laws), relative to evaluating data they did not have strong views about (skin cream). Moreover, those with stronger views were more likely to get the answer wrong.[17]

Why did these participants get different rates of accuracy when evaluating the exact same data? Data which differed only in how it was framed? Remember that these are folks who can easily calculate the right answer, but they give different answers when they have strong opinions about the data. Why? The answer is that when faced with a decision where we have a strong prior, we tend to use that prior to come up with our answer, rather than to engage in the effortful calculation process. The fact that these development professionals, who are contractually obliged to engage in the objective evaluation of data and produce policy reflecting that data, are susceptible to these kinds of biases should make us think. Confirmation bias has an enormous impact on our world.

What all this amounts to, then, is how central our beliefs are in guiding decisions. We might like to think that when we make a decision, particularly a big decision, we are being rational. Very often, it just *feels* as though we have acted rationally. Often, we do what we do because of our perceptions and beliefs, rather than an objective evaluation of data. In our daily lives, and when trying to build a decisive mind, it is essential to keep this in mind. If we think eating a bowl of ice cream is going to have a positive influence on our life, for instance, by making us happy, we will do it. Nobody is going to engage in a cost and benefit analysis over whether a bowl of ice cream is going to make us happy, both in the long and short term. To change our behaviour, we need to create a wholesale change in our perceptions about a given action – we need to believe that ice cream makes us unhappy. We cannot expect ourselves to deliberate over every action, and we cannot expect deliberation to necessarily come up with an accurate view of the facts either.

Know thyself

The evidence above makes clear that we hold biased perceptions about the world in general. But we aren't just wrong about everything around us. We have biased perceptions about ourselves, too.

There are two biases that particularly hamstring our ability to clearly see the world. One is overconfidence and the other is optimism. Overconfidence is our tendency to believe ourselves to have higher ability than we actually do. It can also mean that we underestimate the capabilities of an opponent, the difficulty of a particular task, the risks associated with engaging in certain behaviours, or simply the time it takes to get something done. This, the 'planning fallacy', is something everybody has at some point fallen foul of.[18] How long will it take to move house? At least one day longer than the number of days that you took off from work. Overconfidence is, essentially, the belief that our ability is higher than it actually is. When we think we're better than we are, we don't provide enough effort. We fall short. We will cover how we deal with such inevitable failures a bit later, but for now it is important to note that if we are overconfident, we underestimate the effort required to achieve any particular outcome.

A quick note: overconfidence in this sense is a cognitive bias – a systematic fault in human perception. You are, unfortunately, still subject to it even if you aren't an extroverted type who is happy telling people at parties how great you are.

But why? Why do we overestimate our abilities? One of the most persuasive models is that overconfidence has an evolutionary advantage. In a conflict setting, overconfidence can be advantageous. Imagine a situation where two people, in our prehistoric past, wanted to access the same blackberries growing on a bush that was, itself, growing halfway up a cliff face. One of the people is a significantly better climber than the other. But if the lower ability individual is more confident in their abilities, they would claim the blackberries by leaping at the opportunity to shimmy up the cliff face. The better climber loses out if they cannot perfectly observe their own and their opponent's ability levels. In such a situation, it's obvious that overconfidence becomes a profitable strategy. Furthermore, unlike other species where overconfidence may persist due to natural selection, human beings engage in experimentation, imitation and learning, which can increase overconfidence overall. In other words, overconfidence can be useful because it can boost resolve, persistence and ambition.[19]

But the researchers who demonstrated this insight also noticed something even more fascinating: overconfidence increases when uncertainty increases. The more uncertain something becomes, the more overconfidence seems to emerge. The implication of their model is useful to explain everything from the Iraq War to the response to Hurricane Katrina. Certainly, overconfidence had a role in the 2008 financial crisis, and it is playing a role right now as our climate changes. I often think this happens with the Winter Olympics. Here in Britain, winter sports aren't played very often. And yet, when the Winter Olympics are on the TV, everybody suddenly begins talking as though they are an expert pundit when it comes to the Skeleton Bob or Freestyle Skiing. 'Oh, yes, the Canadian bobsledders look very strong this year,' says your colleague, who two weeks ago knew as much about 'the Canadian team' as they did quantum mechanics. The fact that this effect manifests itself *more* when the scenarios are more uncertain, makes it, potentially, disastrous.[20]

This paints a rather bleak picture. However, because it is so fundamental to understanding how people engage in tasks, there has been a considerable amount of time and effort dedicated to studying overconfidence. Overconfidence has been broken down into three main families, which researchers call overestimation, overplacement and overprecision.[21]

Taking each of the above in turn, overestimation is the most familiar. It is simply defined as overestimating one's own performance in any particular task. Overestimation is the one we will concern ourselves with most because it directly affects individual decision-making. The clearest example is somebody believing they scored higher in a particular test than they actually did. Overestimation also pertains to issues like the level of control one has over the outcome of a situation, or the chance of success one has. Generally, absent other factors, we have a belief about our abilities that is systematically higher than our actual abilities.

Scientists provide a direct test of this effect using a simple trivia task with college undergraduates.[22] They gave participants a quiz consisting of easy, medium and hard questions, and they paid them according to their performance on the task, with higher payments for those that did better. They then asked the participants to guess their performance, with higher payments for those who guessed correctly. Participants *underestimated* their performance on easy quizzes, were accurate on medium quizzes, but they overestimated their performance on difficult quizzes. Proof positive that as uncertainty rises, so does overconfidence.

The second type of overconfidence is *overplacement*. This is primarily social. People consider themselves to be better than others at a given task. Famously, one in eight men believe that they can win a point off Serena Williams in a game of tennis.[23] This is related to overestimation. Those that consider their ability to do a certain thing to be higher than it actually is are more likely to believe that they are better than others at whatever that thing is. Think of our prehistoric rock climbers. It follows that the lower ability climber thought they were better than the higher ability climber, alongside thinking that they had the ability to grab the berries. Overplacement and overestimation are not wholly independent, though of course it's possible to believe that you are better than you actually are, whilst also believing that others are better than you. Still, a series of publications in psychology confirm that most people think that they are above average (or, more precisely, above the median) in given tasks, which is, obviously, not possible.[24]

The final type of overconfidence is overprecision. It's defined by excessive certainty about the accuracy of somebody's beliefs. If you ask somebody to put down a range of possible answers to a particular question, for example, the height of a mountain, the range given is almost always too narrow and contains the correct answer less than 50 per cent of the time. It is very strange, but people tend not to say, 'The mountain is between 0 metres and 7 million metres tall.' They say, 'The mountain is between 2,345 and 2,500 metres tall.' In general, people believe they are more accurate than they are.[25]

So, there is clear evidence that, in general, we are more confident in our own abilities due to our beliefs. We believe ourselves to be of higher ability, more accurate and above average. The next question we deal with here is why these beliefs persist when the rubber hits the road. Imagine somebody being overconfident in delivering a piece of work on time. I know that I can struggle with deadlines but knowing that doesn't necessarily alleviate things. Surely after repeatedly failing we should be able to reason that we are being overconfident and our beliefs should begin to align with reality, right? Wrong.

There's an issue with this line of reckoning. We all maintain some prior belief. Let's say, for instance, that you have a belief about your ability on taking tests. You might have a belief that on the next test, you will score 70. But you take the test and your actual score comes out less than this, let's say 60. Now this actual score constitutes what the literature calls a signal – it's a datapoint that can help you chart where you are. We would assume that you use this signal to update your beliefs about your ability such that the next time you face a test, your new belief should be something closer to 60 rather than your original belief. In other words, this new information, your actual test score, should be used to update your beliefs such that over time, there is no chance of being overconfident because the data forces you to adjust your beliefs appropriately.

But the evidence suggests that because individuals are routinely overconfident in their own abilities, there must be a different form of belief updating going on to the one I laid out above. Specifically, we call this the 'Good News-Bad News effect'. When updating beliefs about our performance, we treat good news (that we did better than we expected) differently from bad news (that we did worse than we expected). An experiment asked participants to undertake a 25 question IQ test, or to participate in a speed-dating exercise. In each case participants were ranked based on their score in the IQ test, or others' evaluation of their attractiveness. This constituted an objective ranking. Then participants were asked to put down where they thought they ranked. Next, they were paired with an anonymous partner and told whether they ranked higher or lower than them. After which they were asked to revise where they thought they ranked. The process repeated until all pairings were exhausted.[26]

What the authors found was striking. When given good news (that they were ranked higher than their partner), participants revised their beliefs accordingly. However, when given bad news (that they were ranked lower than their partners), participants were reluctant to revise their beliefs! The effects were stronger for judgements about beauty than about IQ, but relative to a control condition, both beauty and IQ demonstrated differences in how participants viewed good news versus bad.

When it comes to evaluating factors associated with our self-esteem, we are not at all objective. Because we treat good news and bad news differently, we need a lot more information showing us that we are not as good as we think we are to bring our perceptions in light with reality. On the other hand, we need only a fraction of positive information to reassess and this small morsel of good news can cause us to overshoot in our beliefs. We have a vested interest in believing that we are better than we are. It's beneficial for us; so, we actively do it. But the upshot is we often underestimate the amount of effort it takes to accomplish a difficult task, or the amount of time it takes (specifically, the latter is known as the 'planning fallacy').[27]

A final point on overconfidence is the relatively well-known Dunning-Kruger effect.[28] The basic idea is that we overestimate our performance. But this overestimation is higher for those that are of lower ability. Furthermore, lower ability individuals are less able to recognise competence in others, making it less likely for them to update their skills through learning or mimicry. The less competent you are, the more likely you are to be overconfident. The more competent you are, the more likely your beliefs about your ability align with your actual ability. This is incredibly important when attempting to stick to your goals. At the start of the process, you are likely to be a beginner, meaning that you are incompetent. But you don't know just how incompetent you are, and a consequence of that is it causes you to think that you're better than you are. For instance, you may wish to start blogging. You might look around you and think that it will be easy to get a certain number of followers, whilst pumping out a certain number of weekly articles. But then, when you get started, the followers are slow to follow and the articles are difficult to write. Your overconfidence is suddenly met by reality. Hubris, meet nemesis.

Avoiding overconfidence

Once again, all of this is important when we think about building that decisive mind. Our information about the world is limited and most decisions we undertake are based on an idea of the world that we carry around in our heads, rather than objective reality itself. It's pretty much impossible for us to take in all the information that the world provides. That means we place our attention on some things and our mind filters out other information, leading to a deviation between our perceptions and our beliefs. The decisions that we undertake reflect our understanding of the world rather than the world itself.

Central to this chapter have been the concepts of selective attention and confidence. Confidence is the difference between our actual ability and our perception of our ability. Most of us are over-confident. In addition to this, we have selective attention, meaning that we make decisions based on a limited set of information. We don't perceive our knowledge as limited, however, because we fill in the gaps in our knowledge with our own mental models, which leads to biased and less than ideal decision-making.

Perhaps more importantly, we are also biased in the manner in which we update our beliefs about the world. We are prone to confirmation bias, that is, we have a tendency to selectively seek, process and retain information that confirms our beliefs, rather than perform an objective evaluation of information. Worse still, our beliefs about ourselves and our ability to perform are not objective. We lean towards overestimation in our abilities (particularly in difficult tasks). We overestimate how good we are, which makes it difficult for us to plan our efforts accordingly. Moreover, according to the Dunning-Kruger effect, the less competent we are, the more we overestimate our abilities. Hence, the more difficult a task is for you, chances are the more you believe it is not difficult.

Finally, there's a problem with updating our beliefs when it relates to our self-esteem. We tend to treat good news, signals that we are of higher ability than we actually are, differently from bad news, signals that we are of lower ability than we actually are. This means that overconfident individuals, i.e. most people, update their beliefs very slowly, while underconfident individuals update their beliefs rapidly, yielding the cognitive bias that we observe.

All of this has a huge bearing on building a decisive mind. For the time being, it's worth understanding and gaining a greater deal of awareness about all of this. It is, of course, bad news, which as we now know, you are likely to discount. But I hope that the wealth of evidence I have provided you with here makes it clear that you need to take overconfidence seriously. When planning and executing long-term goals, you are very likely, at the beginning, to set your sights too high. You are very likely to think that you are more capable than you are. And you are very likely going to estimate the time horizons completely inaccurately. Taken all in, this is a recipe for failure.

On the other hand, forewarned is forearmed. Knowing about it does give you at least some defence. It might be worth thinking about moments in the past where you've been prone to overconfidence. The planning fallacy – where we underestimate how long a task will take – is, no doubt, a problem we have all encountered at some point and in some field of our lives.

It may also be worth considering how overconfidence can play out in more subtle ways. For instance, if we set ourselves a diet, we may be very overconfident about how well we'll stick to it. We may overlook the many problems – for instance, going to a restaurant, resisting a chocolate bar at the corner shop, what to do when we're on holiday – that we will face. Yes, on paper, it may seem that you can plan your every meal and eat a balanced diet, including lots of fruit, vegetables and nuts. But that is in the world that you carry around in your head. It is not the world of concrete, and actual, reality. Knowing that what you think you'll do is unlikely to be what you'll actually do may help you bring your planning in line with your capabilities.

Back to Romer

In the aftermath of the article published by the *Wall Street Journal*, Paul Romer was asked to resign from his position. The Doing Business report was replaced by another report and an independent inquiry revealed no evidence of malfeasance, though the individual in charge of the report also resigned. Romer subsequently won a Nobel Prize and continues to be influential in policy circles. One may speculate why it took someone of Romer's stature to uncover the weaknesses of the report, but the story is illustrative of one important point: if we perceive the results of a particular analysis to be correct, we are less likely to look for reasons to the contrary.

So much of our decision-making relies on our perceptions of the information, rather than the information itself. This difference is critical because a lot of the time, we make interventions designed to provide more information. But who cares about the information if, when it tells you something unflattering, you ignore it?

All of the concepts explored in the chapter imply that an individual's perception can differ substantially from reality, making goals more difficult to achieve. Our perceptions can shift our decision classification in a way that makes us feel as though we are making progress, when really, we aren't.

Your perceptions are driving your behaviour. The intention here is not to just provide you with information, which we know that you will look at selectively, but to try to give you a thorough understanding of the mechanism behind this and how these perceptions lead to behaviour. To change behaviour, we need to spend some time reflecting on and changing our perceptions. That's been the focus of these under-the-hood, science chapters. In Part II of the book, we start putting these insights to work by developing our Roadmap.

Box: Your turn!

Assignment # 5

This is an exercise in two parts. First, please consider three moments in which you have been subject to the planning fallacy – where you have underestimated the time that it will take you to do something. Write down (in brief) the situation, the amount of time you thought it would take you and the amount of time it actually took you.

	Describe the situation	The amount of time you thought it would take	The amount of time it actually took
Situation 1			
Situation 2			
Situation 3			

Next, consider the information in this chapter. Being aware of the Good News/Bad News problem, try to internalise the idea that, apart from the things in which you are expert, you are largely overconfident. Putting these two things together, return to the aspirations that you looked at at the beginning of this book. How long did you think they might take to achieve and how hard would they be? Is it worth revising either the goal, the time frame, or the amount of effort you need to put in?

Aspiration 1:

When do you want
to achieve this by
(from Chapter 1)?

Would you like to
revise the timeframe?

When do you want
to achieve this by
(REVISED)?

Why did you decide to
revise or not?

Aspiration 2:

When do you want
to achieve this by
(from Chapter 1)?

Would you like to
revise the timeframe?

When do you want
to achieve this by
(REVISED)?

Why did you decide to
revise or not?

Aspiration 3:	
When do you want to achieve this by (from Chapter 1)?	
Would you like to revise the timeframe?	
When do you want to achieve this by (REVISED)?	
Why did you decide to revise or not?	

References

Romer, Paul M. 'Endogenous technological change.' *Journal of Political Economy* 98, no. 5, Part 2 (1990): S71–S102.

Jayasuriya, Dinuk. 'Improvements in the World Bank's ease of doing business rankings: Do they translate into greater foreign direct investment inflows?' *World Bank Policy Research Working Paper* 5787 (2011).

Kahan, Dan M., Peters, Ellen, Dawson, Erica Cantrell and Slovic, Paul. 'Motivated numeracy and enlightened self-government.' *Behavioural Public Policy* 1, no. 1 (2017): 54–86.

Johnson-Laird, Philip N. 'The history of mental models.' In *Psychology of Reasoning*, pp. 189–222. Psychology Press, 2004.

Becklen, Robert and Cervone, Daniel. 'Selective looking and the noticing of unexpected events.' *Memory & Cognition* 11, no. 6 (1983): 601–608.

Stoffregen, Thomas A. and Becklen, Robert C. 'Dual attention to dynamically structured naturalistic events.' *Perceptual and Motor Skills* 69, no. 3–2 (1989): 1187–1201.

Neisser, Ulric and Becklen, Robert. 'Selective looking: Attending to visually specified events.' *Cognitive Psychology* 7, no. 4 (1975): 480–494.

Simons, Daniel J. and Chabris, Christopher F. 'Gorillas in our midst: Sustained inattentional blindness for dynamic events.' *Perception* 28, no. 9 (1999): 1059–1074.

Driver, Jon. 'A selective review of selective attention research from the past century.' *British Journal of Psychology* 92, no. 1 (2001): 53–78.

Sunstein, Cass R., Schkade, David, Ellman, Lisa M. and Sawicki, Andres. *Are Judges Political? An Empirical Analysis of the Federal Judiciary*. Brookings Institution Press, 2007.

Banuri, Sheheryar, Dercon, Stefan and Gauri, Varun. 'Biased policy professionals.' *The World Bank Economic Review* 33, no. 2 (2019): 310–327.

Kahneman, Daniel and Tversky, Amos. 'Intuitive prediction: Biases and corrective procedures.' In Kahneman, Daniel, Slovic, Paul and Tversky, Amos (Eds.), *Judgment under Uncertainty: Heuristics and Biases*, pp. 414–421. Cambridge: Cambridge University Press, 1982.

Johnson, Dominic D. P. and Fowler, James H. 'The evolution of overconfidence.' *Nature* 477, no. 7364 (2011): 317–320.

Camerer, Colin and Lovallo, Dan. 'Overconfidence and excess entry: An experimental approach.' *American Economic Review* 89, no. 1 (1999): 306–318.

Glaser, Markus and Weber, Martin. 'Overconfidence and trading volume.' *The Geneva Risk and Insurance Review* 32, no. 1 (2007): 1–36.

Howard, Michael. *The Causes of Wars and Other Essays*. Harvard University Press, 1984.

Malmendier, Ulrike and Tate, Geoffrey. 'CEO overconfidence and corporate investment.' *The Journal of Finance* 60, no. 6 (2005): 2661–2700.

Neale, Margaret A. and Bazerman, Max H. 'The effects of framing and negotiator overconfidence on bargaining behaviors and outcomes.' *Academy of Management Journal* 28, no. 1 (1985): 34–49.

Odean, Terrance. 'Do investors trade too much?' *American Economic Review* 89, no. 5 (1999): 1279–1298.

Moore, Don A. and Healy, Paul J. 'The trouble with overconfidence.' *Psychological Review* 115, no. 2 (2008): 502.

Alicke, Mark D. and Govorun, Olesya. 'The better-than-average effect.' *The Self in Social Judgment* 1 (2005): 85–106.

Eil, David and Rao, Justin M. 'The good news-bad news effect: Asymmetric processing of objective information about yourself.' *American Economic Journal: Microeconomics* 3, no. 2 (2011): 114–138.

Kruger, Justin and Dunning, David. 'Unskilled and unaware of it: How difficulties in recognizing one's own incompetence lead to inflated self-assessments.' *Journal of Personality and Social Psychology* 77, no. 6 (1999): 1121.

PART II:

THE ROADMAP

CHAPTER 6

Goals, Goals, Goals . . .
The Science of Goal-Setting

Key lesson: Step # I: SET A GOAL

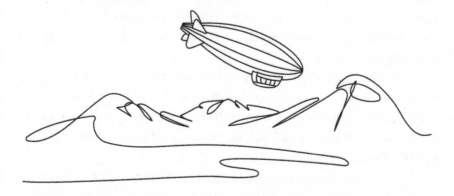

Bedford, England, October 1930. In the small village of Cardington, there is excitement in the air. A crowd has started to gather around to witness an unusual event, not only for this sleepy little village, but for England in general. And, even, for the world. In the early evening, the famous airship R101 would depart from the village to its destination in Karachi, British India, stopping once for refuelling in Ismailia, Egypt. While in Ismailia, the airship will put on a fancy dinner for dignitaries, before heading on its journey. The timing of the flight coincides with the Imperial Conference, held in London in 1930. A successful voyage of the airship had important implications for the British Empire, cutting down the 4,000-mile journey time from 17 days (by sea) to just three by air! To complete the journey while the Imperial Conference was in session was an important demonstration of the capability of the British Empire.

But the airship never reached Egypt.

For the uninitiated, an 'airship' is different to an airplane. Airships are lighter-than-air aircraft that use a lifting gas (typically helium in contemporary times, though hydrogen was commonplace prior to this). Hot-air balloons use the same principle, as heating air makes it lighter than cooler air and hence a balloon filled with hot air rises and can carry small payloads. Prior to famous crashes, hydrogen was used due to its availability and cost-effectiveness.[1]

The trouble with hydrogen is that it explodes.

Prior to the 1940s, many wealthy countries invested heavily in airship research and development, seeking a cost effective and more efficient way to travel. They were widely seen as the future of air travel. The R101 was of the 'rigid' type, meaning it had a solid outer structure that maintains its shape, but the actual lifting gas was contained in internal gasbags that inflate or deflate to gain or lose altitude.

By October 1930, the R101 airship had been flying for just under a year, mainly for the purposes of testing, though many in the Air Ministry had their doubts that testing was the real motive behind the flights. Indeed, Swinfield documented that first officer Noel Atherstone called many of these trips 'joy-rides' for the sake of politicians.[2]

As the sun slowly sank, the crowd became larger and larger, standing at the outskirts of the Royal Airship Workers, to cheer on the R101. The 777-foot-long airship fired its engines in light rain. The airship carried a total of 54 people, including the most important person, both in rank and to the development of the airship itself, the Secretary of State for Air, Lord Thomson.[3]

The presence of Lord Thomson was no mere coincidence. Thomson had been directly responsible for the development of the airship and had a keen interest in its outcome. Also on board were a series of items that would be considered (with the benefit of hindsight), a bit frivolous. Fine dinnerware had been stowed away expressly for the purpose of the dinner to be held in Egypt. Important foreign dignitaries had been invited and Thomson understood that it was critical to communicate the majesty of the British Empire to them, ruling the air just as the navy had ruled the sea for generations; and dining in style all the while. Thomson looked around the ship with an air of satisfaction. It had been fitted elegantly, its stylings reminiscent, perhaps too pertinently, of the Titanic.

Lord Thomson was born Christopher Birdwood Thomson in 1875 in Nashik (near Mumbai) India, into a military family. His father attained the rank of Major-General and his mother was the daughter of another Major-General. Following his father, Thomson joined the Royal Engineers after graduating from the Royal Military Academy. It was during the Second Boer War of 1899 that Thomson had his first brush with aviation. During the war, he was assisting the Royal Engineers Balloon Section. This section had been expressly formed to operate balloons in the field.[4]

Thomson eventually turned to politics and joined the Labour Party. The Labour Prime Minister Ramsay MacDonald wanted Thomson in government and so elevated Thomson to (Baron) Lord Thomson of Cardington and appointed him Secretary of State for Air, in charge of the (recently formed) Air Ministry.

Travel to and from different parts of the British Empire was arduous. The government had been interested in developing an airship scheme for reducing the amount of time it took for individuals and information to arrive from different parts of the empire (most importantly, India, Australia and Canada). In 1922, the Vickers company proposed a scheme for the development of commercial airships with an eye to linking up the British Empire. The original scheme (called the Burney scheme, after its founder Dennistoun Burney) involved six airships to be built and operated by Vickers.[5] The government was in favour of the scheme and appointed an advisory panel to examine the details. The panel included the founder and none other than (the eventual) Lord Thomson.

Thomson had misgivings about the Burney scheme. He worried that it granted Vickers (a private company proposing the scheme) an effective monopoly on the operation of the airships at the cost of the taxpayer. In addition, Thomson also felt that the publicly owned Royal Airship Works in Cardington (his constituency) could produce a better airship than the one proposed by Vickers. When Thomson took charge of the Air Ministry in early 1924, he was given his chance to put his assumptions to the test.[6]

He rejected the Burney Scheme and replaced it with the Imperial Airship Scheme. Under this, the government would fund the construction of two airships, one by the Royal Airship Guarantee Company (a subsidiary of Vickers, managed by Burney), the other by the Royal Airship Works at Cardington. The fact that one of the manufacturers was a private firm, while the other was the government was not lost on the press. The scheme quickly became labelled as a competition between the public and the private sector, with the Vickers Airship (the R100) called the 'Capitalist Airship', while the Royal Airship Works airship (the R101) was dubbed the 'Socialist Airship'.[7]

Both airships were given the goal of completion in one year and trial flights planned six months thereafter. Neither airship met this goal.

As the government had a vested interest in the development of the airship in Cardington, there was no end to public scrutiny. Constant oversight meant that a core purpose of the Royal Airship Works became the provision of positive news about the astounding (albeit untested) capabilities of the R101. Indeed, many brilliant minds were assembled to bring this (increasingly impossible) vision to fruition. But what was a technical challenge was quickly becoming political. Scrutiny came from all sides of the political spectrum – those that had a vested interest in the R101 failing and those that had a vested interest in its success.[8]

In the midst of all this was Thomson. Thomson had a vision for how the scheme would pan out, putting his faith in the ability of information to be shared between the two competitors to the point where the final product, particularly the public version, would be far superior to what could have been achieved by the private sector alone. Thomson's personal credibility was at the centre of this; his reputation among the engineers at Cardington was for being 'overbearing'.[9]

The political aspect of the R101 then saw the airship take on several publicity stunts, with Lord Thomson aboard the second flight in late October. A third flight went over Sandringham House in early November and was observed by King George V and Queen Mary.[10] These flights generated a number of serious technical and safety issues. Corrections were made, even though some of these flights were used to carry several passengers. In what was yet another publicity stunt, Thomson organised a flight for a party of 100 members of parliament. The event was oversubscribed and the ship was unable to handle this many passengers. It remained at the mast, though the officials were invited on board to view the airship. These early flights were not going well.

While these events were occurring at Cardington, the R100 was completed by the team at Vickers (the Capitalist Airship). The R100 departed for Canada in late July of 1930 and returned in mid-August 1930. The team at Cardington had to undertake the flight the same year or risk losing face.[11]

The Air Ministry drew up a schedule to undertake the R101's maiden flight to India in early October, for primarily political (and not technical) reasons. In addition to saving face, the flight to India was to occur during the Imperial Conference to be held in London. The airship was given an airworthiness certificate on 2 October 1930, two days before it was scheduled to depart.

On 4 October 1930, the R101 departed from Cardington on its way to Karachi, via Egypt. Lord Thomson of Cardington, the man whose reputation was inexorably linked with the success of the R101, stood on board awaiting departure. He was instrumental in bringing this moment to fruition and convinced of the success of this flight. He was looking forward to the scheduled dinner in Ismailia. Swinfield writes, with a certain style, that the weight of the food and materials to support the banquet was hefty, but 'the weight of ego that set sail that night is unknown'.[12]

Eight hours after departure, the R101 crashed in Beauvais, Northern France. The airship covered just 200 miles of the 4,400-mile journey. Forty-eight individuals died, including Lord Thomson. Two survivors died from their injuries in hospital shortly thereafter. The number of casualties was higher than that of the famous Hindenburg disaster of 1937. The crash led to an immediate end of the Imperial Airship Scheme and the British Empire's ambitions of this form of air travel. The R100 was similarly scrapped in the aftermath. Later commentators would agree that while the R100 was a triumph of engineering, the R101 was, by contrast, overweight and underpowered, unable to achieve what it was designed to do.[13]

Thomson and setting goals

Many accounts detailed by Swinfield point to Thomson's ambition as a major contributing factor to the crash. He presents a letter from Air Marshal Sir

Victor Goddard, stating that Thomson had aspirations to become the Viceroy of India, in fulfilment of which he deemed it important to return from India before the end of the Imperial Conference as a show of his capability and managerial prowess. This 'personal vanity' directly contributed to a number of decisions that, in Sir Goddard's opinion, directly led to the disaster.[14] When viewed through this lens, there are a number of flawed decisions that seem directly attributable to Thomson and the Air Ministry.

The story of the R101 is instructive for our purposes in several ways. But at the very top, the most important thing illustrated is the importance of setting goals and having autonomy in doing so. Prior to Thomson taking charge of the Air Ministry (and having his own experience from military campaigns to draw upon), the Burney Scheme had nearly granted the design and construction of airships to the Vickers subsidiary (led by Commander Burney). Thomson points clearly to the lack of influence he had on the private organisation in terms of the details on construction, which prompted an additional step to bring development in house. Immediately after the Imperial Airship Scheme was undertaken, the delivery window was set to one year, an extremely optimistic (some might say unattainable) target.[15] Arguably the delays until 1929 could very well be attributed to the Conservative government taking over in late 1924 and with a new Secretary of State for Air (Samuel Hoare, who had previously been in charge of the Air Ministry during the conception of the Burney Scheme). But either way, a goal was set and not reached.

Eventually when Thomson took over the Air Ministry in early 1929, he set out another ambitious goal, for the flight to be undertaken during the next Imperial Conference in just over a year. The conferences were periodic gatherings that were held every two or so years, and so it was important to Thomson to announce his great success in front of important people – it fed directly into his personal ambitions. Note, however, that the goals were set in service to these ambitions and many on the team were unduly instructed to follow suit or to face severe career implications. Again, a goal was set and not reached (in the most tragic circumstances). But the goal was in service to Thomson's ambitions, rather than in service to the creation of a good airship.[16]

This illustrates the importance of both goal-setting and autonomy. Exerting effort in service of a direct immediate goal is much simpler and easier to both think about and execute. For instance, you can imagine feeling hungry and then exerting effort to go to the kitchen and make yourself a meal. This action carries an immediate reward; I was hungry, I took some action, now I am no longer hungry. We do this kind of thing all the time, reacting to immediate needs and exerting effort to fulfil them. Remember our simple model of decision-making:

- Do something if rewards are greater than the costs
- Do nothing if costs are greater than the rewards

But what about aspirations and the effort needed to achieve them? What about the R101s in our own lives? Following the behavioural insights we explored in earlier chapters, the thing to recognise is that action undertaken in service to an aspiration does not necessarily generate an immediate short-term reward. This means that the cost of effort exerted to work towards an aspiration or long-term goal is not directly offset by anything, making the action difficult to undertake.

Setting goals provides a valuable function – it helps us to become aware of the aspiration. The rewards we receive from acting at any given point are largely psychological. If we can reward ourselves psychologically along the way, threading an aspiration to a daily action becomes easier. Or, more concretely, if you know and act on the fact that, yes, even though putting the money you could spend on a coffee into a retirement pot is a little painful in the immediate term, it is in service to an aspiration of retiring early, therefore the later reward of not having to work more than offsets your current lack of caffeine. This is obviously massively simplified, but it gives a sense of what is going on.

The science of goal-setting

In an illustrative experiment on how goal-setting affects behaviour, researchers studied the behaviour of over 1,000 first year undergraduate students at Erasmus University in Rotterdam.[17] Student behaviour is illustrative and useful because students undertake considerable effort during their studies and it is effort that is not always intrinsically motivating – people may not be studying something that they are truly passionate about, but rather doing something that is more a means to an end. Beyond that, studying is hard – even if you like the subject! This is compounded for first year students. During the first year, the courses set are mostly obligatory and hence the likelihood of students being intrinsically motivated to study is low.

In the experiment (and more broadly at Erasmus University) students are assigned a mentor. The mentors are senior students in the same programme as the subjects of the experiment, paid by the university to mentor first year students. Mentors typically oversee about 10 to 15 mentees and are obligated to meet with them. Their role is to be a point of contact with the university, but also to provide study skills and monitor student motivation. The authors conducted an interesting intervention. With a randomly selected subset of mentors, the authors asked them to ask their mentees whether they had a goal in mind for the course they were studying and if not, asked them to set a goal for the upcoming semester. Other mentors were not aware of this intervention and carried on their mentor duties without asking their students to set goals.

The students were asked something quite specific: to set a goal of attaining a particular grade in a course that they were taking. The basic idea is that moving goals from vague and ill-defined (do well in Econ 101) towards being specific and measurable (get an A in Econ 101) increases performance and effort.[18] In effect, when providing individuals with difficult, yet attainable, goals, longstanding research has found that productivity and output increase.[19] The psychology behind this is simple: setting goals, and the effort undertaken to achieving them, is motivating. Remember the issue that long-term goals posed earlier? The idea is that when we exert effort in service to an (attainable) goal, the psychological rewards offset the costs of the effort. This is precisely why long-term goals improve performance. Some scientists label this a 'sense of achievement'.[20]

The study asked the Erasmus students to set a goal for themselves. Students were free to set whatever goals they liked, or to not set any whatsoever. The authors found clear evidence of goal-setting increasing performance: students that were asked to set a goal were more likely to perform better and less likely to drop out of the course. Naturally, the goal here is set by the students based on what they thought was an *attainable* one, contrasting with the unattainable goal set by Lord Thomson when building the R101. Setting a goal that is attainable is hugely important. Setting unattainable goals lead to bad outcomes.

The authors of the Erasmus study added one additional twist, however. Most mentors were told to ask their mentees to set a goal. But some were instructed to go one better and help the mentee set their goal. For those that thought their mentees could do better, they asked the mentors to request a more ambitious goal. They instructed the mentors to ask their mentees to set a goal one full grade above the goal that the mentee set for themselves. It is important to note that not every mentee accepted the raised goal (in fact, the authors report an acceptance rate of about 50 per cent). Nevertheless, they found that those that were asked to set a stretch goal did *worse* than those that were asked to simply set a goal. They found that these mentees fared about the same as the students who didn't have a goal at all!

The importance of goal-setting has a long history in academic literature.[21] But this issue of the attainability of goals has been a more recent addition. A related literature discusses the importance of self-set versus assigned goals.[22] The main point of this work is to show that goals influence behaviour and motivate effort, particularly when they are specific, measurable and attainable. In fact, George Doran first provided a widely used set of criteria for setting goals for performance. He noted that in order to improve performance, S.M.A.R.T., which stand for Specific, Measurable, Achievable, Relevant and Time-related (or timely), goals are best.[23]

Taking each letter in turn:

- The Specific part of a S.M.A.R.T. goal refers to the clarity of the goal. Thinking back to the airship race – was the aim to improve Imperial communications, prove that the public sector was better than the private, or to innovate on airship design? I don't know. Neither did the teams involved. This was a problem. When thinking 'specifics', think 'w' questions – what, where, why, who?
- A Measurable goal is one in which your target is easy to quantify. How much weight do you wish to lose? How many calls do you need to make? Like our undergraduate students, what grade are you aiming for?

- As mentioned above, setting a goal that is Achievable is incredibly important. Make it too difficult and you may as well not have set one at all. When it comes to goal-setting, it's better to aim low and set further goals as you go, rather than aim high and fail.
- Making a goal Relevant is a way of triggering your intrinsic motivation. When thinking about relevance, ask yourself what your goal is in service of – how does it fit in your aspirations? Does it chime with your other goals, desires, wants and needs? If you need to include others in your goal, have you considered their wants and needs? Returning to the story that opened this chapter, Lord Thomson's goal was highly relevant for him, but probably not that relevant for his staff.
- Time-related goals are those that have end points. If you want to lose weight, but you don't set a deadline of how much and by when, it will be very easy, as we have seen previously, to defer the difficult decisions to tomorrow. But time-bound goals are also related to achievability. If Thomson hadn't set so short a deadline, it's possible that R101 could have been a success. We also know how subject we are to the planning fallacy from a previous chapter – as a good rule of thumb, I like to imagine how long I think something will take me and then add half again. So, for instance, if I think I can do it in a month, I'll give myself six weeks.

Taken all in then, our S.M.A.R.T. goal shouldn't be something nebulous like 'lose weight' (we call these aspirations). But rather, 'I would like to go to the gym on the high street twice weekly, with a view to using the rowing machine for 15 minutes, the cross trainer for 15 minutes and doing half an hour in the weights room. In three months' time, when I'm going on holiday to Malaga and will have to wear a pair of swimming trunks, I aim to have lost half a stone.'

Setting a goal is essential for the decisive mind. But whilst it is important to be ambitious and push yourself, it is equally important to be realistic. Hence, while you could easily set yourself the goal of 'lose 200 pounds in two weeks' or 'I want to be a millionaire by the age of 30', the sheer difficulty and unattainability of these kinds of goals actually make them demotivating. Remember, the idea behind a goal is to provide psychological rewards when you exert effort in service to the goal. This reward is used to offset the mental or physical effort that you make which will (by design) carry no intermediate reward. When viewed through this lens, you can easily see that the goal needs to be specific (that is you are able to link your action to the goal) and attainable (your action should matter).

One final point before we wrap up. The importance of *you* setting *your own* goal is critical here. Goals that we receive from others can be motivating if they follow the criteria above, but the reward is also similarly external. If a manager sets a goal for us, we reasonably expect to be rewarded when providing them with evidence of effort in service to that goal. As we saw in Chapter 3, rewards need not be material, just a simple word of encouragement from a manager can be motivating (social rewards). However, if we set a goal *for ourselves*, the psychological reward remains internal and hence is intrinsically motivating. We will discuss this point a little deeper in Chapter 8, but the key point here is that this psychological reward is used to offset the pain of incurring effort along the way. As we do more and more in service to our goals and aspirations, we need additional sources of motivation and hence can look for support from friends and family (social rewards) or can treat ourselves (material rewards), but at the most basic level, setting your own reasonable goal is the necessary first step.

Lord Thomson and the terrible, horrible, no good, very bad goal

Lord Thomson died on the R101 flight to India and took a large number of people with him. The lesson that we learn from his story is one of ambition and hubris, but also of pushing people well beyond what they know they are capable of. Thomson required far too much of his airship, even when those around him tried to say that he was overreaching.[24] The tragedy of the R101 went well beyond the loss of life, however. It put an end to a programme that may have had considerable influence on the way we live today and our impact on the environment. Indeed, because of the massive carbon footprint of contemporary air travel, efforts are underway to revisit the potentially more ecologically friendly lighter than air travel – airships could return to our skies.

Lord Thomson envisioned a future where the path to his personal goal (viceroy of India) was possible only by setting higher and more difficult goals for others. Eight hours into the flight of R101, Lord Thomson's dream ended, as did the British Empire's interest in lighter than air travel. Perhaps his biggest crime was dreaming too big. As we saw from the evidence, setting an unattainable goal is just as bad as setting no goal at all.

Even though there was considerable tragedy, there were also some amazing achievements. The possibility of long distance, commercially viable air travel was achieved in a relatively short amount of time. The R100 was indeed a success, completing its 3,300-mile journey within a decade of conception. Swinfield writes that some argue that were it not for the weather, the R101 would have been a similar success and perhaps given more time, might have changed how we experience air travel today.[25] One important psychological point escaped Lord Thomson, however. For a goal to be motivating, one must experience a reward for engaging in an action in service to the goal. If one believes that the goal set is unattainable, then the action in service to the goal is considered futile. The effort is exerted, but there is no perceptible reward to offset the effort. In subsequent times, individuals will seek to further minimise or eliminate the effort in order to maximise their outcomes.

Relating this back to our framework, at the end of this book, we will set clear S.M.A.R.T. goals. For now, though, remember that the goals that you will set will contribute directly into the decision classification framework. Hence, decisions that contribute to the goal (and hence, your aspiration) will be termed **high impact**. Similarly, decisions that do not contribute to the goal, or do not add anything to us substantially, will get classified as **low impact**. This will be important for us to do two things: identify areas where we can enhance intrinsic rewards and, hence, effort. It will also be important for us to free up resources from other decision-making areas so that we can channel our efforts effectively.

The critical thing to remember is that there is no 'free lunch'. We should not strive to conjure up effort, but rather to channel it away from current activities that do not contribute to our wellbeing and into activities that will, either now or in the future. The vehicle that we will use to determine which decisions are impactful are your aspirations and your goals.

Box: Your turn!

Assignment # 6

In this exercise I would like you to think back over a time when you set yourself a goal, any goal, and failed to achieve it. I'd like you to write down the goal in as specific terms as you can recall and then think about the S.M.A.R.T. goals framework we discussed earlier. Do you see any lapses? Anything you could improve?

Your aspiration:	
What was your goal (be specific)?	
Was your goal Specific? How?	
Was your goal Measurable? How did you measure progress?	
Was your goal Achievable? Why did you think so?	
Was your goal Relevant? How did it contribute to your aspiration?	
Was your goal Timely? What was your timeline?	

Now that you have gone through this, I would like you to take a minute to revise the goal as if you were going to undertake it today. How would you structure and adapt it so that it follows the S.M.A.R.T. framework?

Your aspiration:	
State your goal	
Is your goal Specific? How?	
Is your goal Measurable? How will you measure progress?	
Is your goal Achievable? Why do you think so?	
Is your goal Relevant? How does it contribute to your aspiration?	
Is your goal Timely? What is your timeline?	

References

Swinfield, John. *Airship: Design, Development and Disaster*. Conway, 2013.

Masefield, Sir Peter G. *To Ride the Storm: Story of the Airship R101*. William Kimber, London, 1982.

Van Lent, Max and Souverijn, Michiel. 'Goal setting and raising the bar: A field experiment.' *Journal of Behavioral and Experimental Economics* 87 (2020): 101570.

Locke, Edwin A. and Latham, Gary P. *A Theory of Goal Setting & Task Performance*. Prentice-Hall, Inc, 1990.

Latham, Gary P. and Locke, Edwin A. 'Goal setting—A motivational technique that works.' *Organizational Dynamics* 8, no. 2 (1979): 68–80.

Gómez-Miñambres, Joaquín. 'Motivation through goal setting.' *Journal of Economic Psychology* 33, no. 6 (2012): 1223–1239.

Latham, Gary P. and Yukl, Gary A. 'Effects of assigned and participative goal setting on performance and job satisfaction.' *Journal of Applied Psychology* 61, no. 2 (1976): 166.

Shane, Scott, Locke, Edwin A. and Collins, Christopher J. 'Entrepreneurial motivation.' *Human Resource Management Review* 13, no. 2 (2003): 257–279.

Suvorov, Anto and Van de Ven, Jeroen. 'Goal setting as a self-regulation mechanism.' Available at SSRN 1286029 (2008).

Koch, Alexander K. and Nafziger, Julia. 'Self-regulation through goal setting.' *Scandinavian Journal of Economics* 113, no. 1 (2011): 212–227.

Koch, Alexander K. and Nafziger, Julia. 'Goals and bracketing under mental accounting.' *Journal of Economic Theory* 162 (2016): 305–351.

Anderson, Shannon W., Dekker, Henri C. and Sedatole, Karen L. 'An empirical examination of goals and performance-to-goal following the introduction of an incentive bonus plan with participative goal setting.' *Management Science* 56, no. 1 (2010): 90–109.

Hollenbeck, John R., Williams, Charles R. and Klein, Howard J. 'An empirical examination of the antecedents of commitment to difficult goals.' *Journal of Applied Psychology* 74, no. 1 (1989): 18.

Doran, George T. 'There's a SMART way to write management's goals and objectives.' *Management Review* 70, no. 11 (1981): 35–36.

CHAPTER 7

Why Can't You Be Like Everyone Else? Structuring Feedback

Key lesson: Step # 2: CHECK IN

1951, Swarthmore University, Pennsylvania. A middle-aged scientist hurriedly walks up the steps to his laboratory. He moved to Swarthmore four years ago, but still gets lost from time to time. Today is an exciting day though and he doesn't want to be late. He's already briefed his team and he thinks they have a clear sense of what they need to do, but he'll find comfort going over the protocol with them one more time. He still gets excited on days they conduct studies and he wants to be there to make sure everything goes according to plan. Conducting work in the lab with human subjects is always interesting, but there are many things that can go wrong. A bit like putting on a play, he muses. He walks past Parrish Hall and briefly considers stopping by his office, before continuing to the lab. The scientist is no other than Solomon Asch.

As he is about to enter his building, he has a flashback to when he was seven years old, in Lowicz, Poland. Passover, April 1914. Everyone in his family is tense, but he's not sure why. Family arguments rage every now and again, and in recent months conversation around the dinner table has become increasingly heated, but he is blissfully unaware of the geopolitical causes of this and the crescendo-ing drumbeat of war. His eyes wander over to a single cup of wine sitting on the table. Sensing his curiosity, his uncle asks him whether he knows who the glass is for. He shakes his head.

'The wine is for the prophet, Elijah. He visits each Jewish home at Passover and takes a sip from the wine in the cup that is left out for him.'

Solomon remembers being fascinated by this. He vowed to keep an eye on the cup so as to catch a glimpse of the prophet when he came for his sip. He watches and watches the cup, but no one ever comes; no one touches it. Yet everyone he asks tells him that the wine is for the prophet. He keeps watching the cup with an eagle eye and yet even though he saw no one, eventually he thinks that the level of the wine went down a little. He's sad, and confused, that he missed seeing Elijah.

Outside the steps of the university building, Solomon chuckles to himself. Of course, Elijah never came, and yet he could have sworn that a sip was taken from the wine. The study that he will conduct that day will, potentially, answer the question of why he was able to disregard the evidence from his own senses and believe the stories of his uncle and his family.

At the age of 13, Solomon Asch and his family moved from his native Poland to New York. He was a quiet, shy boy, growing up on the Lower East Side of New York, amid many other immigrant families. At first, he struggled to speak English. He had a small circle of friends, who affectionately yet teasingly referred to him as Shlaym, the Yiddish word for phlegm. Perhaps it was his weak command of English that kept him close to his family for many years. But it also made him quite introspective – he became fascinated by how people made decisions. Many of his psychologist colleagues had similar stories.[1]

Solomon Asch went over the study in his head. He had invited around 50 male students to participate. This particular study was building on previous work regarding how people process visual cues and information.

Asch wanted to know how people made decisions in the presence and influence of others.

Asch was interested in human behaviour at an early age, though he initially studied anthropology. He attended Columbia University in New York, obtaining his masters in 1930 and his doctorate in 1932. Along the way, he was heavily influenced by the Gestalt psychologist Max Wertheimer.[2] Wertheimer became a great friend and although by the day Asch was due to conduct the study he had passed for some time now, Solomon's mind often turned towards him and their various conversations. He had Wertheimer to thank for where he was now.

These sessions required a lot of preparation, more so than any study he had done before. At the centre was a simple idea. Participants are to sit in a room and look at a piece of paper on an easel, at a prespecified distance. On the left side of the paper is a single line drawn vertically of a certain length. On the right side are three vertical lines of different lengths, numbered from one to three. Eight participants are to be brought into the room to sit across the easel. An assistant is to run the study and read instructions aloud for all to hear. The instructions state that the task for the participants is to identify, of the three vertical lines, the one that is closest in length to the one on the left. The participants are numbered from one to eight and for each trial (the term for each piece of paper, as each paper had lines of different sizes), the participants are to name the line that is closest in length, in a clear voice. The assistant is to record the responses.[3]

The set-up is simple, but because it has a few different moving parts, Solomon is nervous. 'You're always this way before sessions,' he mutters to himself as he enters the lab. Volunteers enter and are told that they are participating in a visual perception test. Within each trial, the differences in the three lines are stark enough that anyone paying even a little bit of attention should be able to identify the correct answer within a split second. It was important to set a task that was this simple, to rule out any alternate conclusions.

The assistant was under strict orders to conduct the experiment neutrally, meaning that he shouldn't let the participants know the true nature of the study – they weren't really testing the participants' eyesight. Not at all.

On entering the lab, Asch was greeted by not just his assistant, but seven other individuals. These additional confidants were part of the study. Asch was interested in how people would react when they were a dissenting voice against a unanimous majority. The seven confidants were instructed to provide an incorrect answer to the trial on purpose. Asch predicted that the true participant would ignore their own perception, even on such a simple test, and provide the wrong answer to go along with the group. Just like the young Solomon Asch, they would think Elijah had sipped from the cup just because everyone said that he had.

Solomon instructed the confidants on how they were supposed to conduct themselves during the trials. Given that there were 50 independent participants, the sessions would take some time and it was important that each session was identical to the one preceding it.

Once the instructions were given and the sessions started, there was nothing to do but wait for each session to complete and to debrief the participant. This meant sitting down afterwards with the participant, explaining the true purpose of the study and asking them why they made the decisions that they did.

Asch could not have been aware of the impact his work was going to have on the field of social psychology. An interesting curiosity that stuck with him from his childhood led to the study that he was conducting today, unsure of what the results would be. He spoke with participant after participant, getting more and more excited by the minute.

You see, as with any good experiment, Asch had a control group. The control group underwent the exact same protocol, but they had to submit their answers in writing, so that there was no possibility of influence. The responses were correct 99 per cent of the time, indicating the simplicity of the task.

However, when asked to answer out loud, this accuracy rate dropped to 68 per cent.[4] A considerable proportion of individuals gave the wrong answer to conform with the rest of the group. About one-third of the group provided answers corresponding with the majority opinion at least half the time, while about a quarter never gave an incorrect answer.

This is incredible stuff! Participants ignored the clear evidence in front of their own eyes and went along with the majority opinion. When Asch asked them why they did this, one participant said that it was because he was seated in the middle. Had he been the first to respond he would have answered differently.

At the other end of the spectrum were participants that always gave the correct answer. When Asch probed them for a reason, they said they couldn't help themselves, they had to give the answer that they thought was right, but they wondered whether they had been subject to an illusion that the others were not.

Asch had a sense that these were important findings, but he could not have foreseen just how seminal they would be to the study of conformity and what are now known as social norms. The pressure to comply with the majority opinion is often strong enough that many people conform even though they might know and believe that doing so isn't right.

Asch further wondered how the results might change if he tweaked the protocol. He first changed from one true participant to two true participants, such that the participants would have a partner. He found that errors dropped from 32 per cent in the single variation to 10.4 per cent in the partner variation, indicating that the participants were sensitive to the presence of another dissenting opinion. In another variation of the participant condition, one confidant was asked to always give the true answer. When this happened, error rate further dropped to 5.5 per cent.[5]

Asch's findings were an extremely important contribution to social psychology. Perhaps more importantly in terms of building a decisive mind, they underline the importance of feedback, both in terms of what we ourselves perceive and what others perceive and inform us about. The experiments are striking precisely because people were willing to abandon the evidence to go along with the crowd. Furthermore, the motivation for the participants is also striking. Some of those that thought they were correct could not help but respond correctly, ignoring social pressure entirely. For others, even if they thought they were right, they were willing to go along with the majority. But this effect changes dramatically as soon as they have a single person that is willing to go along with them. Even a small amount of accurate feedback is enough to push people onto the right path.

Structuring feedback

When exerting effort in pursuit of a goal, the role of motivation and belief is critical. While effort itself can be rewarding, it is helpful to link the effort you are making to progress in pursuit of your goal. This progression takes the form of feedback. Feedback doesn't need to be overcomplicated. If your goal is to save money, checking the amount in your savings account is good feedback.

We could stop there, but just as with goals, there's a lot that can be done to improve the way you receive feedback at the margin. Feedback that is benchmarked, or compared to something, is more effective. To take the savings example, you may have a figure in mind that you would like to save at the end of a 12-month period, January to January. For argument's sake, let's say it's £120. Clearly, you know that you need to save £10 per month if you are going to hit your target. Checking in during the summer, if you have only £30, you need to do something! This much is intuitive. However, as we shall see, this type of feedback can be dangerous, yielding both positive and negative effects. Another type of benchmarking is the one we see in Asch's experiment; it's about comparing your outcome with others. In this chapter we will focus on how to structure feedback.

In Chapter 6, we learnt about setting goals to provide direction and motivation. Remember our simple decision rule:

- Do something if rewards are greater than the costs
- Do nothing if costs are greater than the rewards

The effort exerted in service to an aspiration requires some form of reward to offset the costs in the interim. Effort exerted in support of an aspiration gives the effort purpose, or a sense of direction. This sense of purpose is independently motivating as it serves as a small reward.

In Chapter 3, we discussed how giving purpose to tasks increases effort via intrinsic motivation.[6] This means that when the task we are performing is linked to a positive outcome, either now, or in the future, we generate intrinsic (psychological) rewards which help to offset the costs of exerting effort. The use of clearly defined goals allows us to reward our effort through purpose and achievement.

When we get this right, it leads to us, for instance, no longer going to the gym because we enjoy it, but because the action serves a broader purpose and function whose rewards we will receive in the future. Furthermore, in Chapter 4, we discussed the concept of present biasedness, the idea that rewards in the present loom larger than rewards in the future. If I transformed into a man with a chiselled six-pack every time I visited the gym, then I would probably go much more often, even if my six-pack lasted a relatively short time. But in real life, the reward is delayed. The six-pack does not immediately appear. And because we tend to prefer immediate rewards over later ones, we hit the doughnut shop rather than the gym.

So what can we do about this? First, having set an aspiration and a goal, it gives me a bump of pleasure each time I exert effort in service to it. The second point is that this bump in pleasure is probably not enough and will tend to diminish very quickly. Both these points working together tend to lead to us starting lots of projects but not following through. What we need to do is *structure* events in such a way that the reward bumps keep coming, even when the ultimate payoff (the achievement of the goal/aspiration) remains a long way away.

One piece of advice that many behavioural scientists have given is that constructing small interim and consistent steps along the way helps get us to our goal. In popular self-development literature, authors like BJ Fogg in his book *Tiny Habits* have excellent insights into how small changes lead to the development of habits that lead to lasting behaviour change.[7] James Clear in his bestselling *Atomic Habits* has similar insights, as does Katy Milkman in *How to Change*.[8] The idea behind these insights is simple – but it is, of course, devilishly hard to implement these kinds of changes. The strategy works by keeping effort costs low, asking you to do something simple like two push-ups a day and then to build in increasing steps as the initial effort is overcome. These books tend to structure rewards in much the same way. Each time you exert effort, you gain a psychological reward. Over time, the reward stays the same, but the effort required becomes smaller and hence the habit sustains itself. Overall, this is a fine method and doubtless will work for some people.

In building our decisive mind, the idea here is much simpler. Many of us work toward distinct aspirations – writing a book, climbing a mountain, getting fitter – without really wanting to change our habits and our behaviours altogether. What this means is that for many of us, change stops along the way because we don't necessarily want to change ourselves in service to one aspiration. I want to get fitter, but I don't really want to do thousands of push-ups per day or run marathons. There is a difference between wanting to achieve an aspiration and wanting to develop a habit. We are building a system for the former. I would love to see data on people that read James Clear's book back in 2018 and are currently doing thousands of push-ups a day. My bet is there aren't many. Indeed, I would guess that the number of people who stuck long term with the 'push-up habit' was small. The ones that did were highly motivated to and they likely took some enjoyment from doing push-ups because motivation is at the heart of being able to stick with something for a long time.

For highly motivated individuals, small steps generally work well. The sense of achievement experienced when exerting small amounts of effort is supposed to compensate for the pain of the effort itself. With enough repetition, the hope is that the small amounts of effort translate into habits. Essentially, once an action has been repeated so many times, we no longer need to think about it; we don't actively have to decide to do it. It moves the action away from a System 2 style deliberative decision to a System 1 style automatic decision. For many this would seem to work just fine, especially for those that are motivated enough to stick with the process. However, consider the situation where the effort is so low, it isn't plausibly contributing to the goal in any tangible way. The 'little and often' model of behaviour change ceases to be as useful. For instance, you are unlikely to be able to rely on habit to obtain a PhD. It might help get you going, but you're going to need something more. Sometimes intrinsic motivation itself is not enough and needs to be bolstered by other factors. This is the domain of feedback and social incentives.

A series of experiments tested the effects of habits on goal pursuit.[9] The basic idea follows from the behaviour change literature, in that habits are repeated responses that are automatically triggered by contextual cues. For example, you probably have a habit of locking the door when you leave your house. The action of locking the door is triggered upon leaving the house, but not as a conscious decision to protect your belongings. Because habits respond to contextual cues and not to pre-specified goals, they can yield the same outcome even when willpower and self-control, or motivation, is low. This is precisely why the behaviour change literature focuses on habit formation rather than on self-control. Once implemented, because they are not reliant on motivation or deliberation, they can yield positive effects over the long term.

The trouble arises, however, in the habit formation stage. It takes a lot of time and consistency to develop habits and it's much more useful for simple tasks rather than complex ones. Likewise, it's much more useful for people who are already motivated, rather than those who aren't. The decisive mind is different because it does not focus on habit formation. Rather, it's the opposite. We're focused on conscious and deliberate choices to structure our behaviour in service to our goals and aspirations. In this fashion, the Decisive Framework applies to a larger context of actions and situations. Yes, it requires greater mental labour, at least in the short term. But, honestly, hard things are hard. As I said, you aren't going to write a PhD on autopilot – even if you love your subject and really, really want to become a doctor. To say that turning up to the library at the same time each day is going to get you in the 'PhD habit' is an oversimplification of the cognitively demanding decisions that you will need to make once you've done the 'showing up' part.

One psychological theory that is relevant here is called Motivational Intensity Theory, which suggests that commitment to a goal, and the willingness to exert effort, are based on the perception of task difficulty, our ability to do the task and the likelihood that exerting effort will lead to progress.[10] In other words, if the task is too difficult, we can't be bothered. Similarly, if I believe I am not capable of completing the task, then I won't do it. The final point is critical though, which is that I need to be *reassured* that exerting effort is paying off or contributing to my goal. If we believe that our effort is not achieving our aims, then, logically, I'm likely to stop trying.

If my goal, aged 25, is to have a million pounds by the age of 30, saving £2 a day feels like an exercise in futility. Sure, I am inching closer to the goal, but I don't have 500,000 days and I'm going to have to scale up absolutely massively. £2 is a drop in the ocean. As we have seen, the challenge with goals is that they must be attainable. Setting micro-goals and trying to build up violates the principle of realism in goal-setting. That means we're likely to give up and look to put our effort elsewhere. Indeed, the plethora of fad diets is a reaction to exactly this.

A diet needs to make us *feel* we are getting closer to our goal. With some diets, the feedback mechanism (jumping on the scale) allows for exactly this feeling to occur, leading to an increase in the adoption rate. For example, fans of the ketogenic diet (ultra-low carb diets) are likely to adhere to them because they see movement on the scale relatively rapidly, whilst being able to eat food that they might already have enjoyed (high fat content). However, the diet is generally considered unsustainable because once individuals return to their previous eating patterns, as most surely do, the weight returns. Or consider the case of going to the gym. On days when you have high levels of energy, you may well perceive the goal of jogging for five minutes on the treadmill to be so easy that it doesn't tangibly contribute to the goal of getting fitter (it does, a small amount, and you know this rationally, but you may not *feel* it emotionally). This can happen for all manner of effort-based tasks and goals and hence one needs to be conducting a careful balancing act, calibrating the goal and the level of effort required to keep motivation high.

So, how do we do this? Through deft use of feedback. As we embark on an effort journey in pursuit of a goal, calibrations need to occur both on defining and redefining the goal. We need to understand the amount of effort that is required to accomplish individual tasks in service to the overarching goal. The role of feedback, then, is to provide data and evidence for us to conduct these calibrations and to ensure that we stick with the goal and continue to make the effort. Or, more simply, we need to make it hard enough that we feel like we're getting somewhere, but not so hard as to demoralise us. Feedback lets you determine how well you are progressing and whether to revise either the effort input or the goal outcome. Furthermore, feedback itself can be motivating, depending on how it is structured.

The 'when' of getting feedback is critical for motivation. Recall that in Chapter 5 we discussed the notion of a good news-bad news effect.[11] Positive feedback can have a similarly positive effect on motivation, while negative feedback can have a negative effect, up to and including giving up the task entirely.

How might this function in the real world? In an experiment conducted with university students, participants engaged in a complex task with multiple components.[12] The use of complex tasks in laboratory-based experiments ensured that participants couldn't keep track of their performance themselves. They had to rely on feedback to help them calibrate their effort. Participants were asked to undertake the task over five rounds, with each performance feedback being given at the end of each round. The authors recorded a series of psychophysiological measures, including heart rate activity, blood pressure, nervous system activity, and a battery of self-reported data such as mood, motivation and confidence. But, as ever, there was a twist. The experiment directly manipulated the feedback that was provided. Half the participants received positive feedback in the form of improved performance metrics in each round. The other half received negative feedback – it was made to appear that their performance got worse each round.

The authors found that participants receiving negative feedback were more likely to report negative feelings and showed signs of stress. Furthermore, for the group receiving negative feedback, motivation was much lower towards the end of the task relative to those receiving positive feedback. The negative feedback group also saw reductions in confidence and control, consistent with reduced motivation. The authors stated that the trend in the psychophysiological data indicated that those faced with repeated failures were on the verge of disengaging from the task entirely – or, in layman's terms, giving up.

There is an ongoing debate among researchers now as to whether the decline in mental effort during extended or repeated tasks arises from a depletion of mental resources. That is, do we have some sort of mental resource that, once used up, means we can no longer control ourselves? Historically, this was called 'ego-depletion', which we have covered earlier in Chapter 2 concerning mental effort. The counter argument is that a decline in performance over time is not associated with a lack of resources (which implies that people cannot continue exerting mental effort even if they wanted to) but a lack of motivation itself.[13] This is an important distinction because the former theory of resource depletion means that people are limited after a certain point, no matter what the motivation or incentives at stake were.[14] The alternative model is that over time motivation declines and so people choose to stop exerting effort. The recent evidence points toward a model of intrinsic costs associated with cognitive control that need to be balanced with intrinsic rewards.[15] Regardless of the model, however, over time decision-making becomes harder and it therefore needs to be balanced by motivation and rewards. Feedback is a calibration exercise that can be used to enhance and improve motivation.

So, how should we structure feedback to enhance motivation? Well, it depends – different feedback works in different ways in different contexts. For example, a field experiment with a police organisation implemented an 'upward feedback' programme.[16] This meant that supervisors were provided with performance feedback from their subordinates. Some supervisors were randomly assigned to receive written feedback while others were asked to simply rate themselves. The results of the study were startling – there was no overall effect of the intervention. Furthermore, they found that those supervisors who were more cynical about changes in the organisation were less likely to improve, indicating that motivation was a critical mediating factor. Those that were motivated to improve did so when receiving feedback, while those that were unmotivated did not.

A meta-analysis, that's a review of all the literature that's out there, of feedback interventions found that about a third had negative effects on performance.[17] It notes that feedback is 'psychologically reassuring' but people don't seem to seek it when the costs are too high – that is to say, people who on paper most need to be told that they are getting off track are least likely to seek out information that tells them so.[18] However, many people do actively seek feedback and it does have a positive impact. The review suggests a kind of compromise. When feedback moves away from the task itself to the individual doing the task, it has a negative impact. This implies that we should use feedback to calibrate effort, rather than to figure out ability. For instance, if we wanted to improve our cardio fitness, we would be better off tracking how much time we spent running, rather than how far we ran during that time. And we would be better off benchmarking ourselves to how much time we managed the previous week or month, rather than how we stack up against other runners.

Further surveys of the literature find that positive and negative feedback has a differential effect on motivation: positive feedback enhances motivation, while negative feedback reduces motivation.[19] This chimes with the good news/bad news effect discussed earlier.[20] We even perceive positive feedback to be more accurate and acceptable (even actionable) than negative feedback. These perceptions matter: individuals take on board feedback that is consistent with self-appraisals, while feedback that is inconsistent can lead people to give up. Essentially, building from the example above, if you think that you're getting better at running and your feedback also suggests this, you're more likely to keep trying to get better. Conversely, if you think you are getting better at running and your feedback tells you that you're staying the same, you're far more likely to give up.[21]

Recent work has dug deeper into the interplay between self-assessment and feedback. Using both a field and a lab experiment, participants were asked to self-assess prior to exerting effort and receiving performance feedback.[22] The research shows that those that had positive self-assessments and were high performers had the highest level of performance following feedback and the lowest levels of giving up. This was followed by those that had low self-assessments but performance was high. In other words, those that had high self-appraisals were most likely to perform better and least likely to leave the programme. This shows two things – it helps to be good at something that you're doing in the first place. Secondly, not having an accurate view of your competence makes you less likely to improve following performance, even if the feedback you receive gives you good news.

So, structuring feedback is important. It's clear that feedback needs to build you up, rather than run you down. It's also clear that receiving feedback from the wrong person doesn't help. Ultimately, it's best if feedback tells you what you already know. This is counter intuitive. We'd expect the most helpful feedback to tell us where we're going wrong. But that doesn't seem to be backed up by the science at all. Rather, it's better to learn where we are going *right* and to provide positive evidence that affirms our beliefs about ourselves. Essentially, if the feedback you receive encourages you to believe that you're on the right track, you're going to keep heading down the track. This doesn't mean burying our head in the sand and surrounding ourselves with false information. It means measuring things that have a good chance of making you feel confident.

Once again, we can see that effort undertaken in service to a particular goal needs to be offset by rewards. One aspect of intrinsic rewards is driven by motivation itself. If you are motivated to hit your goal, the effort you exert in service of doing so is itself motivating. That's enough to receive all the positive impacts of goal-setting seen in the literature. However, goals that are set need to follow some sort of structure and they need to be achievable. What an achievable goal is, is hard to know ahead of time. So in the early stages particularly, we need to do some calibration of both the goal and the effort that we exert as we go along.

It is here that feedback truly comes into its own. Feedback tells us whether the goal is achievable and whether the effort we are exerting is generating progress. I'd recommend that, if the feedback is telling us that we are falling short, don't change the effort, change the goal. You've set your sights too high; a more modest approach will yield greater benefits over the long haul. Remember, feedback can be both motivating and de-motivating depending on our beliefs. The research shows that it is important to be realistic. If you aren't realistic, if you don't have a good grip on your own abilities, the effect of feedback can be negative – it'll push us back to our old ways.

Asch's to Asch's

Solomon Asch's fascinating experiments in 1951 kicked off a massive and controversial research agenda on social psychology and how the behaviour of other people affects our own. This was an important finding that led to a large body of work that looked at how people behave in groups and how social identities affect our behaviour. Asch continued to have a fascinating career, further building up his work and looking at how humans form impressions of others based on a small set of data. This work led to our contemporary understanding of how humans fill the gaps in our reasoning and information based on previous experiences and perceptions and use this information to drive decisions. As we've learnt in this chapter, when we receive feedback from our environment, it isn't some inherent good. If we get the wrong feedback, just like Asch's undergraduates, it might push us down the wrong path. We are quick to compare ourselves to others and this is rarely helpful.

Feedback is rarely objective. It is often benchmarked against our own internal reference points, or reference points set by others. To be motivating, positive feedback has a better chance than negative feedback, particularly at early stages of goal pursuit. Hence, it is important to bolster feedback by using trusted partners or keeping your expectations low.

Furthermore, the timing on the feedback can be critical. In the same way that jumping on the weighing scale immediately after your first workout is misleading, structuring feedback at the wrong time, or using the wrong source, can have the opposite impact and lead to goal abandonment. It may be important to seek out individuals that you trust to help structure your feedback in the early stages so that you are managing expectations effectively. Practically, what this means is to not seek out feedback too soon; give yourself time to make progress and provide yourself with other rewards to keep you going.

The next chapter focuses on the final aspect of tipping the scale in favour of sticking to a goal: structuring rewards. Once this final piece of the puzzle is in place, we will turn to the Decisive Framework and put everything that we've learnt together in a practical and sustainable way.

Box: Your turn!

Assignment # 7

In this assignment, let's focus on when to seek out feedback. As in the previous chapter, think about a goal that you set for yourself, but did not achieve. Did you seek feedback on that goal in any way? Did you find that motivating or de-motivating?

Think about the last time you received feedback. Perhaps the most common way is the dreaded 'performance review' in a workplace. Thinking about everything that we've learnt in this chapter, consider whether it was effective. Chances are the feedback focused on what you need to improve on. As we have seen, this isn't particularly useful.

Your aspiration:	
What was your goal (be specific)?	
Was your goal Measurable? How did you measure progress?	
When did you seek out feedback?	
Were you satisfied with your progress? Why or why not?	
If you could do it over, how would you change the timing of the feedback you received?	

References

Ceraso, John, Gruber, Howard and Rock, Irvin. 'On Solomon Asch.' *The Legacy of Solomon Asch: Essays in Cognition and Social Psychology* (1990): 3–19.

Asch, Solomon E. 'Effects of group pressure upon the modification and distortion of judgments.' *Organizational Influence Processes* 58 (1951): 295–303.

Corgnet, Brice, Gómez-Miñambres, Joaquín and Hernán-Gonzalez, Roberto. 'Goal setting and monetary incentives: When large stakes are not enough.' *Management Science* 61, no. 12 (2015): 2926–2944.

Gómez-Miñambres, Joaquín. 'Motivation through goal setting.' *Journal of Economic Psychology* 33, no. 6 (2012): 1223–1239.

Fogg, Brian J. *Tiny Habits: The Small Changes That Change Everything.* Eamon Dolan Books, 2019.

Clear, James. *Atomic Habits: An Easy & Proven Way to Build Good Habits & Break Bad Ones.* Penguin, 2018.

Milkman, Katy. *How to Change: The Science of Getting From Where You Are to Where You Want to Be.* Penguin, 2021.

Neal, David T., Wood, Wendy and Drolet, Aimee. 'How do people adhere to goals when willpower is low? The profits (and pitfalls) of strong habits.' *Journal of Personality and Social Psychology* 104, no. 6 (2013): 959.

Brehm, Jack W. and Self, Elizabeth A. 'The intensity of motivation.' *Annual Review of Psychology* 40 (1989): 109–131.

Wright, Rex A. and Brehm, Jack W. 'Energization and goal attractiveness.' In Pervin, Lawrence A. (Ed.), *Goal Concepts in Personality and Social Psychology*, pp. 169–210. Hillsdale, NJ: Erlbaum. 1989

Eil, David and Rao, M. Justin. 'The good news-bad news effect: Asymmetric processing of objective information about yourself.' *American Economic Journal: Microeconomics* 3, no. 2 (2011): 114–138.

Venables, Louise and Fairclough, Stephen H. 'The influence of performance feedback on goal-setting and mental effort regulation.' *Motivation and Emotion* 33, no. 1 (2009): 63–74.

Kool, Wouter and Botvinick, Matthew. 'The intrinsic cost of cognitive control.' *Behav Brain Sci* 36, no. 6 (2013): 697–698.

Hagger, Martin S., Wood, Chantelle, Stiff, Chris and Chatzisarantis, Nikos L. D. 'Ego depletion and the strength model of self-control: A meta-analysis.' *Psychological Bulletin* 136, no. 4 (2010): 495.

Job, Veronika, Dweck, Carol S. and Walton, Gregory M. 'Ego depletion—Is it all in your head? Implicit theories about willpower affect self-regulation.' *Psychological Science* 21, no. 11 (2010): 1686–1693.

Baumeister, Roy F., Bratslavsky, Ellen, Muraven, Mark and Tice, Dianne M. 'Ego depletion: Is the active self a limited resource?' In *Self-regulation and Self-Control*, pp. 16–44. Routledge, 2018.

Kool, Wouter, McGuire, Joseph T., Wang, Gary J. and Botvinick, Matthew M. 'Neural and behavioral evidence for an intrinsic cost of self-control.' *PloS One* 8, no. 8 (2013): e72626.

Atwater, Leanne E., Waldman, David A., Atwater, David and Cartier, Priscilla. 'An upward feedback field experiment: Supervisors' cynicism, reactions, and commitment to subordinates.' *Personnel Psychology* 53, no. 2 (2000): 275.

Kluger, Avraham N. and DeNisi, Angelo. 'The effects of feedback interventions on performance: A historical review, a meta-analysis, and a preliminary feedback intervention theory.' *Psychological Bulletin* 119, no. 2 (1996): 254.

Ashford, Susan J. and Cummings, Larry L. 'Feedback as an individual resource: Personal strategies of creating information.' *Organizational Behavior and Human Performance* 32, no. 3 (1983): 370–398.

Sitzmann, Traci and Johnson, Stefanie K. 'The best laid plans: Examining the conditions under which a planning intervention improves learning and reduces attrition.' *Journal of Applied Psychology* 97, no. 5 (2012a): 967.

Stone, Dianna L. and Stone, Eugene F. 'The effects of feedback consistency and feedback favorability on self-perceived task competence and perceived feedback accuracy.' *Organizational Behavior and Human Decision Processes* 36, no. 2 (1985): 167–185.

Meyer, Wulf-Uwe. 'Paradoxical effects of praise and criticism on perceived ability.' *European Review of Social Psychology* 3, no. 1 (1992): 259–283.

Sitzmann, Traci and Johnson, Stefanie K. 'When is ignorance bliss? The effects of inaccurate self-assessments of knowledge on learning and attrition.' *Organizational Behavior and Human Decision Processes* 117, no. 1 (2012b): 192–207.

CHAPTER 8

What Do I Get Out of It? Structuring Rewards

Key lesson: Step # 3: CASH OUT

2001, Hudson, Wisconsin. Thanksgiving Day. Just after 9am, a middle-aged blonde woman stands outside apartment 104 of a small nondescript complex. It's quiet, especially so because it's a holiday and most people have either been out trying to get the latest shopping deals, attending church services or getting last minute groceries to prepare for the feast yet to come. Thanksgiving is a time to express gratitude, be with family and eat, on average, between 3,000 and 4,000 calories over the course of a single meal. However, on a day we typically associate with happiness and joy, the woman outside apartment 104 was about to experience every parent's worst nightmare.[1]

Liz Woolley felt trepidation. She was there to pick up her son, Shawn, to take him to Thanksgiving dinner at her mother's house. But Shawn had been experiencing difficulties lately. Overall, his life had seemed on the right track until about a week ago. He had a good job with an employer who liked him and thought he was a good worker. He was making enough money to support himself and pay rent on his apartment. He did not have a car, but his work was within walking distance, so he did not seem to need one. Until last week, Liz had thought things were going well, even though, like any parent, she worried about Shawn all the time.

Hudson, Wisconsin, is a small town on the St Croix River, which separates the states of Minnesota and Wisconsin. While Hudson itself is small, it is on the edge of Minneapolis-St. Paul, Minnesota, a reasonably sized city by US standards. The city epitomises a culture of the American Midwest, specifically in terms of how nice and polite people are. People from the state of Minnesota have a reputation for being non-confrontational, to the point of being passive aggressive. There's even a term for this phenomenon: Minnesota nice.[2]

Liz thought about this as she walked up to her son's apartment. She had been there at the very same doorstep just yesterday, knocking on the door. She had needed to come and see him to set up a time to pick him up for Thanksgiving dinner today. But Shawn hadn't answered. She was not the type to show up to the apartment unannounced, not least because Shawn had a habit of not answering his door when he wasn't expecting anybody. But yesterday she'd had no choice.

Liz's mind wandered back to August of 2001. Had she made the right decision? After Shawn had moved out to his own apartment and got a job that he liked, she'd thought things were moving in the right direction. Shawn had been looking great at his elder brother's wedding in July, though he had missed the latter half of the ceremony.

There had been friction, on and off, between Liz and Shawn for a while now. The cause? Video games. Shawn had always loved video games. But things had come to a head in the past year because he was becoming obsessed with one game in particular: *EverQuest*. Shawn and Liz had several arguments regarding his playing, not least because Shawn had suffered a series of seizures during extended bouts of play. Liz had banned Shawn from playing the game at their house, even going so far as to lock up the computer keyboard when she was away. Shawn was now living by himself and things were looking good except for some lapses here and there. For instance, Shawn had missed the second half of his brother's wedding because he snuck back to the house to play his game.[3]

In August though, Shawn called Liz to ask for a favour. Liz was over the moon. Shawn never called her for anything; now he needed her. He said that he had saved up some money to buy a computer. He wanted one so that he could get Microsoft Certified and, therefore, get a job in the IT industry. Shawn said that he had found a used computer nearby but needed a ride to be able to go and pick it up. Liz knew that these certifications were one way that people had broken into the IT industry and she wanted to be supportive of Shawn. She wanted to spend time with him. But still . . . a computer? Getting Microsoft Certified might not be Shawn's only motive. In the end, Liz agreed, but now, as she stood outside apartment 104, she wondered if it had been the right thing to do. Could it be that things had slipped since August?

Shawn worked at a pizza chain company called Papa Murphy's Pizza that had recently opened in the town. He had been working there since May 2001 and had moved into his apartment the next month. Shawn loved his job and Rick Murphy (Shawn's boss) spoke very highly of him and his work ethic. But things seemed to be awry. Liz had last seen him the past Friday, after attempting to speak to him at work multiple times. Each time she called, Shawn had not been there despite having a shift. When Liz finally spoke to Shawn's boss, he said that he had not been in all week and had not called in sick either. This was very unlike him. Murphy expressed concern for Shawn and Liz decided to make a trip over to the apartment to check in.

The visit had not gone well. She had to ask one of Shawn's neighbours to buzz her into the building as Shawn was not responding. Furthermore, he did not answer the door when she knocked either. This prompted Liz to call Shawn's landlord as she feared he might have had a seizure and needed help. The landlord came and unlocked the door, but it could not be opened all the way because of a security chain, which meant that it could be opened just enough to peek through. At this point, Shawn appeared; he had heard the door being unlocked. However, he did not let Liz in, saying the apartment was a mess. Liz offered to help clean it, but Shawn refused. Liz asked why he had not been going to work. Shawn said that he'd quit and got another job at Walmart. Liz asked why he hadn't let his current employers know, to which Shawn responded, 'It doesn't matter anyway.' Liz called up Papa Murphy and had Shawn speak to his boss to inform them that he was quitting. She then asked when she could pick him up for Thanksgiving dinner. Shawn asked her to come by his new place of work on Monday. Liz left but came away with a sense that things were getting bad again. She had a sneaking suspicion that Shawn had not cleaned his apartment since August. Again, August.

Liz waited patiently over the weekend. Early on Monday morning, she stopped by the Walmart in Hudson to see Shawn, as he had asked. Liz walked in, headed to the information desk and asked to see Shawn Woolley. The person at the desk was puzzled; they said they had never heard of a Shawn Woolley. There must be a mistake, said Liz, he just recently started working there. The person said it was possible that they didn't know Shawn because he was new. But then, he was not there that day. She returned the next day – same answer. No Shawn Woolley here. Liz was utterly confused. Had Shawn lied to her? She knew she would have to confront him.

Back to Thanksgiving. Liz's hand shook as she reached for the door. Before she turned the doorknob, she somehow knew that it would open. The door was unlocked, but the chain prevented her from going in. She chastised herself for not intruding more forcefully. Deep down, she already knew the truth. Something terrible had happened. Her hand twisted the doorknob and the door swung ajar. She could see inside, but couldn't go in, the same as before. But now there was an odd smell coming from the apartment.

Liz reached for her phone. She must know what has happened to Shawn. She stopped as she started to dial. If she calls the police, they may not let her in. Gathering all the strength that she could muster, she headed back to her car and drove home. The short drive felt endless. Back at home, she grabbed her toolkit, rooted around for a crowbar and some pliers.

Back at the apartment, Liz broke the chain off the door and ran into the bedroom. There, at the desk, was her son. Slumped on his rocking chair, head against the keyboard. Next to him, a .22 rifle. The monitor was still on. There was a video game on the screen. In big, gold letters, the word: Everquest.[4]

Evercrack

Shawn Woolley's death was the first known suicide directly linked to video game addiction.[5] This is now a real diagnosis. It is typified by a significant impairment of an individual's ability to function due to the compulsive use of video games.[6] The important criterion here is a lack of self-control. Today, it's recognised by the American Psychiatric Association, though it was not a recognised disorder at the time of Shawn's death. Liz Woolley has been an instrumental figure in getting the disorder recognised and now runs an organisation dedicated to providing greater awareness of the malady.[7]

This is a dark and tragic story, a cautionary tale on the dangers of addiction, particularly contemporary ones. But it forces us to confront a question that our society desperately needs to ask: why are video games so motivating as to be addictive?

As a reminder, in Chapter 3, we covered the three main categories of reward:

- Psychological rewards – referring to intrinsic incentives, rewards coming from within. Critical, but unstable.
- Social rewards – referring to social incentives, rewards coming from others in the form of competition, feedback and support. Useful, but can be unstable.
- Material rewards – referring to extrinsic incentives, rewards coming from things that we provide ourselves or others provide for us. Useful, stable, require additional resources.

Video games work on intrinsic incentives (psychological rewards), setting up and structuring rewards to keep individuals coming back repeatedly, without promise of any form of material rewards. Video games have become so good at this that they have become damaging to a not-insignificant fraction of their users. The reward system in our brains is delicate and complex – we abuse it at our peril.

Think that video games are only relevant for a small subset of the population? Think again. The gaming industry has grown up. It's a serious business. According to Newzoo, a dedicated gaming market research organisation, the size of the global gaming industry was estimated to be nearly 160 billion USD in 2020; it overtook the global film industry in 2019. Gaming is no longer restricted to children either: only 21 per cent of US gamers are under the age of 18 – 15 per cent of US gamers are over the age of 55. This means that chances are at least one of your parents is regularly interacting with a video gaming app of some kind. With an estimated 2.7 billion people playing across the world, the growth of this industry is remarkable, especially considering that it is only 50 years old.[8]

How did this incredible growth occur? Of course, there are a lot of reasons, but one of the most important is the role of psychology. There is one thing that gaming delivers more frequently than any other entertainment medium: rewards that are linked to effort. These rewards come in all kinds of different shapes and sizes and I'll only highlight a few major ones. At its core, though, the key idea to remember is that these rewards carry motivational properties. This means that the rewards are often important enough to people that they motivate the individual to continue past the point that they are enjoying themselves.

Arguably the original type of reward that gaming offered was a basic points system. This simple method illustrates the mechanic that a game uses to hook you in. When you perform an action that the game wants, you get rewarded with an in-game currency, the earliest of which were called 'points'. Think coins in *Super Mario*, rings in *Sonic the Hedgehog* or just 'points' in earlier games like *Tetris* or *Pong*. Points are feedback. As we know from the last chapter, feedback helps us chart progress. When you engage in actions that the game wants, you get points – these signal that you should keep doing what you're doing. Just as we learnt in the last chapter, the feedback is positive rather than negative. You get points for doing something well. This incentivises players to continue those actions.[9]

Points basically act like in-game currencies, allowing individuals to measure progress in a simple fashion. They also enable competition, either against oneself or against others. Some of the earliest games utilised sophisticated points systems to keep track of player performance, to give you a sense of how well you are doing. Games like *Tetris*, *Galaga*, *Space Invaders* and *Pac-Man* were not only fun on their own but allowed you to keep track of how well you were doing relative to yourself and to your friends. Beating your past self or one of your friends is meaningful and generates a sense of accomplishment. Points operate the same way as goals do, as discussed a couple of chapters ago. This is simple, but it bears repeating and is worth keeping in mind: points are explicitly linked to an effort you exerted playing the game and doing what the game designers intended you to do. The more you performed the expected actions, the more points you got, which kept you coming back.

Competing against others became more and more important to the gaming industry over time. The simple use of points dominated the video game landscape in the 1980s, but the 1990s ushered in an era of player versus player competition, directly contributing to the establishment of the e-Sports industry as we know it today. An example of a game that exemplifies this phenomenon is *Street Fighter II*, the famous arcade game introduced in 1991, that spawned a series of similar fighting games such as *Mortal Kombat*, *Virtua Fighter* and *Tekken*. In these games the player controls a character and engages in (typically) one-on-one fights with either a computer or a human opponent. The violence in *Mortal Kombat*, in particular, is famous for being at the centre of controversy when the game was first released and is widely credited with introducing ratings guides for video games. Indeed, the release of *Mortal Kombat* was the first time policymakers noticed the potential of danger in games, though it was not their addictive qualities that were coming under the microscope, but their portrayal and glorification of violence. *Mortal Kombat* was banned in Germany until the late 2010s! Fighting games, perhaps more than any other genre of video game, exemplify the importance of competition. In a 'beat 'em up' the competition is very direct – you must defeat a single opponent. In most games, it's less direct – think of *Tetris*.

For somebody who studies reward and motivation, there's something slightly bizarre about video games when you think about them rationally. We pay an organisation for the opportunity to exert effort, with little to no material rewards – so the economics part of the equation doesn't necessarily make sense. Video games only work their magic on us when we consider the importance of psychological rewards. We covered the motivating power of these in Chapter 3, so there is little need to rehash them here, but the important point is the explicit linking of psychological rewards to effort, whether that's for earning points, defeating an enemy in combat or topping a leaderboard. Video games reward you when you offer time and energy. As Chapter 3 explains, when we are aware that effort generates progress towards a particular goal, we experience positive emotions because of exerting said effort.

You should be able to see where we are going with this. But to spell it out to those who are thinking 'this is well and good for people playing video games, but what does it mean in real life?', you should know that these techniques of adding game elements to tasks (known as 'gamification') are already being used extensively in various industries as we speak. Famous examples come from the gig economy, with companies like Uber and Lyft at the forefront.[10] These gaming elements provide workers with feedback that allows them to become more engaged and motivated in the tasks that are set out before them. These mechanisms allow for the implementation of rewards, either material or psychological. Specific elements like leaderboards and competition don't work for everybody universally, so these companies use a suite of interventions to offer feedback and rewards. For our purposes, in building a decisive mind we need to figure out what we might best respond to, and to do so, we need to know that all these interventions exist and that they don't work equally well for all.

There's a final aspect of motivation that bears remarking on. It's the importance of purpose. We get sucked in by a narrative, or story, that motivates us to engage in games. All kinds of games have fantastic storylines – I'm thinking of *Double Dragon*, *Final Fight*, *The House of the Dead* and, most recently, *The Last of Us* and *Elden Ring*. The focus on telling a compelling story keeps players coming back to see it through to the end. Some of these games do not use typical types of currency (such as points), instead they signal progression by using a narrative, giving the actions engaged in by the player a function.

In Chapter 3, I discussed a study that I had conducted where participants were asked to engage in a simple word-decoding task.[11] Even though the task itself was boring and carried little meaning, many participants exerted considerable effort. Others were asked to decode words, but the words themselves became part of a story that participants could unlock. We found that participants increased effort in the task when their effort led to more of the story being revealed. In both cases, the task itself was the same, only the feedback and reward changed.

Most video games, in terms of the task itself, are the same – manipulating a controller to make stuff happen in front of you. But powerful games suck you in with a story and all that joystick waggling suddenly becomes emotional and meaningful. In this sense, there's no wonder video games are now more lucrative than films. Just like films, they tell stories. But unlike films, they reward you by making you the thing that causes the plot to unfold. This behavioural linking is unbelievably motivating and it's this that allows us to keep engaging in a task even when we are having a bad time doing it.

There's a dark side to all of this. *EverQuest* is sometimes referred to as 'EverCrack' – an unsubtle nod to its addictive nature. This game is widely regarded as one of the most influential and ground-breaking games of all time, enjoying unprecedented success upon its release in 1999. The game itself is a massively multiplayer online role-playing game (MMORPG) and while it is not the first of its kind, it introduced mechanics that were extremely addictive. What set the game apart from those that came before it was the use of social elements. The game is built around individuals creating a controllable character that they use to navigate the game world. In the world there are core gameplay loops for fighting beasts and demons, in exchange for experience.[12] Experience is the points system which progresses the character, allowing them to grow stronger and access more parts of the world. However, there is a limited amount of content a player can experience independently and so the game encourages players to link up with one another, making relationships that they otherwise may not in the real world. Woolley and Langel write, 'A person can get sucked into these virtual worlds, and this becomes their new reality.'[13] So it was for Shawn. The social aspect of these games is a very powerful motivator, going well beyond the core gameplay loop.

Does this sound familiar? The tasks that we might engage with when building our decisive mind are also likely to be shot through with a strong dose of purpose. They're likely to be reliant on relationships. Many of our workplaces are structured in a way that is not dissimilar to this – we overcome challenges and gain experience, and as we do so we become stronger and can explore more. Collaborating with others draws us deeper into the narrative and unlocks ever-greater rewards. But we must be careful. Being motivated to do things that we aren't enjoying is, arguably, a crucial factor in whether we will be successful. It's also an obvious route to burnout. Gamifying your life and your goals is helpful . . . until it isn't. The office environment, the football field, your bank balance:

all of these are, in effect, virtual worlds that we have created for ourselves. Don't let them become the totality of your reality.

The science of rewards

Having said that, it's possible to use rewards in a healthy way. As we know, linking rewards to effort is a critical aspect of goal achievement. One of the most influential writers on behaviour change, Katy Milkman, conducted a study with university students over a ten-week period.[14] The study focused on the use of rewards to simulate effort for things that participants were motivated to do, but did not do regularly – exercise, for instance. Through the study, the concept of 'temptation-bundling' was introduced. It's a form of commitment device – something that helps ensure that we do things. A classic of the genre is automating a system whereby every time that you *don't* do something that you intend to do (e.g. go to the gym) a donation is made to an organisation you dislike, for instance, a political party that you oppose. In the study, participants were randomly put into three groups. The control group was simply given some text on the importance of going to the gym and their activity was monitored over a ten-week period. The second group was given a set of audiobook novels that were loaded onto their own personal devices. The audiobooks had been selected based on the taste of the participants – they were books they enjoyed. The participants were told that they should try to listen to these novels when at the gym so as to pair an unpleasant activity (going to the gym) with a pleasant activity (listening to an audiobook). A third group was also given audiobooks, but on devices that were owned by the authors, and participants were required to only use the devices when at the gym and to store them in a locker when they weren't.

The idea here is that if you can pair a pleasant activity (a reward) with an unpleasant activity (effort), then the likelihood of engaging effort increases through the use of immediate rewards. The authors find that gym attendance increased by 51 per cent for the group that was only able to access the audiobooks when at the gym (third group).[15] However, this was when the devices were first introduced and their effectiveness lowered over time. Note that this is a pretty low-cost intervention and that many people do not value audiobooks in the same way, but the main principle of bundling rewards with unpleasant activities is well-illustrated. The take home for our purposes is straightforward. If you love music and hate running, take your headphones with you and listen to your favourite songs, but only when you run. If you need to study and you love coffee, get a cup on the go when you settle down, but only when you study.

A useful review of the literature with contributions from Katy Milkman and Angela Duckworth (who wrote the bestselling *Grit*) separated interventions that are situational, meaning that they attempt to modify the situation you are in, or cognitive, meaning that they attempt to modify how you feel about the situation.[16] Further categories looked at interventions that were self-deployed – meaning the individual took deliberate action to modify their decisions – or other deployed – meaning the opposite, that some other person initiated action on an individual's behalf. In terms of building a decisive mind, we are naturally concerned with the self-deployed interventions, but using others to hold us accountable is also a useful technique that we will deploy. For now, though, note that the temptation bundling technique of pairing audiobooks with exercise is a self-deployed situational technique. Self-deployed techniques are handy for us because, in a sense, this is a 'self-help' book and they are a way to, quite literally, help yourself.

Commitment devices which focus on making it harder to engage in an activity that is unwanted also seem to work well. For example, one study tested a savings device where individuals committed to only having access to savings after reaching a savings goal, or after a preselected date.[17] Savings rates were 81 per cent higher for those that pre-committed. Another form of this may be to make the tempting behaviour more difficult to execute, for example, removing temptations from sight, rather than resisting them.[18] In both instances, it isn't hard to imagine ways that this could map onto anything that we set our sights on. Let's say you have a study goal and you don't want to procrastinate. Turn your mobile phone off and put it in another room. Reward yourself by granting access after a set period.

Self-deployed cognitive techniques are something we've discussed before, because the first and most well-known is goal-setting. The setting of specific, attainable, yet challenging goals have been effective in raising effort levels. Another meta-analysis didn't just show us that goal-setting is effective, but that goals that are set publicly can be even more effective than goals in private.[19] Once again, that gamification is at play, adding another layer of social motivation to enhance our drive. Splitting large goals into smaller sub-goals is also more effective, with the intuition being that the sense of accomplishment increases with each attainment of sub-goals – just like levelling up in a video game.

Further studies highlight the role of planning, mental contrasting (that's visualising a positive outcome and contrasting it with an obstacle that stands in the way), self-monitoring, mindfulness, cognitive therapy and psychological distance as valuable techniques in prompting behaviour change.[20] Again, the broader point here is about considering the costs of effort and looking for sources of motivation to help offset those costs. Commitment devices increase the costs of not complying. Planning and goal-setting maximise psychological rewards. The main takeaway from this literature is that goals can be effectively tackled with a little planning ahead of time. Naturally, this is easier said than done and in Chapter 11, we will discuss the steps to accomplish this.

This research and the growth of the gaming industry tell us that explicitly linking rewards to effort is important. Think about the last time you had to do something that you did not really want to do (such as, perhaps going to the gym, or doing the laundry). Think about our simple decision model:

- Do something if rewards are greater than the costs
- Do nothing if costs are greater than the rewards

The reason why you do these necessary but unpleasant tasks is that you know that there is some future reward to doing so (for example, becoming fitter, smelling nice, etc.). However, when the feedback is not very explicit (you know you will become fitter over time, but right now, you are not sure whether it has any effect), you can use these reward mechanisms to give your motivation a little boost. There are lots of public exercise apps which create social incentives for you. Likewise, there is a reason that many people end up running their first marathon 'for charity' – it imbues all that running with meaning. You might affirm and reward behaviour by buying yourself a coffee from your favourite café after every run or study session. Maybe after a long day of hitting the books, your reward is spending uninterrupted quality time with a loved one.

There are infinite ways to reward yourself when you think creatively. Learning what works for you is a process of trial and error, but it can't be overlooked. You need to hammer home to yourself at every stage of the journey that the effort that you are putting in will get rewarded.

Based on all the above evidence, a clear picture is starting to emerge. The first step towards achievement is to decide on a goal. What is it that you would like to achieve? Next, you need to think through the decisions that directly contribute to the goal. This is a form of planning. You need to think through how the decisions taken on a daily, weekly and monthly basis will help push you further along the path to progress. This component takes effort and time. We have to think through these steps carefully and make sure we are categorising the various decisions accurately. Then, we need to think through feedback mechanisms. How will we know we are making progress towards our goals? And when should we seek out feedback to make sure we are not demotivating ourselves? Finally, how can we go about structuring rewards around decisions?

Remember that decisions made in service to our goals can be painful – they have a lot of effort and typically carry small rewards. So how can we enhance the rewards as much as possible, or reduce the costs of effort? And when can we put these rewards in place? The literature covered in this chapter gives us one consistent rule: implement rewards as close to the action as possible so that we can make the explicit connection between the cost of effort and the reward.

Liz Woolley and the tragedy of Shawn

Liz Woolley paid the ultimate price. She lost a child to a terrible addiction. The worst part is that it was not classified as an addiction at the time, with one doctor simply telling her son to play less games. Liz had even met with Shawn's psychiatrist, who had recommended that Shawn could keep playing the game and that he had made Shawn aware of excessive gaming. Woolley and Langel write, 'To me, this was utterly ridiculous. It was like telling an alcoholic, that if drinking is the only thing you like to do, keep drinking! Or telling a drug addict that if heroin is all you like to do, keep doing it.'[21]

The story of how video games moved from diversion to an actual hobby, undertaken by people of all ages, is one of many different types of gamification operating over time. Games started with simple premises linking actions to feedback systems and then combining them with rewards, at first psychological (target and achievements), social (MMORPGs and social gaming) and finally monetary (e-Sports and tournaments). Along the way, games increased in their levels of addictiveness by offering distinct rewards and overcoming real world and material considerations for a subset of players. Naturally, the thing to think about is that the core gameplay loop (what the game expects you to do in return for the reward) is intrinsically motivating, but the sheer variety of tasks that individuals undertake in modern games combines tasks that individuals find pleasant along with tasks they hate. In research my colleagues and I have conducted, including multiple types of motivational affordances makes a person increase voluntary effort.[22] This means that whatever the task one is willing to undertake, linking it to multiple forms of rewards increases the likelihood that people will actually do it. It is possible to then layer on a series of rewards for the desired activity and link them to either inputs (whenever effort is exerted a reward is triggered) or outputs (whenever a goal is achieved a reward is triggered).

Naturally the unpleasantness of any activity mediates this relationship. The more unpleasant one perceives the task, the more effort (mental or otherwise) the activity requires. The more effort needed upfront, the greater the reward needs to be to offset the cost. Consider Shawn's case of playing EverQuest. Because the core gameplay loop was pleasant, Shawn kept wanting to play more. The world that the game immerses players in gives the actions distinct purpose, further strengthening the reward. Adding to this was a social element. Discovery of a trusted friend that would engage in quests with him and protect his resources when he was not playing, further generating a reward, one that perhaps Shawn found difficult to attain in the real world. Indeed, Woolley and Langel write of Shawn, 'He was a kind and warm-hearted person . . . He liked being a kid, with the kids. He felt more comfortable with the little ones, then with the judgmental, mean adults. He could be himself and not be judged or condemned for it.'[23]

Woolley and Langel note that Shawn's life dramatically changed after playing EverQuest. They write, 'Shawn had been playing computer games for the past 10 years, with no major character or social changes in his life . . . Everquest was one of the first of the "new generation" of video games specifically designed by people with degrees in psychology . . . to make the video games as addicting as possible . . . The gamers cannot leave the game without losing their status in the game. Also, the game is now the place where the gamer's peers are. If they quit the video game they will no longer have contact with their friends.'[24] Woolley and Langel are alluding to how different forms of rewards are implemented by the gaming industry to keep individuals coming back. Since *EverQuest*, even more addictive games have been released, and the addictive gamified architecture has been rolled out in everything from social media to shopping websites and the news.

Perhaps the major takeaway from this chapter is slightly askance. The techniques pioneered and used by the gaming industry have found homes in places where the core effort loop is not nearly as intrinsically rewarding or fulfilling, for instance, in the gig economy. While there are monetary rewards that are utilised, the use of behavioural rewards and gamification have been added to varying degrees. The point is that even when financial rewards become less motivating (for example, when you are working hourly), there are other forms of motivation that keep you going, such as competitions, social motives, status-seeking behaviour, goal-setting and so forth. We should be wary of this and more generally of putting ourselves in the position of endlessly gamifying our already gamified lives. I want you to build a decisive mind so that you can unlock your potential and live a fulfilling life. Not so that you can run yourself into the ground trying to achieve some arbitrary goal. I include Shawn's story as a reminder of this. Whilst his case is unusual, I see echoes of it everywhere. We are hijacking our reward systems and this is not always a good idea.

I think, therefore, that this chapter brings us back to the beginning – to our goals. Whilst it's impossible to say, I'm not sure that Shawn ever actively set the goal to become the best possible *EverQuest* player that he could. I think it's much more likely that *EverQuest* stepped in and took over when he wasn't looking. There's a lesson in that for us, too. If we are mindful about our goals, setting rewards can help us get them. But if our goals are gifted to us, if they are ultimately in service to the people who use our labour or our money for their own ends, we need to watch out. We are enormously complex creatures, but we are very simple, too. Everybody likes a gold star, even if they're a respected member of society with jobs and children.

One final thought on this. There are healthy places where these reward systems are also used. A sports club, a reading or study group, an art class all similarly use a suite of interventions to affirm good behaviour – from the post-game pint to the end-of-year show – clubs and meet-up groups know to link something pleasing to a behaviour you want to cultivate. And they're social, too.

With these preliminaries in mind, the next three chapters detail out the Decisive Framework. I'll provide you with a framework that will help you achieve what you want in the way that you want it.

Box: Your turn!

Assignment # 8

Again, an exercise in two parts. First, I would like you to think back to the goal that you failed to achieve (sorry for bringing this up, I know it's emotionally a little taxing, but it's a good way to help you understand how you can improve). Think about one to three recurring decisions that you needed to undertake in service to the goal. For saving money, this could be things like not buying something you really wanted, or not hanging out with friends at the local pub, etc.

Now, think about every time you made the right choice (in service to the goal) – what rewards did you gain? It is perfectly normal to not think of anything straightaway, but do try to see whether there were any immediate rewards that you gained from this activity. Write these down in the box below.

Goal # 1:		
Decision 1	Whenever I undertook this decision/task, I gained the following reward:	Psychologically: _____ Socially: _____ Materially: _____
Decision 2	Whenever I undertook this decision/task, I gained the following reward:	Psychologically: _____ Socially: _____ Materially: _____
Decision 3	Whenever I undertook this decision/task, I gained the following reward:	Psychologically: _____ Socially: _____ Materially: _____

Alright! Thanks for that. Now, let's pretend this is the goal you are now going to set for yourself going forward. You can set up whatever rewards you like, so please go ahead and plan out your rewards, at least two for each decision. Once you have done that, reflect on whether you would have found the goal more manageable had you thought of these rewards beforehand.

Goal 1 – Reward strategy		
Decision 1	Whenever I undertake this decision/task, I will reward myself by:	Psychologically: _____ Socially: _____ Materially: _____
Decision 2	Whenever I undertake this decision/task, I will reward myself by:	Psychologically: _____ Socially: _____ Materially: _____
Decision 3	Whenever I undertake this decision/task, I will reward myself by:	Psychologically: _____ Socially: _____ Materially: _____

References

Woolley, Liz and Langel, John. 'Your son did NOT die in vain!: A true story about the devastating effects of video gaming addiction.' *Outreach for On-Line Gamers Anonymous*. Kindle Edition (2019).

Atkins, Annette. *Creating Minnesota: A History from the Inside Out*. Minnesota Historical Society, 2009.

Spain, Judith W. and Vega, Gina. 'Sony online entertainment: EverQuest® or EverCrack?' *Journal of Business Ethics* (2005): 3–6.

Griffiths, Mark D., Kuss, Daria J. and King, Daniel L. 'Video game addiction: Past, present and future.' *Current Psychiatry Reviews* 8, no. 4 (2012): 308–318.

Hamari, Juho, Koivisto, Jonna and Sarsa, Harri. 'Does gamification work? A literature review of empirical studies on gamification.' In *2014 47th Hawaii International Conference on System Sciences*, pp. 3025–3034. Ieee, 2014.

Banuri, Sheheryar, Dankova, Katarina and Keefer, Philip. *It's Not All Fun and Games: Feedback, Task Motivation, and Effort*. No. 17–10. School of Economics, University of East Anglia, Norwich, UK, 2017.

Milkman, Katherine L., Minson, Julia A. and Volpp, Kevin G. M. 'Holding the hunger games hostage at the gym: An evaluation of temptation bundling.' *Management Science* 60, no. 2 (2014): 283–299.

Milkman, Katy. *How to Change: The Science of Getting From Where You Are to Where You Want to Be.* Penguin, 2021.

Duckworth, Angela L., Milkman, Katherine L. and Laibson, David. 'Beyond will-power: Strategies for reducing failures of self-control.' *Psychological Science in the Public Interest* 19, no. 3 (2018): 102–129.

Ashraf, Nava, Karlan, Dean and Yin, Wesley. 'Tying Odysseus to the mast: Evidence from a commitment savings product in the Philippines.' *The Quarterly Journal of Economics* 121, no. 2 (2006): 635–672.

Duckworth, Angela L., White, Rachel E., Matteucci, Alyssa J., Shearer, Annie and Gross, James J. 'A stitch in time: Strategic self-control in high school and college students.' *Journal of Educational Psychology* 108, no. 3 (2016): 329.

Epton, Tracy, Currie, Sinead and Armitage, Christopher J. 'Unique effects of setting goals on behavior change: Systematic review and meta-analysis.' *Journal of Consulting and Clinical Psychology* 85, no. 12 (2017): 1182.

PART III:
THE DECISIVE FRAMEWORK

The Tyranny of Small Decisions . . . Misclassification Based on Impact

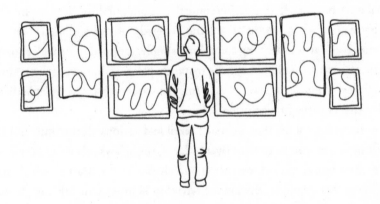

Unlike the hard sciences, where laws abound, social science tends to be a bit . . . smudgier. Physical laws, like gravity, are consistent. You know that when an apple becomes detached from a branch, it's going to head down towards the earth. If you are a physicist, you can even figure out how long it will take. But in social science, everything operates probabilistically. Social science can't guarantee that a phenomenon will occur with certainty, it only models the probability of some behaviour.

Still, we often use the term 'law'. You may have heard of Parkinson's Law, named after Cyril Northcote Parkinson, a relatively obscure academic historian who wrote in *The Economist* in 1955, 'work expands so as to fill the time available for its completion.'[1] He followed this up with Parkinson's law of triviality, wherein both individuals and groups tend to focus on the little things rather than the big picture. Parkinson illustrated the principle by way of a story of a committee deciding how to build a nuclear reactor, which spent far too much time on the bicycle shed.[2] Both laws are meant as satire, inspired by Parkinson's time in the military during World War II. But they set the tone for the laws of social science.

Similar laws abound. For example, Sayre's Law states, 'In any dispute the intensity of feeling is inversely proportional to the value of the issues at stake.'[3] The quip was termed by one Charles Phillip Issawi, who was discussing academic politics, which, as I can attest, tend to be vicious.[4]

Alfred Kahn, a notable American economist, penned an essay in 1966 called the 'Tyranny of Small Decisions'. In it he explained that many decisions are made in ignorance of their wider context. They might be rational at the individual level, but they lead to an outcome that is undesirable.[5] We saw this effect at play earlier when we discussed the 'Tragedy of the Commons' and Lin Ostrom. Kahn was describing something simple: stripped of its wider context, a decision made in isolation may be instantly pleasing, but over time and with enough repetition, it can have devastating consequences. It's a principle that we are looking at throughout this book.

So, these laws show that we make terrible decisions all the time. But they also hint at a reason as to why. By and large, these laws rely on us conserving our mental resources and rewarding ourselves over the short rather than the long term. For example, the law of triviality is important for our purposes because it states that a disproportionate amount of our precious time is spent on trivial tasks. That's because the reward we give ourselves for completing a task tends to be the same (that sense of satisfaction – *yes*, I finished!) regardless of what the task is. That means that if the effort we need to accomplish the task is low, it's attractive to us. Anybody who has ever made a To Do List with item 1 being 'write to do list' knows what I'm talking about! It's the same principle at play in the example of the bike shed versus the nuclear reactor. The effort required to build a nuclear reactor is far, *far* greater than the effort required to build a bike shed. But if (from the managers' perspective) the reward is equivalent, then effort on the bike shed seems more rewarding because the costs are so low.

When thinking about the tyranny of small decisions, it's the same idea again. The principle was that many decisions are made in ignorance of the wider context. They might be rational at the individual level, but they lead to an outcome that is undesirable. Imagine eating a doughnut. In isolation, a good decision. However, if you ate a doughnut every day, you would fall foul of your doctor's advice very, very quickly. Small decision that is rational in isolation: doughnut. Wider context: doctor's advice.

Alright, fine. We know the science on rewards and mental energy quite well at this point. But where does this leave us and our decisive minds? How can we improve our decision-making?

How can we, in essence, not eat all the doughnuts?

Impact misclassifications

First, let's quickly recap the framework. In Chapter 1, we introduced the idea of four types of decisions, along the impact (low to high) and frequency (low to high) dimensions. Each decision we make can be classified into one of these four categories. The figure below illustrates this. The trouble is that we tend to misclassify. How, and why, do we do this?

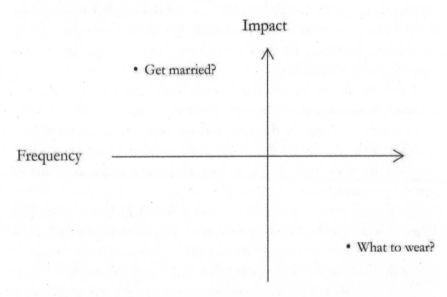

Next, let's recap our behavioural insights. In Chapter 2, we discussed the issue of mental effort – we want to preserve cognitive resources. Sometimes, when making a hard decision, we don't think twice, and we should. I will tend to use the word 'deliberate' here – I simply mean 'think twice'. For most decisions, however, we actually *want* to use our gut. We need to preserve these same mental resources. But, again, if we misclassify, we get hung up on deliberating over something we don't need to. Either way, making decisions costs us, and the more decisions we need to make, the higher the costs become.

In Chapter 3, we discussed rewards and how our motivation influences rewards. If we are intrinsically motivated to do something, the mental satisfaction we get is higher than when we aren't. Suppose you are a shift worker at a factory because you need the money. It's unlikely that you'll go the extra mile on the factory floor without further payment. You need an extrinsic reward – money. Alternatively, think of a musician. While the money associated with being a performer can be very good, the musician exerts effort due to intrinsic factors – they love making music. Effort is costly, but the way we think about rewards, due to our own motives, can increase the level of effort when costs are high.

In Chapter 4, we discussed the importance of time and how rewards that happen now seem bigger than rewards we get later. This means our perceptions of rewards change the further away they become. For example, imagine writing a novel. Many a writer gives up about a third of the way in, after the initial flush of creativity has faded. The costs incurred for plodding on are high and the rewards gained are distant.

Finally, in Chapter 5, we discussed the role of our perceptions and how they shift to suit our behaviour. An example of this was confirmation bias, where we exert effort to seek answers that agree with our beliefs. Another example was about how we perceive ourselves to be above average and readily incorporate evidence that confirms this belief, but disregard evidence that disconfirms this belief (overconfidence!).

So, putting everything that we've learnt in Part I (behavioural insights) together, let's return to that simple framework. The easiest way to think about any decision that we make is that we do a quick (often unconscious) comparison of the costs and benefits (rewards) of undertaking an action. We'll be bothered to do something if the benefits of said action exceed the costs of the action, but we won't be bothered otherwise. Here again is the general rule that we all tend to follow:

- Do something if rewards are greater than the costs
- Do nothing if costs are greater than the rewards

Now two things to note here with the above: rewards and costs are usually not *real* rewards and costs, but *perceived* rewards and costs. This means that our decisions are not based on objective data or objective reality, but rather, what we think is going on. This is both a blessing and a curse. But it's precisely this fact that the framework will be able to help us with.

So, what does this mean for our framework? Let's begin by considering the low frequency decisions (TYPE II – Korean or Chinese or TYPE III – Vegan or Carnivore). Within this larger category, we find low and high impact decisions. We often misclassify these two.

But what does *impact* mean in this context? Well, for the purposes of this book, **a high impact decision is one which aligns with your goals. A low impact decision is one which does not.**

We need to be a bit careful at this juncture because it is important to recognise that just because something does not align with a goal does not mean that it is not going to affect your welfare overall. Indeed, many people find that when in pursuit of some goal (like, in my case, finishing this book), other welfare-enhancing decisions may fall by the wayside (like, again, in my case, eating healthily). Hence, while we can classify any decisions that are not in line with the goals that you set at the outset as low impact, this does not mean that they should be ignored altogether. With that caveat in place, let's move on.

Low frequency and impact

What constitutes a low frequency decision depends largely on how you look at things, but let's consider (for the sake of definition) a decision that you do not have to make on regular basis (we can think of regular as being at least once a month, just to fix ideas). Decisions such as making mortgage payments, or what shirt to wear, get classified as high frequency, and we will cover them a little later. However, low frequency decisions may be things like where to go on a holiday, shopping for an anniversary or special event, engaging in home repairs, joining a gym, buying a big-ticket item such as a house or a car, selecting an electricity provider and so on.

The first thing to note about low frequency decisions is that they tend to require effort and deliberation. This is usually because of the unique circumstances surrounding them. The context of making a low frequency decision is different enough from a high frequency decision that we tend not to have simple rules of thumb to help us. As you'll remember from Chapter 2, one way in which we reduce the costs of decision-making is to shift decisions away from System 2 processes (which are deliberative) to System 1 processes (which are intuitive). The use of heuristics, what we call rules of thumb, are an easy way to accomplish this.

Gerd Gigerenzer, an important psychologist working in cognitive psychology, illustrates our use of heuristics by describing things like catching a ball. On the face of it, catching a ball is quite a complex calculation, involving a series of variables including speed, trajectory, height, direction, wind resistance and so on. However, many of us do this all the time without engaging in any sort of calculations. Coaches teach children by giving them a few rules, such as keeping their eyes on the ball and keeping their head still as they run to meet the ball. These rules are called heuristics. They are less precise than the actual calculations, but they work most of the time. We can use heuristics to catch a ball, but not to land a spacecraft on the moon. Through a series of trials and repetitions we can train ourselves to engage in an everyday action with minimal effort.[6]

However, since low frequency decisions often do not have associated heuristics in place, like landing a spaceship on the moon, individuals often find the need to deliberate to make better decisions. Simply stated, as there are no easy rules of thumb accessible, people do not have the requisite 'practice' to make the decision. What tends to happen, therefore, is that they either deliberate, which means that the cost of effort increases, or they go with their gut feelings and intuition, which increases their chances of making mistakes. Finally, they can also put off making the decision by delaying and procrastinating. To sum up, we either deliberate, guess or delay.

If you are intrinsically motivated to make the decision, you are much more likely to deliberate because the perceived reward is higher. For example, imagine you are deciding where to book your holiday. Most of us will engage in quite an extensive search based on a variety of factors and preferences. We will make sure to exhaust each option before booking our flights. The reason why we do this is not because the impact on our life would be greater by finding the optimal trip, but because it is interesting and fun to learn about all the options available and plan the trip. Do I go to Spain, or do I go to Italy? Spain has tapas, but Italy has pasta. The remarkable modern architecture of Barcelona, or the Roman ruins? We can lose whole days trying to make this kind of a decision. Similarly, I have trouble selecting a laptop, making sure to exhaust all possible options before undertaking a decision. The effect on my life were I to purchase a laptop that was marginally less than optimal is basically negligible, yet I will compare machines down to the last kilobyte of memory. The time I wasted on trying to make this decision far outstrips any benefits that I accrued by purchasing a laptop that was 'good enough'.

Now let's consider trying to make a less pleasing decision. Imagine you need to buy travel insurance to go with your lovely holiday. Chances are, unless you're extremely into insurance plans, you won't deliberate too much, but rather just go with your gut ('this one's cheapest and I went with them last time'). Likewise, you may delay the decision ('I'm a bit short this month, I'll wait until I get paid . . .'). You might even delay and delay and not quite get around to doing it. Why does this happen? The perceived reward from undertaking deliberating is low, so you choose to either avoid the decision or pick one pretty much at random.

Whether you go to Spain or Italy, you'll probably have a good time. Spending ages researching the relative merits of both destinations probably won't have a major impact on your experience. If you went to Spain rather than Italy because the flights were cheaper and you enjoyed it the last time you were there, it's unlikely that you will have a life-changingly terrible time. Using the exact same heuristic (cheaper, went with this last time) to choose your holiday insurance, on the other hand, could end up being a life-changing mistake. So, what is going on here? Why do we misclassify the impact that a decision might have?

The simple answer is how we perceive rewards. We usually set goals so that we exert effort in things that we are not currently doing. For example, if you love playing football and get enjoyment from doing it, you will not need to set goals to practice . . . you're already practicing! It's happening naturally. However, if you absolutely hate exercise of all forms, you may need to set a goal to get yourself to play football on a regular basis for health reasons. Once we have set a goal, many decisions we undertake surrounding the goal become high impact – they help us progress towards it. Unfortunately, we often delay or avoid undertaking them because we aren't motivated. And it's hacking our motivation that is at heart of this book.

What about misclassifications in the other direction? Why do we spend so much time on (seemingly) trivial decisions that may not affect us all that much in the long run? The example that we looked at above was deciding on a vacation, but there are a limitless number of examples that we can consider. The short answer is again: motivation. Because we enjoy deliberating in areas that are intrinsically motivating to us, it stands to reason that we subconsciously classify these decisions as high impact, and we'll often engage in ex-post rationalisation and justification when casting our eye over the time and effort that we've spent. It's fun to think about where you're going to go on holiday!

This matters hugely. As we remember from the behavioural insights, deliberating always costs us energy. If we are exerting all our effort on decisions that don't have any impact on getting us towards our goal, this makes it less likely that we'll exert effort on those decisions that really do make a difference. In other words, even if we are aware that we need to go to the gym *tonight* if we are going to achieve our goal of losing some weight ahead of our beach holiday, it's much harder to lace up our trainers and head out the front door if we've wasted lots of mental energy earlier on that evening trying to decide between a Spanish or Italian beach holiday. You become much more likely to think, 'Ah, it's ok, I can go tomorrow' – delaying. You might not make the link at the time; you may engage in rationalisation ('I'll get more out of it tomorrow') but that's what's going on under the bonnet.

In sum, when it comes to low frequency decisions, we can be confused over what's important. The rewards associated with a high impact decisions are often perceived to be low and therefore action or decisions are not undertaken or are delayed. Similarly, due to wasting effort in undertaking low impact decisions, the costs of high impact decisions suddenly loom larger.

High frequency and impact

We've covered low frequency decision-making. Next, let's look at high frequency decisions. These are the decisions that you make regularly – more than once a month. Some are very regular, every day. Others might be weekly and fortnightly. The important thing to note is that high frequency decisions often have a range of heuristics that are triggered to minimise mental effort. These are decisions that we are well-practiced in making. What this means is that we will seldom deliberate, often choosing to rely on intuition and gut feelings instead.

I'm trying to make you see that not all decisions are equal. High and low impact dimensions are distinct. It's much better to deliberate in the high impact domain and not bother in the low impact domain. This reduces the impact on resources for decisions that are not in service to our goals.

When it comes to frequency, misclassification means deliberating when you don't need to and using your gut when you do. In general, we expect there to be less deliberation for high frequency decisions. That should be obvious – you don't tend to deliberate too much over whether you want a coffee or are going to clean your teeth. The exception though is when somebody is intrinsically motivated by a decision they make all the time. For instance, someone may spend lots of time deciding what to wear because the process of picking and choosing outfits is pleasing to them. The downside to this, just as with low frequency decisions, is that mental effort is being wasted. The inverse is true, too. We might not want to engage with a high impact decision because we can't see how, or when, we'll be rewarded. So, we don't bother deliberating.

The thinking here is straightforward and follows directly from the reasoning we saw above for low frequency decisions. High frequency decisions tend to rely on System 1 processes precisely because they're high frequency. The repetition has caused us to develop heuristics to aid in decision-making thereby minimising effort costs. We only use more deliberation if we are intrinsically motivated because we perceive a higher reward for undertaking an action (deliberation) than the effort we exert. In this way something that is low impact (and hence not worthy of deliberation) can be perceived as high impact (and hence worthy of deliberation). Which is a waste of time and effort. Similarly, and often more importantly, something that is high impact may be perceived as low impact and not deliberated upon. For instance, we may not think that it's important to deliberate much over our weekly shop, but it's precisely this kind of deliberation that will help us reach our goals if we are trying to eat healthily.

Overall, what this means is that misclassification occurs due to two main reasons, in line with the framework discussed above. Either the perceived rewards are too low, or the costs of deliberation are too high. In low frequency cases (where simple heuristics are not accessible) the rewards are important because most decisions have high costs associated with them. Costs go even higher when we choose to spend our energies elsewhere, but the main issue is the perception of reward. In high frequency cases, rewards still matter, but since easily available heuristics are implemented, the costs of deliberation can loom large and so again the perceptions of rewards become critical. On the other hand, if you can create a good heuristic for yourself through mindful deliberation – for instance, if your weekly shop contains all the foods you need to have a balanced diet – you can implement it repeatedly without any costly thinking.

Social laws

Before we move on, let's recap what we've learnt in this chapter whilst thinking about how we might begin to put these learnings into action.

Misclassification along the impact dimension happens in both directions, depending on our motivation (Chapter 3): if we think an activity as intrinsically rewarding, we tend to classify it as a high impact activity (it is important to me, hence I do it), while an activity that carries little intrinsic rewards might be classified as low impact. These are classifications based on our *perceptions* of the activity, not the reality. When we discipline our perceptions by considering our goals, we may alter the perceived rewards and costs.

For example, consider the decision to consume a sugary snack. With System 1 thinking, feedback from consuming the snack is evaluated positively. The activity is intrinsically motivating because it makes me feel good. System 1 thinking *also* makes me evaluate this decision in isolation, leading me to think that this decision provides an immediate benefit with no associated costs to long-term health. All this means that we *think* we are making a TYPE I decision (Apples or Oranges). But we aren't. We are making a TYPE IV decision (Crisps or Nuts). We think this decision has no impact, but that's a trick of our perception. If we discipline ourselves to be aware of what decisions we are really making and align them with our goals, we are much more likely to be able to make the right one. In this case, we need to force ourselves to deliberate. Or, we need to remove the option of being able to choose a sugary snack so that we would have to deliberate instead whether to actively go out and get one. Most of the time, we won't be bothered.

As another example, let's consider the case of buying a washing machine. There is no simple automatic thinking process that I can rely on to help with this decision because I don't often buy washing machines. We perceive ourselves to be making an important decision that we must deliberate hard over. But, if we get a washing machine that's within budget, the magic of consumer capitalism means that one £200 washing machine is pretty much the same as another £200 washing machine. Unfortunately, it's easy to spend extraordinary amounts of time on a decision of this kind – even though the impact on your wellbeing is minimal, or possibly even negative. Again, there is a need for a disciplining process based on your goals. For instance, if I have a goal of saving money, classifying this decision as TYPE III (Vegan or Carnivore) is appropriate (£200 is a lot of money, can you get a cheaper one?). However, if I have other goals, this decision would be classified as TYPE II (Chinese or Korean) and hence requires little effort and deliberation (you've set a budget of £200 and it doesn't matter how long the spin cycle lasts). When it comes to washing machines, you can go with your gut to minimal ill-effect. In the unlikely event of a problem, there's always the returns policy.

Because mental resources require effort, deliberating over low impact decisions causes us to defer or delay high impact decisions. That's, potentially, a big problem. It means we're focusing on the wrong thing. Worse still, we know that when the impact is higher, people are less likely to deliberate anyway for fear of making the wrong choice – they are more likely to rely on automatic thinking (or 'go with their gut'). Automatic thinking is fine for low impact decisions, but potentially disastrous for high impact decisions. Often you end up treating a high impact decision as if it is a low impact decision, even when you know otherwise ... because you wasted all your valuable mental resources on low impact decisions that you misclassified!

The incorrect classification of decisions reduces the extent to which we make tricky decisions well. Limitations on time and mental resources make for bad decisions. If you're going to engage in poor quality decisions, do so when it doesn't matter for your wellbeing.

Underpinning this framework are the earlier chapters on motivation and effort. That's the key that unlocks why we misclassify decisions based on impact. We want to achieve the highest of highs, as quickly and as easily as possible. Life doesn't work like that. Some things are hard. You are more than capable of making the right choices, but you must give yourself the best shot at doing so. You'll only be able to do so if you figure out what's important and focus your energies there. Remember, decisions that are easy to make can be perceived as important, while decisions that are hard to make might be relegated to obscurity. Both misclassifications come with serious long-term consequences.

Box: Your turn!

Assignment # 9

For this exercise, I would like you to think about low and high impact decisions and try to match them up. I would like you to write down one goal and three decisions that you currently undertake that do not contribute to your wellbeing. I would like you to replace those decisions with decisions that are currently in service to your goal. For example, you might consider replacing something that brings little value to your growth and development (watching random videos online) with something that is in service to the goal that you specify. Don't worry about this taking up some time – it is meant to be a difficult exercise. Do try to highlight three decisions.

Think about low impact decisions that you have a habit of deliberating too much over. In this chapter, we've discussed purchases, but it may be that before you settle down to study you spend long hours deciding on a place in which to do it. Library or café? At home or at school? By the time you've chosen, you've wasted mental energy that could have been given over to studying. It's worth deliberating hard over where, most of the time, the best place to study is. But only once. Not every day. The café may be more pleasant than the library, but you may be more easily distracted. Apply your goals (getting an A in maths) to this decision and pick the place that you think is most likely going to nudge you further along the path. Then, only go there when you study. With time, this decision becomes a heuristic, something that you don't think much about. This is just an example, but regardless of what your goal is, you can certainly make a good decision once and consistently apply it. Deliberate, and make a better decision next time. Then, through repetition, route that decision to cruise control.

Goal # 1:		
Decision		Decision details
Decision 1	I currently do this:	
	I would like to replace it with this:	
Decision 2	I currently do this:	
	I would like to replace it with this:	
Decision 3	I currently do this:	
	I would like to replace it with this:	

References

Parkinson, C. N. *Parkinson's Law and Other Studies in Administration*. Houghton Mifflin Company, Boston, 1957.

Homer, Frederic D. and Levine, Charles H. 'Triviocracy: Sayre's law revisited.' *Review of Policy Research* 5, no. 2 (1985): 241–252.

Issawi, Charles Philip. *Issawi's Laws of Social Motion*. Hawthorn Books, 1973.

Kahn, Alfred E. 'The tyranny of small decisions: Market failures, imperfections, and the limits of economics.' *Kyklos* 19, no. 1 (1966): 23–47.

Marewski, Julian N., Gaissmaier, Wolfgang and Gigerenzer, Gerd. 'Good judgments do not require complex cognition.' *Cognitive Processing* 11, no. 2 (2010): 103–121.

CHAPTER 10

I Want to Join a Gym!
Misclassification Based on Frequency

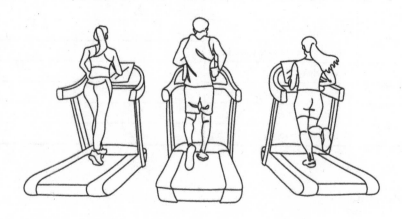

Vic Tanny was in his early 20s, living in his native New York and working as a schoolteacher. In his spare time, he was a bodybuilder. Vic identified the need for a gym and opened one in his parents' garage, charging other weightlifters to come and use it. This was a less-than-successful venture and Tanny eventually closed shop and moved to LA to get a teaching degree. While at the University of Southern California, Tanny (along with his brother) opened a more official gym, called West Coast Tanny. Over the next 30 years, the Tanny gym empire exploded, expanding into nearly 100 locations all across North America.

Tanny is legendary in the fitness world for pioneering the modern gym club, along with membership arrangements. After trying (and failing) to get his businesses going, he noticed a few patterns about the demand for fitness. Gyms had traditionally catered to three types of clientele: bodybuilders, housewives and celebrities. Gyms typically catered to each group exclusively. Tanny wondered why there weren't any gyms that catered to *all* groups simultaneously. He attempted to establish precisely this, often pairing workout machines with other attractions, such as bowling alleys and skating rinks.

But Tanny's real innovation was not the attractions above, but his introduction of the annual membership. Eventually the idea of the annual membership proliferated throughout the whole fitness industry, but his implementation of it was what led to the further expansion of the business. Tanny noticed that many casual users cited the expense of joining a gym as the main reason that kept them out and he thought about a way to solve this problem. Annual memberships worked in his favour because he would use the advance revenue generated to obtain loans and expand.[1]

There are routine spikes in gym memberships in January, tapering off consistently afterwards every year – it's so predictable that behavioural science has given it a name, the Fresh Start effect.[2] This effect can be found in many aspects of consumer behaviour but is particularly visible in the domain of health and fitness. However, much of the spike in post-holiday traffic dies down considerably by February–March. What if there was a way to extract money from these infrequent members without them actually using the facilities?

Tanny's great innovation was to set up membership contracts by inflating the price of month-to-month contracts, while keeping annual contracts reasonably inexpensive. This would allow for a greater share of individuals to undertake annual contracts, even though many of them would not visit the gym enough to make it worthwhile. He would then sell the contracts in multi-year packages. Eventually, these annual memberships became structured as loans, rather than monthly fees. In this manner, when people came to sign up, they would be signing up for a multi-year contract, even though they might not use the gym for more than a month. Because the fees were scheduled as a loan, breaking the contract carried negative consequences, like damaging your credit rating, which served as a major deterrent to members who wanted to leave.

Gym cancellations became so notoriously difficult that there are dedicated websites aimed at making sure consumers use regulation to their advantage. A case in point is the government of Western Australia, who developed the 'fitness code' which sets out certain regulations for any business working in the fitness industry. The code lays out a series of regulations including membership cancellations, where it specified that 'details on how to cancel a membership, and how to do it electronically, must be in all membership agreements.'[3]

High impact and frequency

Think about the decision to join a gym. The typical consumer decides to join a gym because of a perceived need to get into better shape. Gym memberships typically spike during New Year, when resolutions are being made. At this point a person (let's call them 'Sam') decides that the easiest way to get into shape is to start exercising. Since exercise equipment is expensive, Sam decides that the answer is to go to the gym. He decides to sign up for membership or undertake a trial period at the local gym. This is a great decision, Sam believes, because this is the one thing that has been holding him back; access to the equipment that will help him get fit. Sam knows that there is hard work ahead but believes that without this crucial first step, he can go no further.

The gym industry is huge, boasting nearly 200 million members globally and generating revenue of nearly 100 billion USD in 2019. In the US alone, 64.2 million individuals hold a gym membership.[4] The gym industry knows you are coming and knows why you are there. The gym industry also knows that you have *no idea* how frequently you will actually use the gym. And it gets just one opportunity to bring you into its fold.

But, you might ask, why the heck is this the case? Surely people have the foresight to estimate the number of times they will realistically attend the gym and then sign a contract that provides them with the highest benefit for the lowest cost, right? Right?

Not quite. Indeed, in a landmark study, researchers studied the decisions of over 7,000 gym members in the US over a three-year period. Specifically, they were interested in the type of contract people chose and the benefits (as measured by the number of gym visits) that they undertook. The paper studies the decisions of individuals, particularly on their choice of contract when joining the gym.[5]

You see, when you go to the gym, you will typically get presented with two, sometimes three, main contracts. One is a pay-as-you-go contract, which typically costs more at the time of the visit. A second contract (which salespeople will push you towards) is a membership, usually a monthly membership, or the third, which is a discounted annual membership. In the study, people had a choice between these three contracts. The annual contract required an upfront payment of ten months, and the monthly contract contained monthly fees that automatically charged individuals and were set to renew automatically, while the pay as you go fees were the highest. Or so it seemed.

For the monthly membership to work out to be cheaper than pay-per-visit, members would need to visit the gym at least eight times per month. The authors find that people on average went to the gym fewer than five times per month, meaning that they were paying a whole lot more on the monthly contract. Furthermore, the authors found that people on this rotating contract also kept their contracts for longer than a year, while on the annual contract (which requires manually renewing) most did not. So, chances are Sam isn't losing his 'dad bod', but he sure is losing money regularly for the next couple of years!

When you think about this, it doesn't sound like it can be true. Surely people can see that they are not going to the gym often enough to make their contract worth it and they should cancel. Why don't they? The monthly contract is more likely to be taken up than the annual contract, even though the annual contract is cheaper up front. The first phenomenon I described is usually chalked up to overconfidence: people believe they will go to the gym more often than they actually do.[6] Their membership is a binding contract (sometimes called a commitment device) which will force them to go, as they are paying money and want to get value. But the problem is the human mind doesn't work that way. Once we have incurred the cost of the gym, we seem to completely disregard it.

So, Sam decided to get fitter. This led to his decision to join the gym. This was a costly and emotionally taxing decision, but he made it. The salesperson said that the contract was very cost-effective if he went to the gym 15 times a month. So, Sam made the seemingly rational decision, that if he was paying to go 15 times a month, he would go 15 times a month. But then he didn't. He went twice.

The decision to get fitter leads to the decision to join the gym. But that needs to lead to multiple further decisions to actually *go* to the gym. And a whole host of other decisions around going to the gym, too – decisions to pack Sam's bag, decisions to take the bus that goes to the gym, rather than the bus that goes to his house, decisions around what time of the day and which days of the week to go. All of these further decisions, the ones that add up to actually going to the gym, culminates in the 'Intention-Action gap'. This is a well-known finding in behavioural science, that well-intentioned individuals struggle to undertake actions that they want to. The motivation is there, but somehow, they do not follow through.[7]

Let's put this situation a slightly different way. Think about the decision model we discussed earlier. Simply put:

- Do something if rewards are greater than the costs
- Do nothing if costs are greater than the rewards

For a decision to be made, the rewards must outweigh the costs. Now consider the decision to take on a gym membership. The reasoning goes, that the cost of each individual visit becomes the lowest it can possibly be, so that the decision to go to the gym has a higher chance of success. So far so good. Furthermore, as the cost has already been incurred, we might assume the cost of each visit is zero. Hence, the only cost to consider is the effort cost – the actual, 'ok, I'm going to lace up my trainers and go to the gym' effort.

Unfortunately, effort costs are not observable up front. We can't tell in the present how much effort we need to muster up in the future to go to the gym. Your motivation isn't really observable up front either – you can't figure out how much you're going to need to bribe yourself to get off the sofa when it's pouring rain outside and you can't be bothered to get yourself down the gym. You make the decision to join the gym without complete information, thinking that the cost will spur you to action. But costs that you have already incurred don't spur you to action. You don't lie in bed at night thinking about a coffee you bought six months ago that you didn't need. You don't lie in bed at night thinking about your gym membership that you don't use. You worry about the payment you need to make *now*.

The thing is, the gym industry saw you coming. They know that most people that sign up for the gym (especially around New Year's) are not going to come back with high frequency. So, when you actually make a rare visit to the gym, they need to make sure they get as much money out of you as they can.[8] Why do they know this? Over years of studying human behaviour (implicitly) they have discovered that most users make the decision to go to the gym emotionally, weighing perceived costs and benefits and ultimately concluding that they will 'start going tomorrow'. And tomorrow never comes.

Going the other way

In the previous chapter, we looked mainly at high impact decisions. The basic idea was that high impact decisions often are more difficult to undertake. They carry large effort costs and while the payoff accumulated over a lifetime can be large, the immediate reward is small. Hence, we choose to avoid such decisions (or don't bother) because in the moment, they cause pain and carry little reward.

Still, we know that these high impact decisions are good for us, so we want to take some sort of action on them. It's very common, therefore, to do something like New Year's resolutions: undertake a difficult decision once and then not follow through. The gym industry capitalised on this aspect of human behaviour by contracting our intentions and betting on the intention-action gap.

So, what about low impact decisions? These decisions don't matter all that much in the long run, but neither do they contribute to our goals. How do these work along the frequency dimension?

Well, let's take the decision to go to the pub. This is arguably a much more pleasant experience than going to the gym (at least for a lot of us!). For many in the UK, this decision happens quite frequently, and while it may well have a high impact in a general sense (after all, spending time with friends and family helps our mental state a lot), it would get routinely classified as low impact as it doesn't typically have a direct contribution to our goals. Hence, decisions like these have the opposite effect; there is a low effort cost, some monetary costs, but high rewards in terms of the wonderful experience in the pub itself. When faced with a decision to go to the pub, it is easy to say yes.

Let's take another example, the decision to go shopping. For those that enjoy the experience of shopping, the decision carries high rewards and generally low effort costs, even more so online. Monetary costs are also similarly variable, they can be high or low, but since this is a pleasurable activity, most of us are happy to go shopping on a regular basis.

Now both these activities (or any number of similar things) carry high intrinsic rewards and so we engage in them on a regular basis. Rather than keep this to a low frequency decision, we turn it into a high frequency decision. We end up going more frequently than may be optimal and at this point these innocuous activities start to tip into negativity. Consider the individual going to the pub every day. While going occasionally is certainly good for mental health and wellbeing, going every day may bring about diminishing returns. So, you may start wanting to go even more to get that now-more-elusive wellbeing boost. By going every day, and sometimes nipping in at lunch time, you manage to keep the reward high. Years pass and you've developed a drinking problem. Along with the many health concerns, the impact that going to the pub every day has had on your finances is devastating. Let's say you go to the pub every day for a chat and drink only mineral water. Even then, you'll almost certainly never get around to writing that screenplay or running that marathon. The innocuous things that we decide to do are important when they eat into the impactful things that we do.

Overall, the key aspect to consider is the immediate reward of engaging in actions relative to the long-term reward. As we have discussed in Chapter 4, individuals tend to be hyperbolic discounters, meaning that immediate rewards have greater weights on them than long-term rewards. This makes activities that carry long-term benefits challenging to engage in.

For those decisions that we do not enjoy, but which carry a high impact, we tend to fool ourselves into reducing their frequency. We trick ourselves into believing that *joining* a gym somehow carries the same benefits as *going* to the gym because the effort cost of making those decisions is incurred once, rather than multiple times, while the rewards are similarly infrequent.

Therefore, for low impact decisions, the role of motivation is critical: if the process or outcome is pleasurable, we are inclined to dedicate more time and mental resources to making such decisions. We are also inclined to turn low frequency decisions into high frequency decisions because we enjoy doing whatever it is that we decided to do. Take the decision to purchase tickets to an expensive concert. The process of purchasing tickets is fun, regardless of the outcome. That is, for many of us, the action of gathering information about the concert, listening to the music that we will hear, texting our friends to see who's available, as well as thinking about the bar we want to go to afterwards, is pleasurable. Certainly, it's more pleasurable in comparison to other things that we could be doing, for instance, catching up on our emails.

Making the decision to buy concert tickets is fun. Because of this, we are induced to spend more resources than are warranted.

This is a key point: because we find pleasure in the process of undertaking a particular decision, we tend to increase the frequency with which we undertake similar decisions. Our automatic thinking processes evaluate the effectiveness of the decision in terms of how much pleasure it provides, especially in the absence of observable feedback on the decision's impact.

If we think something is low impact (I walk past the doughnut shop every day, today I'm going to go in and get myself one. It's just one, after all), we will rely on emotional thinking to guide us. We reason that we do not need to spend resources on such low consequence decisions. Using the instant feedback that we receive, emotional thinking increases the frequency of the decision (boy, that doughnut was delicious, maybe I'll get another one when I walk past this place tomorrow).

For perceived high impact decisions, as we laid out earlier, the role of motivation is critical. First, if we perceive a decision to be high impact, we are more likely to use deliberation to evaluate decisions. Second, the feedback received on the impact of the decision is important – it can have a substantial impact on our emotional state. As earlier, if the outcome is in our favour, we derive pleasure from the decision. But if the outcome is against us, we derive pain. This is an important point: if we know the decision is difficult and that feedback is likely to be negative, we have a strong preference for reducing the frequency of such a decision.

Hence, for typical high stakes decisions, we want to make *one* choice (join a gym, buy a diet book) rather than make a choice over and over (go the gym, steamed vegetables not mac and cheese). Since we know this is a difficult decision and feedback is likely to be negative, our inclination is to reduce the frequency of the decision (join the gym, as opposed to go to the gym), to preserve resources.

Looking over this and the last chapter, you need to remember something: this is never going to change. If you find it difficult to go to the gym, you're going to find it difficult going to the gym. You can't suddenly become a new person. If you have always hated swimming, you won't suddenly love it just because you paid for an annual pass at your local pool. But knowing how to classify the decisions that you are making and taking steps to shift them around – so a low impact decision becomes high impact, or a low frequency decision becomes high frequency – goes a long way to mitigating the negative effects that get us off task. Doing so is key to building a decisive mind – you are losing distractions and getting the most juice from the lemon day-to-day.

Box: Your turn!

Assignment # 10

Have you ever made a New Year's Resolution? Have you ever bought a diet book and then proceeded to not stick with the diet? Joining a gym may have caused you to deliberate because you don't join a gym every day. It may have felt like a big step towards your goal. But if you don't go to the gym, it was a low impact decision – it wasn't worth thinking about. It did nothing. Identify moments in your life where you've done this and start thinking about areas in your life where you can eliminate these wasteful, low stakes decisions.

Next, look at the time you waste with low impact high frequency decisions – scrolling on your phone is an absolute classic. The whole world of social media is built around causing you to make high frequency, low impact choices. It feels like you are doing something. But you aren't. Try to identify areas of slack where you are wasting time and mental energy on stuff that doesn't drive you towards your goal.

Goal # 1:		
Decision		Decision details
Decision 1	I currently do this:	
	I would like to replace it with this:	
Decision 2	I currently do this:	
	I would like to replace it with this:	
Decision 3	I currently do this:	
	I would like to replace it with this:	

References

Black, Jonathan. *Making the American Body: The Remarkable Saga of the Men and Women Whose Feats, Feuds, and Passions Shaped Fitness History*. University of Nebraska Press, 2013.

Dai, Hengchen, Milkman, Katherine L. and Riis, Jason. 'The fresh start effect: Temporal landmarks motivate aspirational behavior.' *Management Science* 60, no. 10 (2014): 2563–2582.

DellaVigna, Stefano and Malmendier, Ulrike. 'Paying not to go to the gym.' *American Economic Review* 96, no. 3 (2006): 694–719.

Moore, Don A. and Healy, Paul J. 'The trouble with overconfidence.' *Psychological Review* 115, no. 2 (2008): 502.

Sheeran, Paschal and Webb, Thomas L. 'The intention–behavior gap.' *Social and Personality Psychology Compass* 10, no. 9 (2016): 503–518.

Carrera, Mariana, Royer, Heather, Stehr, Mark and Sydnor, Justin. 'Can financial incentives help people trying to establish new habits? Experimental evidence with new gym members.' *Journal of Health Economics* 58 (2018): 202–214.

CHAPTER 11

Let's Do This!
Building and Implementing Your Plan

Back to the beginning.

You might think that you are at the end of this book and therefore 'finished'. You aren't. The battle is only just beginning. You now understand all the science that goes into making a decisive mind. In this chapter, we are going to work together, put a plan into action and finally build one.

Firstly, let's remind ourselves of the decisive framework. Our framework classifies decisions into four categories, based on the frequency with which the decisions are made and the impact of those decisions on our lives and to our wellbeing.

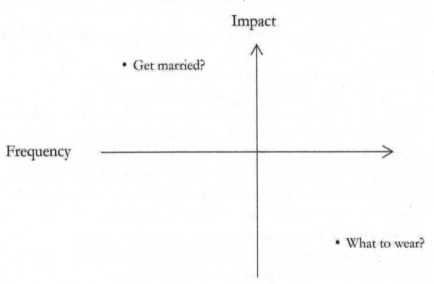

Perhaps the most important insight this book has given you is that we are bad at classifying our decisions and you need to get better if you're going to pursue your aspirations. Now, you could potentially take stock of each and every decision that you make, but this would be very unwieldy! So, we need some time to work through a few key decisions, the better that we might route them to a more automatic process in time.

In each chapter I asked you to undertake an assignment, putting the ideas from that chapter into practice. If you have been engaging in the assignments, you are already most of the way there. In this chapter, we will revisit those activities and put them together. Feel free to refer to your answers to those assignments and put them here as we go along. However, given that you are now armed with the behavioural insights and the Roadmap, this is also a good moment to review and revise.

Let's recap those insights:

Behavioural insights	
Insight # 1:	Decisions take effort
Insight # 2:	Why am I doing this? The role of motivation
Insight # 3:	When do I want it? The power of now
Insight # 4:	Perceptions shape decisions

Quick reminder of the insights we learnt in Part I: The first important insight in the science of decision-making, which virtually all behavioural science books will talk about, is that of the System 1 and System 2 processes of decision-making. We called this automatic and deliberative systems of thinking, with System 1 as the former and System 2 as the latter. The distinction between these two systems is largely the effort required to make decisions. System 1 decisions are taken emotionally and reflexively, with little to no mental resources going towards them. System 2 decisions are deliberate and rational, undertaken with significant levels of effort and thought. We outlined various examples, but a classic one might be that System 1 decisions are decisions that you make without thinking about them – things like brushing your teeth in the morning. Day-to-day stuff. System 2 decisions take time and effort, like selecting a house or choosing which breed of pet dog you would most like.[1]

The other thing to remember is that human beings are built to preserve resources. For many of us, we prefer to be sedentary instead of working out. We prefer to lounge around in our pyjamas instead of doing housework. We prefer to mindlessly watch *Love Island* than read Immanuel Kant. Both physical and mental resources are exactly that: resources. The human being has a background fear that it's going to run out of things. It preserves these resources so that it can deploy them at a critical moment. The phrase 'cognitive misers' applies to many of us.[2] Let's keep this in mind. Anytime we need to act in pursuit of our goals, it requires effort, and effort is something our mind doesn't do for nothing.

We can use this to put together a simple strategy for how we undertake decisions. Remember:

- Do something if rewards are greater than the costs
- Do nothing if costs are greater than the rewards

Costs must be outweighed by benefits. But costs and rewards depend on your perception. Hence, *perceived* costs must be less than *perceived* rewards.

Not engaging with a decision has consequences. It means that we default to the automatic form of thinking and either avoid the decision or do whatever we feel like doing in that moment. An overreliance on System 1 decisions is likely what made you turn to this book in the first place. You are engaging in actions that feel good in the moment but are ultimately hurting you and your wellbeing. Too many doughnuts, not enough greens. Too much mindless scrolling, not enough focused learning. Too many contributions to your local pub, not enough contributions to your pension plan.

Remember that the reason you are not already financially secure (to use an example I've put forward) is because the many decisions that it takes to become financially secure have so far proven too painful and arduous to undertake. They have required too much effort. They have brought you too few rewards. We are going to change that. But it takes real forethought and real engagement.

Each decision that you take in service to your aspirations is going to cost you (in terms of effort). But it will also bring about some rewards. The rewards can be material, or psychological, or social, or some combination of all three. But it is important to recognise that the reason why you have not been engaging in this activity in service to your aspirations to begin with is because the costs that you perceive are too high and the rewards you perceive are too low. You must change something about these costs and rewards with your decisive mind. So, let's revise your decision calculus and give you your best shot at achieving what you aspire to.

Throughout this chapter, I will ask you to do a few things. As before, you actually have to do them. This is an essential step in committing to your plan, so while it seems as if just doing the actions in your head is the same thing, you will get far, *far* more out of this chapter and book if you follow along and take the appropriate steps. So please grab a pen or pencil and get ready to mark up this chapter extensively.

Just to give you a summary of what's to come, we will follow the following steps as we build towards your decisive mind:

The 7-Step Decisive Mind Programme
Step 1: Write down your aspiration
Step 2: Write down concrete goals that feed into your aspiration
Step 3: Break up the goal into a series of repeating decisions
Step 4: Classify decisions according to whether they are low or high frequency
Step 5: For each high impact decision, specify a low impact decision
Step 6: Structure rewards (i.e. cash out)
Step 7: Set out your feedback and revision plan

STEP 0: Knowing yourself

First, let's get to know yourself a little bit. I call this Step 0 because, I hope, reading this book has caused you to gain in self-awareness. Gaining in self-awareness doesn't stop, after all, and people change. Change, and understanding yourself, is a constant part of the process. I want you to engage in a few short activities designed to inform you about yourself a little better. Please answer as honestly as you can for these (no one is looking besides you!).

Getting to know you # 1: In the box below, thinking about your typical day. Try to detail the times when you believe you have the highest amount of energy and the times you have the lowest amounts of energy. By energy I mean generally the times when you feel like you want to get things done (high energy) or feel sluggish or tired (low energy). These will be the times to capitalise or avoid decision-making.

Energy timings catalogue (most days)		
Time of day	Energy levels (circle one)	
Early morning (6am to 9am)	LOW	HIGH
Late morning (9am to noon)	LOW	HIGH
Early afternoon (noon to 3pm)	LOW	HIGH
Late afternoon (3pm to 6pm)	LOW	HIGH
Early evening (6pm to 9pm)	LOW	HIGH
Late evening (9pm to midnight)	LOW	HIGH
Early night (midnight to 3am)	LOW	HIGH
Late night (3am to 6am)	LOW	HIGH

Getting to know you # 2: In the next table there is a series of trivia questions. Please don't worry about why we are doing this at the moment, just answer as best you can, and please don't look up the answers!

Trivia time!	
Q1. An average hen lays how many eggs in a year?	Your response: _____
Q2. What is the height (in metres) of the Eiffel Tower?	Your response: _____
Q3. What is the length of the Colorado River (in miles)?	Your response: _____

Next, please answer the following questions regarding your answers above. For each question, please rate how confident you are that the answer you gave is within ten units of the right answer:

Trivia time!	
Q1. (Eggs) How confident are you about the answer you gave?	Not at all confident Somewhat confident Very confident
Q2. (Eiffel Tower) How confident are you about the answer you gave?	Not at all confident Somewhat confident Very confident
Q3. (Colorado River) How confident are you about the answer you gave?	Not at all confident Somewhat confident Very confident

This simple test will give you a sense of your overall level of confidence. Most people do not know the answers off the top of their heads. However, many people think they have a sense of the answers and generally feel confident that they are close. If you felt like you were Somewhat or Very confident in being close for any of the questions above, you should probably consider yourself to be overconfident.[3]

It is worth understanding if you are the type that is over or under confident. Underconfident types tend to have low expectations, but research shows that most of us tend to be overconfident (men more so than women[4]). Indeed, overconfidence is a distinct bias that we covered in the perceptions chapter (Chapter 5). This matters because it affects how you perceive effort. If you're overconfident, you're going to think that you don't need to put in as much effort as is required to do whatever it is you need to do. That means reality is going to slap you in the face in a few months' time, making it very likely that you'll quit.

Controlling for your overconfidence avoids this fate. If you do end up progressing quicker than you had initially planned, great!

Getting to know you # 3: For this next part, please answer the two questions honestly on a scale of 0 to 10:

Time preferences catalogue	
Q1.Are you generally an impatient person or someone who always shows great patience?	0 = Very impatient; 10 = Very patient Your response:_____
Q2.Are you generally an impulsive person?	0 = Not at all impulsive; 10 = Very impulsive Your response:_____

Please note down your responses. You should consider yourself a generally impatient person if you responded with a 5 or lower to question 1 and an impulsive person if you responded with a 5 or lower to question 2.[5]

Ok, with that done, let's recap. Based on the information above, you now know what times of the day you should try to time your high impact decisions. You should also now know whether you are generally classified as an **OVERCONFIDENT** person, an **IMPATIENT** person and an **IMPULSIVE** person.

Done getting to know thyself? Let's move on.

STEP I: Write down your aspiration

Let's go back to the very beginning – setting out your aspirations. The reason we set those out at the beginning was to give us the opportunity to revise them as we went along. Now we want to be focused. This means we want to engage our decisive mind on one aspiration and one aspiration only. You are free to go back and redo these exercises for multiple aspirations later on, but let's just keep our focus on one for now. As you will see, this will get overwhelming very quickly, so it's easier to keep things neat and clear. Which aspiration you select is up to you, but try to focus on the one that you think will be the most instrumental to your wellbeing.

How do you choose? I'll leave up to you, but I would encourage you to pick the one that you believe is most important for your wellbeing and improving your life. An alternate strategy might be to pick something that you know will be specific and measurable and hence easier to track.

Please go ahead and put that down here and try to fill out the rest of the box with a fresh perspective:

Aspiration:	
What do you want to achieve?	
Why do you want to achieve this (how will it change your life)?	
When do you want to achieve this by?	

STEP 2: Write down your goals

Great! We are well on the way! Now let's take this a step further: we need to set goals. In Chapter 6, we discussed the need for you to set your own goals, precisely because they are motivating in and of themselves. Goals specified by somebody else and prescribed to us have less of an impact and are less likely to be achieved.

So, jot down a goal that flows from your aspiration. Be as specific as you possibly can, giving a timeframe by which you would ideally like to achieve the goal and how you would know that you have achieved it. How would you measure completion? Is there something quantifiable that you can use? Next, think about how attainable the goal is. Remember, it's much better to aim low (especially if you're generally overconfident, but even if not!).

Think about *why* you want to achieve this goal. Can you link it to some narrative that you are telling about yourself? Does it have a purpose that you can draw on from within (I want to lose weight because I want to live a long, healthy life so that I'm the best parent and, at some point, grandparent that I can be) rather than from without (I want to lose weight so that people think I look good when I'm at the beach)?

Here is why you need multiple goals: breaking down an aspiration into small chunks gives you different ways of observing your progress. For aspirations like losing weight, this can be fairly easy. Your goal might be to go to the gym once a week for six months and to weigh yourself every month for six months.

For other aspirations, for example, trying to be less stressed at the work, this can be complicated. Think about whether you require the help of another individual that can give you objective (but positive!) feedback. The system of feedback depends on the goal or aspiration. Whatever the case is, take time to think through your aspiration and take a moment to break it into mini chunks. I'd recommend reviewing the relevant chapters (6 and 9) here to make sure that you have a framework for doing this. Try to be as detailed as possible and try not to skimp on any details. Each component is important for this journey.

Feel free to go back to step 1 and revise the aspiration as much as you like and to return to this step to break it down into numerous goals. For instance, your aspiration may be to learn French. You may have written this down as your aspiration at the start. But knowing what you now know, breaking it down into a whole host of specific goals is the way to get you over the line. Here's an example of how I'd structure this:

Aspiration: Learn French.

- Goal 1: Use a language app daily for at least five minutes. Revise after six months.
- Goal 2: One hour lesson per week with a tutor or self-directed learning. Revise after six months.
- Goal 3: Pass the end of unit test in the course book provided by the Institut Français. Attempt as least once per month. Revise after one year.
- Goal 4: Take a language test from a certified authority. Attempt at least once a year. Revise after one year.
- Goal 5: Pass the fluency test within three years.

Note how each of the goals have their own timescales and feed directly from the aspiration. Be sure to keep referring to the aspiration. Always ensure that each of the revised goals really are in service to the aspiration. You don't want to get lots of momentum taking you in a direction that you never hoped for.

Remember, use the S.M.A.R.T. principle that we covered in Chapter 6.[6] Let us remind ourselves the key characteristics of a well-set goal:

- Specific: Is the goal clear?
- Measurable: Can the goal be quantified and/or measured?
- Achievable: Is the goal too difficult?
- Relevant: Is the goal in line with your aspiration?
- Timely: Does the goal have an end point?

Remember, the S.M.A.R.T. goal shouldn't be something nebulous but concrete. Less 'lose weight' and more 'Mondays, Wednesdays and Fridays I will go to the gym for at least one hour for the next six months'. Try to write down at least one goal that has a clear end point. You can add more goals as you do this, but you need a minimum of one. Remember that whilst it is important to be ambitious and push yourself, it is equally important to be realistic.

Goal I	
State your goal	
Is your goal Specific? How?	
Is your goal Measurable? How will you measure progress?	
Is your goal Achievable? Why do you think so?	

Is your goal Relevant? How does it contribute to your aspiration?	
Is your goal Timely? What is your timeline?	

Goal 2	
State your goal	
Is your goal Specific? How?	
Is your goal Measurable? How will you measure progress?	
Is your goal Achievable? Why do you think so?	
Is your goal Relevant? How does it contribute to your aspiration?	
Is your goal Timely? What is your timeline?	

Goal 3	
State your goal	
Is your goal Specific? How?	
Is your goal Measurable? How will you measure progress?	
Is your goal Achievable? Why do you think so?	
Is your goal Relevant? How does it contribute to your aspiration?	
Is your goal Timely? What is your timeline?	

All done?

Not so fast! Are these goals *really* achievable, knowing everything that you know about yourself? Have you been overconfident? If so, take a moment to look over these goals whilst being genuinely, even brutally, honest with yourself. Make sure to take your confidence into account and revise your goal accordingly. Do take time to seriously consider revising because this is precisely the step where things go awry. If you are overconfident, and most of us are, consider setting a lower bar with an aim to revise the goal upon achievement. Don't worry about setting the bar too low, worry about setting it too high.

Not quite done yet. Are you impatient? Are you impulsive? Then look at the goal again and revise the timeline if you need to.

Once you are done, we can move on to step 3. Take your time with this step, it is critical.

STEP 3: Break up the goal into a series of repeating decisions

Next, we need to think about every single decision that you are likely to make that feeds into these goals. This part is hard. It will take some time and you might have to come and revise this list as you go through the rest of the chapter, or indeed once you get going and discover that there are more decisions than you bargained for.

But for now, I would like you to take one goal that you put down above and focus on that. Take this one step at a time, super-simple and straightforward, before moving into anything more complex. This simplicity might feel a bit annoying to start with, but it will work out in your favour over the long run, so stick with it.

What are the decisions that you'll be making when trying to achieve your goal?

The goals have a series of decisions that are essential components. I would like you to write down as many decisions as you can think of that will contribute to the goal (and hence the aspiration). As an example, let's take the aspiration of achieving financial security and, for argument's sake, let's say that you set a goal of developing a portfolio of £500,000 including property over the next 50 years.

There are going to be a lot of decisions. Some you won't be able to predict, but lots of others are much more straightforward. At the most basic level, you would need to decide to open a savings account. Included in that, you would need to decide *which* savings account to open. You would need to decide to put money into the account. You may decide that setting up a direct debit is going to be more effective than contributing funds on an ad hoc basis. Next, you might also consider decisions like researching investment accounts, researching stocks, bonds and mutual funds. Then you may need to make a decision on opening an investment account, or portfolio allocations, or retirement funds. You may need to decide to go back to university so that you can obtain a better paid job later on. You may have to consider where and when to buy property. That means mortgages, solicitors, insurance and so on. You also have to decide how to budget. That means deciding, every day, whether to buy a coffee at the café or to use a French press at home.

What I'm driving at is that having a goal is full of decisions. Most of the time, we don't think in advance about the very many decisions, some of them tough, that we will need to make. This is the point of this exercise. To think carefully about all the choices that you are making and how they advance or distract from your goal.

Be creative and brainstorm as many decisions as you can think of. At this point, you shouldn't worry about whether or not you think you are capable of doing all this stuff, or if it's unrealistic, just put down everything that you think *might* feed into your achieving the aspiration. In the above financial example, perhaps you know you aren't going to return to university to get a higher paying job any time soon. Even so, it's worth imagining, were you to have unlimited time and resources at your disposal, what you would do differently. This may spur you to spot high impact decisions that you could be making.

Be patient at this stage. It's a bit like cleaning the kitchen. You have to take everything out of the cupboard first, thereby making a mess, before you can tidy everything away again. Major life goals involve many steps and many decisions. This is perfectly normal. Just write down as many as you can think of. When you are ready, let's move on to classification.

Goal 1	
State your goal	
What is the key decision that you need to make?	
When does this key decision occur?	
Why might you choose not to take this decision?	
Any additional decisions that you need to take?	

Goal 2	
State your goal	
What is the key decision that you need to make?	
When does this key decision occur?	
Why might you choose not to take this decision?	
Any additional decisions that you need to take?	

Goal 3	
State your goal	
What is the key decision that you need to make?	
When does this key decision occur?	
Why might you choose not to take this decision?	
Any additional decisions that you need to take?	

STEP 4: Classify decisions according to whether they are low or high frequency

Now that this step is completed and you have listed down all the decisions that feed into goal and aspiration achievement, it sure looks daunting, doesn't it? The next step that we will undertake is to organise all these decisions and put them into the Decisive Framework. The way that we will do this is to classify the decisions that are made frequently and the ones that are made infrequently. As I've put it, you only ever really make four types of decisions. Knowing what kind of decision you're making is half the battle.

Note that so far, we have not laid out any guide as to what decisions are made frequently or infrequently. A lot of this tends to depend on the type of goal/aspiration we are talking about because some goals have more low frequency decisions, while others have more high frequency decisions. In general, having more low frequency decisions tends to be a good thing as you can ensure that you put a lot of effort into a low frequency decision and then, hopefully, reap the dividends in the future. Again, using the above financial example, setting up a monthly direct debit that puts a set amount of money from into a savings account is a low frequency decision. But by automating the process of putting money aside, you save yourself relying on willpower when the time comes.

Let's make things a little more concrete. As most of us live on a monthly cycle, splitting frequency based on whether a decision is made once a month or more is a useful way to think things through. If you find that this is not as useful, other ways to think about the split are daily vs not daily, or weekly vs not weekly. In general, though, anything occurring more than a once a month would be reasonably considered frequent.

Split the list of decisions that you wrote down into either TYPE III (high impact, low frequency – Vegan or Carnivore) or TYPE IV (high impact, high frequency – Crisps or Nuts) decisions. Since these are high impact decisions they feed directly into your goals, these are the ones that you need to focus on. The purpose of putting down the goal was precisely to define decisions along the impact dimension. These are the TYPE III and IV decisions that you need to build into your life. Let's classify them now, in the table below. As an example, the list of decisions that I laid out above, I will classify into TYPE III and

TYPE IV decisions:

Goal: A portfolio of £500,000 including property over the next 30 years.

TYPE III (low frequency) decisions:
- Start a savings account
- Research investment accounts
- Research stocks, bonds, mutual funds
- Open an investment account
- Research portfolio allocations
- Research retirement funds
- Decide on a skill to learn.

TYPE IV (high frequency) decisions:
- Move money to savings accounts
- Look for a new job
- Study to learn a new skill
- Apply for jobs
- Look for networking opportunities
- Stick to a daily, weekly and monthly budget for everyday expenses.

Decisions catalogue		
Goal/Decision	Summary	Frequency (circle one)
Goal 1 – Decision 1		LOW HIGH
Goal 1 – Decision 2		LOW HIGH
Goal 1 – Decision 3		LOW HIGH
Goal 2 – Decision 1		LOW HIGH
Goal 2 – Decision 2		LOW HIGH
Goal 2 – Decision 3		LOW HIGH
Goal 3 – Decision 1		LOW HIGH
Goal 3 – Decision 2		LOW HIGH
Goal 3 – Decision 3		LOW HIGH

So far, so good. Remember that at this point these decisions are very rough guides. They're intended to help you with the upcoming series of decisions afterwards. This will seem like a monumental task at this point because you have not completed the rest of the process. Don't worry and don't get disheartened – things will become clearer as we get through the remainder of the steps. You've done great to get this far.

Ok, brilliant. You have a sense of all the high impact decisions that you need to make. How are you going to start making them?

Now, with these preliminary steps complete, here comes the trickier parts.

STEP 5: For each high impact decision, specify a low impact decision

In Chapter 1, we discussed the story of Bill W. and his alcoholism, and in Chapter 2 we talked about Marvin Renslow, the pilot of the ill-fated Continental Flight 3407. Both these cases have a common thread: decision fatigue.[7] Having to exert mental resources over and over again on various tasks depleted their resources to the point that they were no longer able to make the right decision. This led to deadly consequences. But in both cases, the ultimate decision that carried those dire consequences should not be taken out of context. Bill refused several drinks leading up to the one that lost him everything. Marvin had performed the action that stabilised the plane many times before. They made the wrong decision due to the overwhelming fatigue they had whilst making the final, disastrous choice. Bill didn't think one drink would hurt; Marvin didn't think the plane would crash. The perception of the reward was too low and the effort cost was too high. Stress on the word *perception* there.

Consider our simple model of decision-making:

- Do something if rewards are greater than the costs
- Do nothing if costs are greater than the rewards

But consider: *why* was the cost of the effort too high? It was because of the context surrounding the decision. Bill had already spent resources on decisions leading up to the ill-fated one. Marvin had already spent resources on tasks before the ill-fated one. The cost of the effort was so high because of the high levels of costs that had already been incurred leading up to it. Hence, the first thing we must consider is how one is to *lower* the costs of effort to undertake decisions that work towards your goals.

By far, the easiest way to lower these effort costs is to consider what you might give up instead. For this, we now need to consider decisions that are low impact (TYPE I decisions – Apples or Oranges and TYPE II decisions – Chinese or Korean). These need not be driven by any overarching goal, in the same way that the high impact decisions are, but they need to be articulated and written down. This is because an important part of the framework is what I like to call the 'No Free Lunch' principle. Here the idea is that effort in service to your goals cannot simply be conjured up as if by magic. You are already spending your life on a series of activities that are contributing to who you are. For this reason, you need to look and understand where the effort that you will exert will come from. The framework will not rely on 'doing more' but rather on 'doing different'.

Why is this the case? The way that you use your time is based on who you are. Some of us engage in more leisure time than others. Person A might consider Person B's leisure time a waste, but if Person B did not have that leisure time, they would not feel happy and mentally fulfilled. Think about the time that you are spending on various activities throughout a given day, week and year, and ask yourself what you are really benefiting from.

An illustration of what I'm talking about is Steve Jobs' famous preference for wearing the same outfit each day. Other famous individuals (Albert Einstein, Barack Obama) have undertaken the same strategy.[8] Why? So as to not have to waste mental resources on deciding what to wear each day. These resources are then redeployed elsewhere. These people knew how important their mental resources were to them and their work and so they looked to cut costs everywhere.

However, this particular strategy (wearing the same outfit everyday) is not as easily deployable for others. Firstly, it's for individuals that do not perceive any benefits or rewards based on how they look. They find it unreasonable to justify the costs of effort for no perceived benefits (using our formula above) and so they decide on a strategy that allows them to no longer need to make this decision (obviously they still need to dress themselves, they just have the multiple versions of the same outfit, something this author has done himself on many occasions).

For each of the decisions you have laid out above in service of the goals, we now need to articulate decisions that correspond to the same time frame (daily, weekly, monthly, yearly) but are low impact decisions – that is, not in service to your goal – that you will replace with high impact decisions. Note that the list that you put down does not need to correspond exactly, but you should try to find decisions that correspond in terms of frequency, that you are willing to give up to service the decisions that feed into your goals (high impact). Note also that you need not match them on frequency either. For example, if you are a daily gamer, you might consider skipping just an hour or two here and there so you can add in a high impact decision once a week.

This is probably the most difficult exercise and something that you might need to revisit. You'll probably learn that something you gave up was more critical to your wellbeing than you previously thought. Likewise, you may be surprised by the extent to which you don't miss certain activities and were doing them simply out of habit. Nevertheless, try to follow the replacement principle here and replace those activities that are not in service to your goals with activities that are.

There are likely several high frequency, high impact decisions that you can automate, thereby turning them into low frequency choices. For instance, from the financial planning list above you can set up a direct debit to move money into a savings account automatically. You can set up a profile on a career app and have it automatically send notifications of jobs within a certain set of parameters. In terms of budgeting, you can give yourself the best opportunity of not spending money on, for instance, coffees during your commute by investing in a thermos and filling it before you leave the house. Or you can do your shopping online and have it delivered, thereby ensuring that you make the decision related to household and grocery purchases in a controlled environment and at a time that works for you, rather than at the end of a long day in an environment that is designed to grab your attention and part your money from you. These are just examples, but it's always the case for whatever goal that there is some leeway for you to move high frequency decisions into low frequency ones.

Decision replacement guide – Goal 1				
Decision	Frequency		To-do	Decision details
Decision 1	LOW HIGH		I will do more of this:	
	LOW HIGH		I will do less of this:	
Decision 2	LOW HIGH		I will do more of this:	
	LOW HIGH		I will do less of this:	
Decision 3	LOW HIGH		I will do more of this:	
	LOW HIGH		I will do less of this:	

Decision replacement guide – Goal 2				
Decision	Frequency		To-do	Decision details
Decision 1	LOW HIGH		I will do more of this:	
	LOW HIGH		I will do less of this:	
Decision 2	LOW HIGH		I will do more of this:	
	LOW HIGH		I will do less of this:	
Decision 3	LOW HIGH		I will do more of this:	
	LOW HIGH		I will do less of this:	

Decision replacement guide – Goal 3				
Decision	Frequency		To-do	Decision details
Decision 1	LOW HIGH		I will do more of this:	
	LOW HIGH		I will do less of this:	
Decision 2	LOW HIGH		I will do more of this:	
	LOW HIGH		I will do less of this:	
Decision 3	LOW HIGH		I will do more of this:	
	LOW HIGH		I will do less of this:	

One final point to think about once you have done this is that if you are feeling fatigued, you will find it difficult to make decisions. The fatigue need not stem from any one source, but it is important to know that when we are tired, the cost of effort looms ever larger and the likelihood of ignoring the decision or of procrastinating becomes higher. You've got to time your decision-making right. Practically, this means if you are a morning person, you might be better off doing your 15 minutes a day of language practice as soon as you get up. Similarly, if you are a night owl, structure your decisions in the evening to try to capitalise on your energy. Regardless of circadian rhythms, if you have a very resource-demanding job, it's important to try to structure decisions before the workday rather than after the workday.

Having said that, I have an intuition, however, that you have different types of effort resources. Highly motivated people who work in cognitively demanding jobs may find that they enjoy working out after work because it helps them 'blow off steam'. Once again, the benefit (blowing off steam) has to outweigh the cost. 'Blowing off steam' tends to be the physical yin to the day's cognitive yan. It's rare to find somebody who goes to work all day as a financial analyst and 'blows off steam' by some other highly demanding cognitive activity like playing chess or studying a new language. Either way, the point I'm making is that you'll need to experiment with this slightly. It may be that structuring your day around different types of activity leaves you with more headroom than you might expect because the contrast between two types of activity is a kind of reward.

In the box below, for each decision you specified, please put down a target time during which you aim to do these activities. Keep a note of your high energy timings and try to match these up as much as possible to maximise the amount of high energy you can expend on yourself.

Timings guide		
Goal/Decision	Summary	Target time
Goal 1 – Decision 1		
Goal 1 – Decision 2		
Goal 1 – Decision 3		
Goal 2 – Decision 1		
Goal 2 – Decision 2		
Goal 2 – Decision 3		
Goal 3 – Decision 1		
Goal 3 – Decision 2		
Goal 3 – Decision 3		

This part may feel like a minor point. Many people when confronted with two choices, A and B, would like to pick the third option: both. That's not sustainable. A degree of sacrifice is necessary if you wish to achieve your goals. That means cutting yourself some slack and giving yourself more resources to spend on activities related to your goal. The truth is, you are only one person and you can't spread yourself too thin. Still, the decisions that you are replacing do not have to occur at the same time. It is important to time your decisions so that the perception of effort does not loom larger than the actual effort required. As an example, take going to the gym. Notwithstanding what I said regarding 'blowing off steam', for the average unenthusiastic gym-goer, it is going to be much more difficult to go to the gym at the end of a tiring day than it is at the beginning of a tiring day. To the extent possible, try to structure the decision to capitalise on your resources as much as possible.

STEP 6: Structure rewards

This step is essentially about detailing the rewards that you would gain when undertaking a decision that is in line with your goals. We will undertake a series of exercises to get there. Keep in mind our simple model of decision-making:

- Do something if rewards are greater than the costs
- Do nothing if costs are greater than the rewards

We can think of structuring rewards in three ways: psychological, social and material.

Before we do this, however, we also need to get a sense of how high you might perceive the effort cost to be. We get a sense of how high you perceive the costs by gauging your motivation to undertake the decisions and goals that you set for yourself. It is important here to try to think of the motivation as close to the decision that is required as much as possible. For example, you may be very motivated with the aspiration (getting in shape, for example), but very unmotivated with the decisions required to achieve the aspiration (going to the gym, for example). One way to measure your psychological motivation is to answer a series of questions that have been adapted from the Intrinsic Motivation

Inventory.[9] Respond to them as honestly as you can when you think about the decisions required to achieve your aspiration:

Intrinsic motivation guide – Goal 1		
Decision	Question	Response
	I think I would describe this decision as very enjoyable	Disagree Agree
Decision 1	I think I would find this decision very interesting	Disagree Agree
	I think this decision would be fun	Disagree Agree
	I think I would describe this decision as very enjoyable	Disagree Agree
Decision 2	I think I would find this decision very interesting	Disagree Agree
	I think this decision would be fun	Disagree Agree
	I think I would describe this decision as very enjoyable	Disagree Agree
Decision 3	I think I would find this decision very interesting	Disagree Agree
	I think this decision would be fun	Disagree Agree

Think about each of the decisions you would have to undertake and respond honestly to each question. If most of your answers are 'disagree' then you would roughly classify your psychological motivation as low. If most of your answers are 'agree' then you would roughly classify your psychological motivation as high.

Note that these questions give you a rough understanding of how motivated you are to undertake the decisions at hand. Chances are that for many of the decisions you have laid out, the motivation for you to perform them is low. If your motivation was high, you would probably already be doing them. Still, it's important to gauge this for all decisions because some decisions you might like (such as the act of shopping around for a gym) versus others you won't (actually working out at the gym). This matters because you need to consider how to scale your reward appropriately to ensure that you undertake the right decision when it matters.

Let's now go ahead and classify the motivation for engaging in each decision as you currently see it. In the table, go through each decision and circle whether the perceived rewards are going to come from the decision and the decision alone (don't think about the reward coming from achieving the aspiration, that comes later).

Rewards Catalogue (Preliminary)				
Goal/Decision	Perceived rewards (circle all that apply)			
Goal 1 – Decision 1	None	Psychological	Social	Material
Goal 1 – Decision 2	None	Psychological	Social	Material
Goal 1 – Decision 3	None	Psychological	Social	Material
Goal 2 – Decision 1	None	Psychological	Social	Material
Goal 2 – Decision 2	None	Psychological	Social	Material
Goal 2 – Decision 3	None	Psychological	Social	Material
Goal 3 – Decision 1	None	Psychological	Social	Material
Goal 3 – Decision 2	None	Psychological	Social	Material
Goal 3 – Decision 3	None	Psychological	Social	Material

Now that we are done cataloguing the rewards that come from undertaking the decision and nothing else, we need to specify the rewards that we will intervene with. This means our next task is to take each decision and bolster it with rewards, preferably from the categories we currently do not have. Try to structure at least two types of rewards for any decisions that currently do not have any.

One further point on the rewards is to bring them as close as possible to the effort that you are going to undertake. Remember the chapter on time preferences? We naturally prefer rewards earlier rather than later. But now you also know whether you are impatient and/or impulsive. If you are either of those things, try to bring the reward as close to the decision as you possibly can.

Since the long-term reward, our aspiration, is very far off in the future and conditional on undertaking a series of tasks, it is important to build in interim rewards along the way to alleviate the pain of exerting effort.

So, what should these rewards look like? It's up to you, and it requires some calibration to make sure they work for you, but the broad principle is nicely covered by the temptation bundling experiment[10] we discussed in Chapter 8. The idea is to pair up an activity that you do not enjoy (going to the gym) with an activity that you do (listening to an audiobook) to give you an incentive to offset the displeasure of the task. This is, of course, an example of a material reward and demonstrates the principle quite nicely, especially timing the reward as closely as possible.

The other thing we learnt from the study was to use this type of reward sparingly, so to deploy it only when the task is being undertaken, or just afterwards, otherwise the reward is no longer linked with the effort provided, undercutting its efficacy. In other words, if you are going to use material rewards such as temptation bundling, use them as close to the unpleasant activity as possible and make the reward *salient*, meaning conditional on the action. Let's stick with that audiobook example. Your headphones go on the moment you start working out, not before and not afterwards.

We focus on three main categories of reward to keep things simple: psychological, social and material. Psychological rewards are gained in the process of engaging in the activity. Once you have the decisions described that you will use to achieve the goals, each time you engage in effort on each of the tasks, you will experience some sense of achievement, however small, associated with getting closer to your goal. This can be intrinsically motivating. However, reliance on this type of motivation is risky, as it will only offset the effort costs in cases of very low effort. Hence, while the science on goal-setting makes it clear that psychological rewards increase output and performance, this is not universally true. It is much more likely to help in cases where motivation tends to be high to begin with.

Let's imagine you're an elite level 10,000m runner. You have been running for many years and you love it. You happen to also be very good at it. Setting a goal to qualify for the Olympics in 16 weeks' time is likely going to be motivating for you. You already have bags of intrinsic motivation and now there's an external motivator, too. Contrast this with somebody who hates running. Setting a goal to run a 10K in 16 weeks' time might just about get you to tip over the line to go for a ten-minute jog in week one. But, by itself, it may not carry you that much further.

A second form of psychological reward comes from feedback which exceeds expectations. This is why the timing of feedback is so critical. When progress towards the goal is easily measurable (such as in the case of losing weight), then feedback on progress should ideally be sought once feedback is likely to exceed expectations, rather than when feedback does not exceed expectations. This means two things. The first is to keep expectations low (easier said than done, especially if you are overconfident) and second, to keep reminding yourself that you are in this for the long haul and only expect to see results after some realistic timeframe. Again, in the case of weight loss, it is important to give your body time to adjust to your new regime before using feedback to motivate yourself.

If, like most people, you are overconfident, you need to temper your expectations accordingly. A rule of thumb might be to halve whatever progress you expect to see at the first milestone. This way you can try to ensure that feedback is more likely to be motivating rather than unmotivating.

Feedback is important to seek out, not just from a motivation perspective. It is important to use it to calibrate your goals and your decisions, to make sure you are making progress and to see whether the goal that you have set for yourself is realistic. You will be motivated to seek out feedback to chart your progress. Just make sure it works for you, not against you. Give yourself enough time and manage your expectations accordingly.

The other aspects of rewards are social and material. The material rewards are obvious, but bear repeating. Do what you can to treat yourself periodically and make that treat conditional on exerting effort. It is important that the reward does not work counter to the goal itself (for example, don't eat doughnuts after a workout). Ideally, it should be something that you enjoy for the sake of it but may not ordinarily do. For example, spending time watching videos online does not often work as a salient reward because this activity is so accessible and prevalent. Good rewards for high frequency, high impact decisions might include spending quality time with loved ones, going to see a movie, or reading a novel (at least for me). Is there a way that you can schedule your workout so that you 'earn' going to the movies with friends right afterwards?

Social rewards are similar. Work with somebody that you trust to keep you accountable and to cheer you on when you engage in the effort needed. You're probably familiar with the concept of gym buddies. The motivation of the gym buddy and the emotional support acts as another reward. If you wish to take up exercise, joining a club might be a good way to offload a lot of the thinking around rewards. Clubs naturally have social rewards, and utilise competition, to keep you motivated. Think back to the story of Bill and Alcoholics Anonymous (Chapter 1) – AA meetings are, of course, done in a group rather than in a one-on-one setting. The same is true with learning new skills – join a study group or sign up to a course. Perhaps with more private goals, financial ones, for instance, social rewards may be harder to come by. But a loving partner, or even a parent or sibling, will surely be there to cheer you on and encourage you through the ups and downs. Asking someone to hold you accountable to your plan increases the cost of reneging – it's a form of commitment device.

Now, take a moment to think through some of the main decisions that you outlined earlier, and decide upon a reward and feedback strategy. Note that you do not have to fill out all rewards but try to have at least two (which can be in the same category of rewards). This is to reduce the likelihood that the reward itself becomes unmotivating.

Goal I – Reward strategy		
Decision I	Whenever I undertake this decision/task, I will reward myself by:	Psychologically: _____ Socially: _____ Materially: _____
Decision 2	Whenever I undertake this decision/task, I will reward myself by:	Psychologically: _____ Socially: _____ Materially: _____
Decision 3	Whenever I undertake this decision/task, I will reward myself by:	Psychologically: _____ Socially: _____ Materially: _____

STEP 7: Set out your feedback and revision plan

Finally, let's lay out an assessment, or feedback schedule. While you are doing this, please do not forget to check back on your confidence level and adjust accordingly (overconfident types, please set a date further in the future than you think is appropriate).

Feedback schedule	
Goal/Decision	Date
Goal 1 – Decision 1	I will commit to seeking feedback on my progress on this date:
Goal 1 – Decision 2	I will commit to seeking feedback on my progress on this date:
Goal 1 – Decision 3	I will commit to seeking feedback on my progress on this date:
Goal 2 – Decision 1	I will commit to seeking feedback on my progress on this date:
Goal 2 – Decision 2	I will commit to seeking feedback on my progress on this date:
Goal 2 – Decision 3	I will commit to seeking feedback on my progress on this date:
Goal 3 – Decision 1	I will commit to seeking feedback on my progress on this date:
Goal 3 – Decision 2	I will commit to seeking feedback on my progress on this date:
Goal 3 – Decision 3	I will commit to seeking feedback on my progress on this date:

Thank you for sticking with it so far. If you have followed each step as it came, you are well on your way towards your aspirations. Remember that it is hard to expect yourself to adhere to your schedule every single day for the rest of your life. Life happens and things will conspire to derail you. But whenever they do, return to your plan. Start again and stick with it. Remind yourself of what you aspire to and how much closer you are to achieving it.

We put down multiple aspirations at the beginning of our journey but followed through on only one of them. Focusing on one aspiration at a time works in your favour because there are fewer things to worry about. Fewer decisions and actions, fewer things to remember. However, this framework is general enough to work with a series of aspirations, so if you believe that you can manage it, please do so. I would say that, until you get the hang of thinking in this way, you should try to complete just one aspiration at a time. I'd recommend returning to this chapter once you are relatively stable and working towards achieving that first aspiration.

In review, here are the steps to follow for all subsequent goals:

The 7-Step Decisive Mind Programme
Step 1: Write down your aspiration
Step 2: Write down concrete goals that feed into your aspiration
Step 3: Break up the goal into a series of repeating decisions
Step 4: Classify decisions according to whether they are low or high frequency
Step 5: For each high impact decision, specify a low impact decision
Step 6: Structure rewards (i.e. cash out)
Step 7: Set out your feedback and revision plan

Throughout, be aware of your motivation, your (over)confidence, and keep your high energy timings handy. This is incredibly useful information and will help you with your journey. Use it to tailor your strategy. As time goes by, you'll find that you naturally start to revise your strategy along the way. Keep coming back and considering whether the effort you are making is yielding the progress that you would like to see. Whether the goal is getting closer, and whether you are happy going without the things that you gave up. These steps will make for a happier, healthier, more peaceful you.

Best of luck building your decisive mind. I am cheering for you.

References

Kahneman, Daniel. *Thinking, Fast and Slow*. Macmillan, 2011.

Fiske, Susan T. and Taylor, Shelley E. *Social Cognition*. McGraw-Hill Book Company, 1991.

Stanovich, Keith E. *What Intelligence Tests Miss: The Psychology of Rational Thought*. Yale University Press, 2009.

Ortoleva, Pietro and Snowberg, Erik. 'Overconfidence in political behavior.' *American Economic Review* 105, no. 2 (2015): 504–535.

Niederle, Muriel and Vesterlund, Lise. 'Gender and competition.' *Annual Review of Economics* 3, no. 1 (2011): 601–630.

Vischer, Thomas, Dohmen, Thomas, Falk, Armin, Huffman, David, Schupp, Jürgen, Sunde, Uwe and Wagner, Gert G. 'Validating an ultra-short survey measure of patience.' *Economics Letters* 120, no. 2 (2013): 142–145.

Doran, George T. 'There's a SMART way to write management's goals and objectives.' *Management Review* 70, no. 11 (1981): 35–36.

Shenhav, Amitai, Musslick, Sebastian, Lieder, Falk, Kool, Wouter, Griffiths, Thomas L., Cohen, Jonathan D. and Botvinick, Matthew M. 'Toward a rational and mechanistic account of mental effort.' *Annual Review of Neuroscience* 40 (2017): 99–124.

Schwartz, Barry. 'The paradox of choice: Why more is less.' New York: Ecco, 2004.

Amabile, Teresa M., Hill, Karl G., Hennessey, Beth A. and Tighe, Elizabeth M. 'The work preference inventory: Assessing intrinsic and extrinsic motivational orientations.' *Journal of Personality and Social Psychology* 66, no. 5 (1994): 950.

Milkman, Katherine L., Minson, Julia A. and Volpp, Kevin G. M. 'Holding the hunger games hostage at the gym: An evaluation of temptation bundling.' *Management Science* 60, no. 2 (2014): 283–299.

Man vs Mountain

Polepole

My ascent of Kilimanjaro was an inspiration for this book. Was summiting Kilimanjaro impossible? No. Was it something that many try, but few succeed? No. The truth is most people make it to the top. It's hard, but achievable. In just the same way, most of us really can save regularly, get fit and maintain the good practices that bolster our mental and physical health. Most of us can quit smoking or curb excessive drinking.

Kilimanjaro was a challenge for me. I wasn't sure what to expect, I was terribly unprepared and the temptation to quit, with each painful step and each excruciating breath, was very real.

And yet, I prevailed.

But I didn't do it alone. I had help. I had support. I had a very obvious goal. I was motivated. I received feedback. I had my reward. And above all, I had Emmanuele. Each time I wanted to get feedback, I could ask Emmanuele. When I wanted a pat on the back, I asked Emmanuele. When I wanted to know what the consequences of quitting were: Emmanuele.

As I said right in the beginning, I wanted to write a book that would serve as your Emmanuele. That would help you get on the right path and stick with it. Using my knowledge of cutting-edge behavioural science, I have attempted to develop a practical guide for you to use and come back to repeatedly to help you stay on track. Just like me on Kilimanjaro, when you need a pat on the back, some feedback, come back to this book.

I'm not going to overpromise here. *The Decisive Mind* is not about achieving the impossible. I'm not going to say that you can become the next Lionel Messi or Marie Curie if you simply follow the steps in this book. But that's not the point. The point is that you can achieve a difficult aspiration for *you*. Life is hard and people are different. But *The Decisive Mind* will help you achieve what you want within the scope of the possible. If you want to get a promotion, or lose a few pounds, or put your financial house in order, you absolutely can. *Polepole polepole*. Slowly, slowly.

The insights that are here in the book are not from my time on Kilimanjaro. They come from my research. However, I am not a disinterested researcher totally removed from practice. I was able to put these principles and insights to the test during the writing of this book. Like climbing Mount Kilimanjaro, most people, I would say, can write a book if they really try. But that is not to say that it is easy. Trust me, it isn't! A decisive mind is a prerequisite. You need to decide you want to do it and you need to go at it.

A long project like this needs considerable time, patience and dedication. Over the course of writing this book, I suffered from a series of pandemic-related health scares, including a six-month battle with long covid, as well as the birth of my first child. Each event was enough to derail this project. But, *polepole*, I kept coming back and got there in the end. To finish, I want to take a moment to walk you through the steps that I used, to show you how they helped me put this book in your hand.

The 7-Step Decisive Mind Programme	
Step 1:	Write down your aspiration
Step 2:	Write down concrete goals that feed into your aspiration
Step 3:	Break up the goal into a series of repeating decisions
Step 4:	Classify decisions according to whether they are low or high frequency
Step 5:	For each high impact decision, specify a low impact decision
Step 6:	Structure rewards (i.e. cash out)
Step 7:	Set out your feedback and revision plan

My decisive mind:

First some preliminaries. As we've learnt, knowing yourself, gaining self-awareness, respecting the biases you're prone to, is a key part of success. For me, I am overconfident. I routinely suffer from the intention-action gap and my estimates regarding my abilities are often crazily optimistic. I regularly fall foul of the planning fallacy.

I am impatient. Any time I start something I want to get it done as quickly as I can to move on to the next task. And I need positive reinforcement to keep going.

Finally, I am impulsive. I have certain moods when I like to get things done (and am super productive when the mood strikes), but equally, there are times when I don't want to do anything, or at least engage in less productive activities.

So, all the troublesome criteria that anybody might suffer from.

I also have clear high energy timings. I have high levels of energy in the mornings, which taper off in the afternoon. My energy levels pick up again in the evenings and spiral down quickly in the late evening. I would characterise them thusly:

High timings:
6–9am
3–6pm
6–9pm (sometimes)

Ok, with that in place . . .

Step 1: Write down your aspiration

Aspiration: Write a book called The Decisive Mind.

Step 2: Write down concrete goals

Goal 1: Write one chapter (5,000 words) per month.

Goal 2: Spend one day (eight hours) per week researching background material for the chapter.

Goal 3: Spend four hours per week writing without interruptions.

Do the goals fit the S.M.A.R.T. criteria?

Are they Specific?

Goal 1 specifies the chapter and words needed. Goal 2 specifies the day and hours needed. Goal 3 specifies the hours needed.

Are they Measurable?

Yes, all three goals have criteria that can be measured (word counts and time spent).

Are they Achievable?

Yes, I believe so. They fit the type of writing I have done in the past and I am able to block out the time in my schedule.

Are they Relevant?

The words and time spent all contribute towards the end product of the decisive mind, so yes, they are.

Are they Timely?

Yes, the distinct end point is when the book is completed, but I set a year to get it done (12 chapters).

Step 3: Break up goals into a series of repeating decisions

Goal 1: Write one chapter (5,000 words) per month.

Decision 1: Check on progress in the middle of the month.

Decision 2: Report back to editor about my progress for the month.

Goal 2: Spend one day (eight hours) per week researching background material for the chapter.

Decision 1: Each Monday schedule time for research and write down the questions for the week.

Decision 2: At the scheduled time, revise the questions you would like to answer.

Decision 3: In the last 30 minutes of the scheduled time, write down what you have learnt so far and what the next steps are.

Goal 3: Spend four hours per week writing without interruptions.

Decision 1: Each Monday, check on progress and schedule time to write for the week.

Decision 2: At the scheduled time, shut out all distractions, including email notifications, and put the phone on silent.

Decision 3: At the scheduled time, write at least one paragraph within the first 15 minutes.

Step 4: Classify decisions based on frequency

Goal 1 – Decision 1 – Low Frequency
Goal 1 – Decision 2 – Low Frequency
Goal 2 – Decision 1 – Low Frequency
Goal 2 – Decision 2 – High Frequency
Goal 2 – Decision 3 – High Frequency
Goal 3 – Decision 1 – Low Frequency
Goal 3 – Decision 2 – High Frequency
Goal 3 – Decision 3 – High Frequency

Step 5: Specify low impact decisions that are replaced by high impact decisions

For all low frequency tasks: Skip afternoon coffee on Mondays and drink tea at desk

Covers Goal 1 – Decision 1; Goal 1 – Decision 2; Goal 2 – Decision 1; Goal 3 – Decision 1

For high frequency tasks:

High impact – Goal 2 – Decision 2: At the scheduled time, revise the questions you would like to answer.

Low impact – Goal 2 – Decision 2: Cancel weekly meetings on certain projects (ask team to contact me over email).

High impact – Goal 2 – Decision 3: In the last 30 minutes of the scheduled time, write down what you have learnt so far and what the next steps are.

Low impact – Goal 2 – Decision 3: Shop online, read video game reviews, check on the news, etc.

High impact – Goal 3 – Decision 2: At the scheduled time, shut down all distractions, including email notifications and put the phone on silent.

Low impact – Goal 3 – Decision 2: Shop online, read video game reviews, check on the news, etc.

High impact – Goal 3 – Decision 3: At the scheduled time, write at least one paragraph within the first 15 minutes.

Low impact – Goal 3 – Decision 2: Do not browse websites for 'inspiration'.

Step 6: Set rewards

On completing low frequency tasks: (Material) Watch an episode of Frasier *(I love* Frasier!*).*

On completing writing time: (Material) Grab a tasty snack (I love snacks!); (Psychological) Write down words completed and subtract them from the target; (Social) Brag to my partner about how much I got done.

Step 7: Set up the feedback and revision plan

At the end of the month check on word count and read through chapter. Revise schedule based on quality of work completed.

Check in with editors and publishers on deliverables and discuss timeline.

And that's it. Easy!

Well . . . Not really.

I would be lying if I told you it all went smoothly. There were many, *many* roadblocks. Chief among them was long covid, which gave me headaches to the point where I was unable to function and left me so tired I was in bed for weeks at a time. My child or my spouse or I got ill from time to time, putting various things behind schedule. There were setbacks, over and over again. And yet, returning to the plan that I had originally set myself, and bolstered by tasty snacks and episodes of *Frasier*, I kept coming back to what I had done, looked at how much I had to go, and slowly but surely, I got it done. I also had the support of my editors and publishers, who were understanding and helped me revise timelines when necessary. I stuck with it and you hold in your hands the result.

Each project I work on, it's the same. I sit down and figure out where I can find the time to do the activities that need doing. My life as an academic has been built around the ebbs and flows of different projects. I am not always successful, certainly not right off the bat, but I keep coming back. That is the main upshot of a decisive mind. Once you sit and think through these steps, you can revise each of them as needed. But if you keep coming back, reminding yourself that each step you take is one step closer, you will get there. I promise you; you will get there.

I hope that I have convinced you of the potential contained within you. We have flaws, and whilst there are many books that look at how you can become a 'better person', I urge you to do the exact opposite. Building a decisive mind doesn't mean becoming something you're not. It means owning up to your shortcomings, recognising them and realising that you can work with them to do hard stuff. Lose weight, save money, change job, study for a test, quit the fags, write a book. Whatever it is, I hope *The Decisive Mind* has helped put you on the right path and I hope that you use it to accomplish whatever it is that you seek. No magic, no secrets, no shortcuts, just honest, hard work optimised. Using the framework in this book, working through the exercises in Chapter 11, will get you to the end as efficiently as your limitations allow. You are beautiful, with all your blemishes, because they are what make you, you. So, no matter what anyone says, you *can* do it . . . as long as you know that it's you, the real you, that has to do the doing.

Kilimanjaro, Uhuru Peak – I'm right there, second from the right
Photo credit: Emmanuele

Notes

I Just One More Drink . . .

1 *Pass It On*, p. 56.
2 *Pass It On*, p. 91.
3 *Pass It On*, p. 92.

2 Long Shifts and Fatal Errors

1 Details of the Continental Airlines Flight 3407 crash have been obtained from the official Accident report filed with the National Transportation Safety Board (NTSB) of the US. The full report is accessible on the NTSB official website here: https://www.ntsb.gov/investigations/AccidentReports/Reports/AAR1001.pdf
2 For more details on the Wielinski family see https://www.legacy.com/us/obituaries/buffalonews/name/douglas-wielinski-obituary?id=4712152
3 For details of the crash from the ground, see https://buffalonews.com/news/local/crime-and-courts/flight-3407-s-crash-into-family-home-is-detailed/article_fe730120-05da-5d2c-9ddd-c502035fa537.html
4 The family arrived at a settlement with Colgan air 13 years after the crash: https://buffalonews.com/news/local/crime-and-courts/wielinski-family-agrees-to-settlement-in-flight-3407-trial/article_979e41ab-ec11-5adc-91ae-360c53918594.html
5 For more details on Marvin Renslow, please see: https://www.nbcnewyork.com/news/local/pilot-of-doomed-flight-described-as-by-the-book/1882835/
6 Details of Captain Renslow's activities have been researched and documented in the Accident report issued by the NTSB. https://www.ntsb.gov/investigations/AccidentReports/Reports/AAR1001.pdf

7 See Renslow's colleagues' testimonies here: http://www.aero-news.net/index. cfm?do=main.textpost&id=2381cff5-cbb0-48ba-9190-1dce7aded551

8 NTSB accident report, p. 8.

9 NTSB accident report, p. 9.

10 Ibid.

11 NTSB accident report, p. 85.

12 See Hull (1943), p. 293.

13 See Smith (1776), Book 1, chapter 5.

14 See Kool et al. (2010).

15 See Westbrook, Kester, and Braver (2013) for more details.

16 See McGuire and Botvinick (2010) and Botvinick, Huffstetler, and McGuire (2009) for similar experiments and findings.

17 For details on dual process models of thinking and cognition, see Posner and Snyder (1975), Stanovich and West (2000), Kahneman (2003).

18 See Kahneman (2003) or Evans (2008).

19 Ibid.

20 See Frederick (2005) for more details on the cognitive reflection test.

21 See Price and Wolfers (2010).

22 In related work, Banuri, Eckel and Wilson (2022) ran an experiment with undergraduate students at Rice University. Students were asked to participate in a game requiring trust. Students were in the role of either a manager or a worker. Managers could choose between a higher ability worker from a different dorm (residential college) or a lower ability worker from the same dorm as them. Half of the managers chose the lower ability worker with a shared identity, simply because they trusted them more. Lower ability workers compensated managers by working harder. It is an example of an in-group bias, but one where the bias actually pays off.

23 See Pope, Price and Wolfers (2018).

24 In a related study, Axt, Casola and Nosek (2019) asked undergraduate students at the University of Virginia to evaluate academic profiles for admission to an honour society. Participants were given both relevant information (grade point average, interview scores) and irrelevant information (through the use of applicant pictures: attractiveness, and racial group). Over the course of seven experiments, they found that participants that were explicitly asked to avoid a particular bias showed reductions in said bias, but showed no effect on other biases. In other words, if participants were asked to avoid being biased due to the attractiveness of the applicant, they showed a reduction in biases arising out of attractiveness, but no reduction in biases arising from group membership. Taken together, these findings, while point towards the importance of awareness, also point to how difficult it is to avoid subjective judgements.

25 Psychologists Susan Fiske and Shelley Taylor introduced the term 'cognitive miser' in their book *Social Cognition* (1984). This term relates to the tendency of human

beings to minimise mental effort in the same way they minimise physical effort. This concept provides evidence for why people engage in mental shortcuts, regardless of intelligence or ability. That is, if the same reward can be achieved at lower costs of (mental or physical) effort, the human mind tends to choose the less costly action.

26 For more details on the Federal Aviation Authority rule changes go here: https://www.pbs.org/wgbh/frontline/article/faa-issues-new-pilot-fatigue-rules/

27 More details here: https://www.aerotime.aero/articles/23034-flight-completely-changed-aviation-safety

3 Wisdom of the Crowds . . .

1 For more details about the fascinating life of Sir Francis Galton, see Brookes (2004).

2 See Galton (1907).

3 See Herzog and Hertwig (2014) for a discussion of Galton's findings.

4 For more on Aristotle and collective wisdom, see Landemore and Elster (2012).

5 See Reagle (2020) for more on the creation of Wikipedia.

6 See Reagle (2020), chapter 1.

7 Ibid.

8 See Reagle (2020), chapter 5, p. 71.

9 For more about Maslow's theory, see Maslow (1943) or McLeod (2007) for a useful summary.

10 See Alder (2001).

11 See Deci, Olafsen and Ryan (2017) for a useful review.

12 See Smith (1962) for an early lab experiment on market behaviour.

13 See Smith (1976) for more details on induced value theory, a central tenet of lab experiments in economics.

14 See, for example, Fehr, Kirchsteiger and Riedl (1998).

15 See DellaVigna and Pope (2018) for details on this experiment.

16 See Banuri and Keefer (2016) for more details on the experiments in Indonesia.

17 See Banuri, Keefer and de Walque (2018) for more details on these experiments.

18 See Ariely, Kamenica and Prelec (2008) for details.

19 See Banuri, Dankova and Keefer (2017) for details.

20 Ibid.

4 Good Things for Those Who Wait . . .

1 For more on the tragedy of the commons, see Ostrom (2008), and for more details on governance of the commons, see Ostrom (1990).

2 See Ostrom (2000).

3 See Nordman (2021), p. 31.

4 For more on Ostrom in her own words, see her Nobel Prize biography: https://www.nobelprize.org/prizes/economic-sciences/2009/ostrom/biographical/

5 Ostrom Nobel Prize biography: https://www.nobelprize.org/prizes/economic-sciences/2009/ostrom/biographical/

6 From Ostrom's lectures, discussed in detail here: https://ian.umces.edu/blog/the-triumph-of-the-commons-no-actually-it-can-happen/

7 See Ostrom (1990).

8 More specifically, her work was in sharp opposition to Harding's (1968) highly influential work on the commons problem.

9 From Ostrom's Nobel Prize biography, accessible at: https://www.nobelprize.org/prizes/economic-sciences/2009/ostrom/biographical/

10 Full disclosure: Lin Ostrom's student Rick K. Wilson went on to a professorship in political science at Rice University. He served on my dissertation committee and is one important reason why Lin was so influential for me.

11 See Mischel, Shoda and Rodriguez (1989).

12 There is a series of papers written about the Marshmallow experiment. See Mischel (1958), Mischel (1961), Mischel, Shoda and Rodriguez (1989) for more details.

13 See, for example, Shoda, Mischel and Peake (1988) and Shoda, Mischel and Peake (1990).

14 See Sutter et al. (2013).

15 See Schnitker (2012).

16 Ibid.

17 Studies show that patience is predictive of credit card borrowing and financial literacy (Meier and Sprenger, 2010), smoking and alcohol consumption (Khwaja, Sloan and Salm, 2006); and better nutrition (Weller et al., 2008).

18 Schnitker (2012) reports that a psychological training intervention was effective in increasing patience. The intervention was composed of cognitive behavioural therapy, meditation and emotional regulation. Note that while the study shows that this is possible, the literature is still in its infancy, and so I am less confident about describing techniques to alter patience. The focus here is on awareness and how patience helps with goal achievement.

19 See Chabris et al. (2008), who use a time preference measure first introduced by Kirby, Petry and Bickel (1999).

20 See O'Donoghue and Rabin (1999).
21 See Augenblick, Niederle and Sprenger (2015).
22 Studies show more patience for monetary rewards, than for food (Odum, Baumann and Rimington, 2006), alcohol (Odum and Rainaud, 2003), candy and soda (Estle et al., 2007), primary goods, such as sugar or beef (Ubfal, 2016).

5 Did You See the Gorilla?

1 See more about Paul Romer here: https://www.nobelprize.org/prizes/economic-sciences/2018/romer/facts/
2 For more on Romer's seminal work, see Romer (1990).
3 See https://www.wsj.com/articles/nobel-in-economics-goes-to-american-pair-1538992672
4 For access to the discontinued Doing Business Reports, visit https://www.world-bank.org/en/programs/business-enabling-environment/doing-business-legacy
5 See, for example, Jayasuriya (2011), which reports positive effects of the Doing Business report, particularly for developed countries.
6 More on the independent evaluation of the report here: https://www.reuters.com/business/external-review-finds-deeper-rot-world-bank-doing-business-rankings-2021-09-20/
7 The Wall Street Journal article: https://www.cgdev.org/blog/chart-week-3-why-world-bank-should-ditch-doing-business-rankings-one-embarrassing-chart
8 The post by the Centre for Global Development on recalculating Chile's rankings: https://www.cgdev.org/blog/chart-week-3-why-world-bank-should-ditch-doing-business-rankings-one-embarrassing-chart
9 Statement by the World Bank on the discontinuation of the Doing Business report: https://www.worldbank.org/en/news/statement/2021/09/16/world-bank-group-to-discontinue-doing-business-report
10 See Kahan et al. (2017) for more details on confirmation bias and how political beliefs affect the interpretation of data.
11 For more on mental models, see Johnson-Laird (2004).
12 See, for example, Becklen and Cervone (1983) or Stoffregen and Becklen (1989).
13 See Neisser and Becklen (1975) or Simons and Chabris (1999).
14 See Driver (2001) for a review of the literature on selective attention.
15 See Sunstein et al. (2007).
16 See Kahan et al. (2017).
17 See Banuri, Dercon and Gauri (2019).
18 See Kahneman and Tversky (1982).
19 For more on the evolutionary benefits to overconfidence, see Johnson and Fowler (2011).

20 Researchers have pointed to the role that overconfidence plays in events like wars, financial crises and stock market bubbles (Camerer and Lovallo, 1999; Glaser and Weber, 2007; Howard, 1984; Malmendier and Tate, 2005; Neale and Bazerman, 1985; Odean, 1999).

21 See Moore and Healy (2008).

22 Ibid.

23 Discussion of the YouGov poll here: https://www.thecut.com/2019/07/poll-1-in-8-men-think-they-can-beat-serena-williams.html

24 See, for example, Alicke and Govorun (2005).

25 See Moore and Healy (2008).

26 See Eil and Rao (2011).

27 For more on the planning fallacy, see Kahneman and Tversky (1982).

28 For more on the Dunning-Kruger effect, see Kruger and Dunning (1999).

6 Goals, Goals, Goals . . .

1 For more details of airships in general, and for a meticulously researched history of British airships, see Swinfield (2013).

2 Swinfield (2013), chapter 6.

3 Swinfield (2013), chapter 9.

4 For a detailed biography of Lord Thomson, see Masefield (1982).

5 Swinfield (2013), chapter 7.

6 Ibid.

7 Ibid.

8 Ibid.

9 Swinfield (2013), chapter 8.

10 Masefield (1982), p. 133.

11 Swinfield (2013), chapter 8.

12 Swinfield (2013), chapter 9.

13 Historian Douglas Botting, via Swinfield (2013), chapter 9.

14 Swinfield (2013), chapter 9.

15 Swinfield (2013), chapter 8.

16 Swinfield (2013), chapter 9.

17 See van Lent and Souverijn (2020).

18 For more background on the theory of goal setting and performance, see Locke and Latham (1990).

19 See Latham and Locke (1979).

20 For more on a sense of achievement, see Gomez-Minambres (2012).

21 See, for example, Latham and Yukl (1976); Shane, Locke and Collins (2003); Suvorov and Van de Ven (2008); Koch and Nafziger (2016); Koch and Nafziger (2014); Anderson, Dekker and Sedatole (2010), among many others.

22 See, for example, Hollenbeck, Williams and Klein (1989).
23 See Doran (1981).
24 Swinfield (2013), chapter 9.
25 Ibid.

7 Why Can't You Be Like Everyone Else?

1 See Ceraso, Gruber and Rock (1990), p. 3.
2 See Ceraso, Gruber and Rock (1990), pp. 7–8.
3 See Asch (1951) on more details of this landmark experiment.
4 Asch (1951).
5 Ibid.
6 See Corgnet, Gomez-Minambres and Hernan-Gonzalez (2015) and Gomez-Minambres (2012) for more on goal setting and motivation.
7 See Fogg (2019) for more.
8 See Clear (2018) and Milkman (2021) for more on this topic.
9 See Neal, Wood and Drolet (2013).
10 See Brehm and Self (1989) and Wright and Brehm (1989) for more details on Motivational Intensity Theory.
11 For more on the good news-bad news effect, see Eil and Rao (2011).
12 See Venables and Fairclough (2009).
13 See Kool and Botvinick (2013) on the debate between ego-depletion and motivation-depletion. Ego depletion indicates a lack of mental resources. Motivation-depletion states that the decline in performance over time is not associated with a lack of resources (which implies that people cannot continue exerting mental effort even if they wanted to) but on a lack of motivation itself. For examples of the latter, Hagger et al. (2010) and Job, Dweck and Walton (2010).
14 See Baumeister et al. (2018) for evidence in favour of resource depletion.
15 See Kool and Botvinick (2013) and Kool et al. (2013).
16 See Atwater et al. (2000) for more details on the upward feedback experiment.
17 See Kluger and DeNisi (1996).
18 See Ashford and Cummings (1983) for a psychological explanation of why individuals that need feedback the most are the least likely to seek it out.
19 See Sitzmann and Johnson (2012a).
20 Eil and Rao (2011).
21 See Stone and Stone (1985) and Meyer (1992) for evidence on perceptions, feedback and task abandonment.
22 See Sitzmann and Johnson (2012b).

8 What Do I Get Out of It?

1 Woolley and Langel (2019), chapter 6, p. 84.
2 For more about Minnesota's culture, see Atkins (2009).
3 Woolley and Langel (2019), chapter 5, p. 73.
4 Woolley and Langel (2019), chapter 6, p. 86.
5 For more details on the context surrounding Woolley's death, please see Spain and Vega (2005).
6 See Griffiths, Kuss and King (2012).
7 Online Gamers Anonymous (OLGA). More here: http://www.olgahon.org/home
8 More on the gaming industry can be found here: https://newzoo.com/global-games-market-reports
9 For a review on gamification technology and impact on effort, see Hámari, Koivisto and Sarsa (2014).
10 More on gamification in the gig economy here: https://www.bloomberg.com/news/features/2022-05-27/how-uber-and-lyft-gamify-the-gig-economy
11 For more on this, please see Banuri, Dankova and Keefer (2017).
12 See Spain and Vega (2005).
13 Woolley and Langel (2019), chapter 5, p. 72.
14 See Milkman, Minson and Volpp (2014) or Milkman (2021).
15 See Milkman, Minson and Volpp (2014).
16 See Duckworth, Milkman and Laibson (2018).
17 See Ashraf, Karlan and Yin (2006).
18 See Duckworth et al. (2016).
19 See Epton, Currie and Armitage (2017).
20 See Duckworth, Milkman and Laibson (2018).
21 Woolley and Langel (2019), chapter 4, p. 66.
22 See Banuri, Dankova and Keefer (2017).
23 Woolley and Langel (2019), chapter 2, p. 35.
24 Woolley and Langel (2019), chapter 3, pp. 52–53.

9 The Tyranny of Small Decisions . . .

1 Please find the article on Parkinson's law here: https://www.economist.com/news/1955/11/19/parkinsons-law
2 For more on Parkinson's Law, see Parkinson (1957).
3 See Homer and Levine (1985) for more on Sayre's law.

4 See Issawi (1973).

5 See Kahn (1966).

6 See Marewski, Gaissmaier and Gigerenzer (2010) on a detailed discussion of using heuristics to solve complex problems.

10 I Want to Join a Gym!

1 For more on Vic Tanny and the fitness industry, see Black (2013).

2 For more on the Fresh Start effect, see Dai, Milkman and Riis (2014).

3 More details on Western Australia's fitness code here: https://www.commerce. wa.gov.au/sites/default/files/atoms/files/fitnessindustrycodeofpractice.pdf

4 Figures for the gym industry can be found here: https://www.ihrsa.org/publica-tions/the-2020-ihrsa-global-report/

5 See DellaVigna and Malmendier (2006) for more details.

6 See Moore and Healy (2008) for more details on overconfidence and its effects on behaviour.

7 For more details on the Intention-Action or the Intention-Behaviour gap, see Sheeran and Webb (2016).

8 More information on overconfidence and gym attendance can be found in Carrera et al. (2018).

11 Let's Do This!

1 For a great primer on the topic of System 1 versus System 2 thinking, please see Kahneman (2011).

2 For more on the topic of cognitive misers, see Fiske and Taylor (1991) or Stanovich (2009).

3 The simplified test for overconfidence has been adapted from Ortoleva and Snowberg (1995).

4 For more on gender, competition and overconfidence, see Niederle and Vesterlund (2011).

5 More details about the simple measure of patience can be found in Vischer et al. (2013).

6 For more about the S.M.A.R.T. goals criterion, see Doran (1981) or see https:// www.projectsmart.co.uk/smart-goals/brief-history-of-smart-goals.php

7 For more on mental effort and decision fatigue, see Schwartz (2004) or Shenhav et al. (2017).

8 More details on famous people dressing the same can be found here: https://www.forbes.com/pictures/efkk45klli/steve-jobs/?sh=5c8d715e7998

9 Details on the Intrinsic Motivation Inventory can be found in Amabile et al. (1994).

10 More details on the temptation bundling experiment can be found in Milkman, Minson and Volpp (2014).

Acknowledgements

A deep, deep thank you to my wife, Khadija, who has always pushed me to do better and always kept me honest and sane. My mother, Arfa, has been my biggest influence and an inspiration. My father, Ather, taught me the importance of charm and levity, which I hope shine throughout this book. My sister, Wajiha, and brother, Haider, are the reasons why I have tried to be a role model, and in that I hope I have seen some success.

A heartfelt thank you to my wonderful editor, Jack Ramm, without whom none of this would be possible. I would also like to thank Huw Armstrong, Harriet Poland and Izzy Everington, who have all been absolutely amazing throughout this process, and to whom I owe many great debts and many more apologies.

Finally, I must thank my grandparents, P. B. Gilani and Munawer, who taught me all these lessons long before science came along.